Releasing Resources
to Achieve Health Gain

Releasing Resources to Achieve Health Gain

Edited by

Christopher Riley
Associate Director
Welsh Health Planning Forum
Cardiff

Morton Warner
Executive Director
Welsh Health Planning Forum
Cardiff

Carolyn Semple Piggot
Operations Manager
NHS Relations
Glaxo Pharmaceuticals (UK) Ltd

and

Amanda Pullen
Executive Director
International Advisory Board
Project Hope

with a Foreword by

John Wyn Owen

RADCLIFFE MEDICAL PRESS
OXFORD AND NEW YORK

Radcliffe Medical Press Ltd
18 Marcham Road, Abingdon, Oxon OX14 1AA, UK

Radcliffe Medical Press, Inc.
141 Fifth Avenue, New York, NY 10010, USA

British Library Cataloguing in Publication Data

A catalogue record for this book is available from the British Library.

ISBN 1 857750 18 7

Library of Congress Cataloging-in-Publication Data is available.

Typeset by AMA Graphics Ltd, Preston
Printed and bound in Great Britain by Redwood Books

Contents

vi   Contents

List of contributors

Dr Mona Abdalla
Health Services Research Unit
University of Aberdeen
Polwarth Building
Foresterhill
Aberdeen, AB9 2ZD

Dr Janet Askham
Deputy Director
Age Concern Institute of Gerontology
King's College London
Cornwall House Annex
Waterloo Road
London, SE1 8TX

Dr Jim Beattie
Health Services Research Unit
University of Aberdeen
Polwarth Building
Foresterhill
Aberdeen, AB9 2ZD

Dr Ken Buckingham
Health Services Research Unit
University of Aberdeen
Polwarth Building
Foresterhill
Aberdeen, AB9 2ZD

Dr Harry Burns
Director of Public Health Medicine
Greater Glasgow Health Board
112 Ingram Street
Glasgow, G1 1ET

Gaynor Bussell
Womens Health Dietitian
University College London Hospitals
Grafton Way
London, WC1E 6AU

Dr Peter Brambleby
Consultant in Public Health
East Sussex Health Authority
Rutherford Business Park
Marley Lane
East Sussex, TN33 0EZ

Michael Chapman
Chapman's Chemist
8 East Reach
Taunton
Somerset, TA1 3EN

Judy Clark
Pharmaceutical Advisor
Public Health and Health Policy
NW Anglia Health Commission
St John's
Thorpe Road
Peterborough, PE3 6JG

Dr Jeremy Corson
Chief of Public Health and Information
Health Promotion Wales
Ffynnon-las
Ty Glas Avenue
Llanishen
Cardiff, CF4 5DZ

Andrew Dawson
Consultant Obstetrician and Gynaecologist
Nevill Hall and District NHS Trust
Nevill Hall Hospital
Brecon Road
Abergavenny
Gwent, NP7 7EG

Dr Peter Donnelly
Consultant in Public Health Medicine
South Glamorgan Health Authority
Temple of Peace and Health
Cathays Park
Cardiff, CF1 3NW

Dr Graham Douglas
Thoracic Medicine Unit
City Hospital
Urquhart Road
Aberdeen, AB9 2YS

Neil Drummond
Senior Research Fellow
Public Health Research Unit
University of Glasgow/
Greater Glasgow Health Board
1 Lilybank Gardens
Glasgow, G12 8RZ

Dr James Friend
Thoracic Medicine Unit
City Hospital
Urquhart Road
Aberdeen, AB9 2YS

Tom Galloway
Specialist in Podiatric Surgery
Day Surgery Unit
Herefordshire Community Health NHS Trust
Belmont Abbey
Belmont
Hereford, HR2 9RZ

Sue Gardner
Consultant Clinical Psychologist
Psychological Services
Upton Hospital
Oak House
Albert Street
Slough, SL1 2BJ

Nick Gilbert
Specialist in Podiatric Surgery
Day Surgery Unit
St Mary's Hospital
Burghill
Hereford, HR4 7RF

Dr Geoff Hackett
Department of Primary Health Care
North Staffordshire Hospital
Thornburrow Drive
Hartshill
Stoke-on-Trent, ST4 7QB

Dominic Harrison
Preston Health Promotion Unit
Preston Health Authority
Watling Street Road
Fulwood
Preston, PR2 4DX

Dr Bill Holmes
General Practitioner
Sherwood Health Centre
Elmswood Gardens
Sherwood
Nottingham, NG5 4AD

Dr Joe Legge
Thoracic Medicine Unit
City Hospital
Urquhart Road
Aberdeen, AB9 2YS

Professor Richard Lilford
Chairman
Institute of Epidemiology and Health
   Services Research
34 Hyde Terrace
Leeds, LS2 9LN

Dr David Lyon
General Practitioner
Castlefields Health Centre
Chester Close
Castlefields
Runcorn
Cheshire, WA7 2HY

Dr Gillian McIlwaine
Consultant in Public Health Medicine
Greater Glasgow Health Board
112 Ingram Street
Glasgow, G1 1ET

Professor Klim McPherson
Professor of Public Health Epidemiology
Health Promotion Sciences Unit
Department of Public Health and Policy
London School of Hygiene and Tropical
  Medicine
Keppel Street
London, WC1E 7HT

Professor Vincent Marks
Professor of Clinical Biochemistry
University of Surrey
Guildford,
Surrey, GU2 5XH

John Wyn Owen
Director-General
New South Wales Health Department
73 Miller Street
North Sydney, NSW 2059
(Formerly: Director
NHS Wales
Welsh Office
Cathays Park
Cardiff, CF1 3NQ)

Dr Donald Pendlebury
Medical Director
Eastbourne and County Healthcare NHS Trust
Grangemead
1 Hawthylands Road
Hailsham
East Sussex, BN27 1EU

Dr Chrissie Pickin
Health Gain Consultant
Salford Health Authority
8th Floor
Peel House
Albert Street
Eccles
Salford, M30 0NJ

Wayne Richards
Dental Practitioner
77 Mansel Street
Swansea, SA1 5TW

Dr Barry Robinson
Unit General Manager
Lyme Community Care Unit
Lyme Community Care Centre
Uplyme Road
Lyme Regis
Dorset, DT7 3LS

Dr Sue Ross
Health Services Research Unit
University of Aberdeen
Polwarth Building
Foresterhill
Aberdeen, AB9 2ZD

Patricia Rouse
North Staffordshire Maternity Hospital
Hartshill Road
Newcastle
Stoke-on-Trent
Staffs, ST4 6QG

Professor Ian Russell
Director of Research and
  Development in Wales
Welsh Health Common Services Authority
Crickhowell House
Pierhead Street
Cardiff, CF1 5XT

Clive Smee
Chief Economic Adviser
Department of Health
Skipton House
80 London Road
London, SE1 6LW

Dr Jack Solomon
General Practitioner
69 Queens Walk
Ruislip
Middlesex, HS4 0NT

Michael Spencer
Pharmacy Department
University Hospital of Wales
Heath Park
Cardiff, CF4 4XW

Dr Kevan Thorley
General Practitioner
Higherland Surgery
3 Orme Road
Poolfields
Newcastle
Staffordshire, ST5 2UE

Sarah Twaddle
Health Economist
Greater Glasgow Health Board
112 Ingram Street
Glasgow, G1 1ET

Dr Morton Warner
Executive Director
Welsh Health Planning Forum
Portland House
22 Newport Road
Cardiff, CF2 1DB

Dr Denys Wells
General Practitioner
Northgate Medical Centre
15 Northgate
Walsall, WS9 8QD

Nesta Williams
Primary Health Care Team
Developmental Manager
First Community Health
Mellow House
Corporation Street
Stafford, ST16 3PX

Professor Graham Whitehouse
Department of Radiodiagnosis
University of Liverpool
Johnston Building
PO Box 147
Liverpool, L69 3BX

Foreword

John Wyn Owen

This book emerged from a conference that was held in Cardiff in March 1994. The issues it addressed are extremely topical and relevant to all involved in health care delivery and in every country aiming to get from the available resources the maximum health improvement for its population.

The key theme is effectiveness; what works. It is accordingly quite appropriate that we met in Cardiff, because it is in South Wales that Archie Cochrane, who has had one of the greatest impacts in the field of public health, did some of his research. It was he, of course, who penned probably one of the most important one-liners which influences health thinking today: 'all free health care must be effective'. I am sure that we would all concur with this; but I am sure, too, that we would admit there is a very long way to go before we come even close to meeting the challenge.

The idea for the conference sprung from work undertaken in Wales, and some background on the Welsh approach may be of interest in setting the scene. Effective use of resources is one of the three strategic themes of the NHS in Wales's approach to tackling major health challenges. The other themes focus on achieving better health and making services more responsive to the needs of individuals. Much of the early thinking on this approach has been undertaken by the Welsh Health Planning Forum, since designated as a WHO Collaborating Centre for health strategy and management development in Europe.

All health authorities in Wales develop their own plans for improving health and health services. These are the basis for local action plans and they address the period to the year 2002, covering 10 health priority areas ranging from cancer and heart disease to mental health and physical disability. These local plans are informed by the Protocols for Investment in Health Gain[1], developed by the Planning Forum and colleagues from across Wales. At the heart of each of the health gain protocols is an assessment of significant health interventions, each of which has been given a rating – 1 if of proven effectiveness, 4 if of no benefit, and a rating of 2 or 3 if the evidence of effectiveness is not clear cut. In Wales I was the

Accounting Officer for the expenditure on health services of somewhere in the order of £2bn of taxpayers' money; and I believed, and continue to believe, that there is an ethical responsibility on all those involved, myself and others, to spend that sort of money wisely, or perhaps I should say effectively.

We take four lines of approach to the use of resources in tackling the key task of managing our health service. The first thing is to *eliminate basic inefficiencies*, and whether that is good old-fashioned cost-improvement programmes or field market testing or the like, this is an important management challenge in its own right.

Second, we look at *eliminating unnecessary activity*. I think it would be right to say that in the past, 'value for money' work has looked mainly at non-clinical areas, but the Forum's work has highlighted opportunities to be better informed by clinical research and development. Certainly, work on clinical audit and the Department of Health's effectiveness bulletins, are going to lead the way in reviewing the clinical areas. Change is certainly needed in some areas. Diagnostic D & Cs[2] in women under 40, for example, are now regarded as examples of ineffective care, and the procedure was described as diagnostically inaccurate and therapeutically useless by the *British Medical Journal* as recently as January 1993; yet rates in the United Kingdom have been six times as high as in the United States.

The third line of attack is *doing things differently*. Often what should be done can actually be done more cost-effectively, for example, in the primary sector, rather than in big acute hospitals. There are now opportunities to undertake work in outpatient departments that previously might have been done on wards. We have many examples of clinical practice that can be undertaken safely on a daycase rather than on an inpatient basis. The aim should be to support developments which allow a similar quality of clinical outcome to be achieved using a lower level of resources, or better quality of outcome with similar resources.

The fourth approach is *acting now to prevent problems later*. This calls for well-targeted health promotion and prevention, using proven techniques. It also requires good support systems and follow-up to reduce unplanned readmission to hospitals, and tackling problems like hospital acquired infections and pressure sores, which are both costly and avoidable.

Others might have added a fifth approach – rationing – but I endorse the view which has been propounded by Robert Brook of the Rand Corporation, who has argued that if we home in on ineffective and inappropriate care, the need to ration services is much reduced, though not completely eliminated. Rationing should be the last thing we look at, certainly not the first.

The purpose of this book is to meet three challenging aims:

- to focus on where we can achieve real improvement in health – health gain
- to explain ways to release resources from existing activities
- to give publicity to practical examples on how this can be done.

I hope it will be of interest and of value.

John Wyn Owen
1995

References

1   Welsh Health Planning Forum. *Protocols for Investment in Health Gain; Cancers* (1990); *Cardiovascular Diseases* (1991); *Maternal and Early Child Health* (1991); *Physical and Sensory Disabilities* (1991); *Respiratory Diseases* (1992); *Injuries* (1992); *Mental Handicap* (1992); *Pain Discomfort and Palliative Care* (1992); *Oral Health* (1992); *Mental Health* (1993); *Healthy Living* (1993); *Healthy Environments* (1993); Welsh Office/NHS Directorate, Cardiff.

2   Coulter A, Klassen A, MacKenzie I *et al.* (1993) Dilatation and Curettage: Is it used appropriately? *British Medical Journal.* **306**: 236–9.

Acknowledgements

In March 1994 a conference, co-sponsored by the Welsh Health Planning Forum and the King's Fund, was held in Cardiff on the theme echoed in the title of this book. The many speakers at the meeting agreed generously to contribute papers for publication based on their presentations and the discussions that followed. Our thanks go to all involved in organizing and attending the conference for their support and ideas.

Throughout the difficult gestation of this book we have benefited from the help, advice and support by our editors at Radcliffe Medical Press. This was both welcome and necessary!

A huge debt is also owed to the administrative and secretarial staff of the Planning Forum for their hard work in organizing the conference and in preparing the book.

Both the conference and the book have been supported through educational grants from *Glaxo PLC*. This is in line with Glaxo's goal of working closely with health care professionals to improve the standards of patient care. The appropriate and effective use of quality medicines, supported by disease management information and education helps achieve the best possible outcomes for patients – the goal of all those involved in the provision of health care.

Finally, our thanks are due to the NHS in Wales.

Christopher Riley
Morton Warner
Carolyn Semple Piggot
Amanda Pullen
1995

List of abbreviations

ACEI	angiotensin-converting enzyme inhibitor		**HACV**	Home Antenatal Care in the Valleys
AFP	alphafetoprotein		**HALO**	Health and Leisure Organization
AIDS	acquired immune deficiency syndrome		**HIV**	human immunodeficiency virus
ATU	alcohol treatment unit		**HNA**	health needs assessment
BBD	benign breast disease		**HRT**	hormone replacement therapy
BMI	body mass index		**HSPI**	hospital sector price index
BTS	British Thoracic Society		**ICD**	International Classification of Diseases
CABG	coronary artery bypass graft			
CHD	coronary heart disease		**IHD**	ischaemic heart disease
CIAS	Cardiff Integrated Antenatal Care Scheme		**IVP**	intravenous peritograms
			LBW	low birth weight
CNO	Chief Nursing Officer		**LCCU**	Lyme Community Care Unit
CNS	central nervous system		**MRI**	magnetic resonance imaging
CT	computed tomography		**NBW**	normal birth weight
CVD	cerebrovascular disease		**NEBDSA**	National Examining Board of Dental Surgery Assistants
D&C	dilatation and curettage			
DES	diethylstilboestrol		**NHS**	National Health Service (of the UK)
DHA	district health authority			
DSA	dental surgery assistant		**NIC**	net ingredient cost
DUE	drug use evaluation		**PBMA**	programme budgeting and marginal analysis
ECMO	extra corporeal membrane oxygenation			
			PEFR	peak expiratory flow rate
ECR	extra-contractual referral		**PHCT**	Primary Health Care Team
ENT	ear, nose and throat		**PID**	pelvic inflammatory disease
FCE	finished consultant episode		**PRS**	patient record system
FCH	First Community Health		**PTA**	percutaneous transluminal angioplasty
FEVI	forced expiratory volume in one second			
			RCOG	Royal College of Obstetricians and Gynaecologists
FHSA	Family Health Services Authority			
			RDS	respiratory distress syndrome
GMS	General Medical Service		**RHA**	Regional Health Authority
GP	general practitioner		**SGA**	small for gestational age
GRASSIC	Grampian Asthma Study			

SMR	standardized mortality ratio	**UCLH**	University College
SSRI	selective serotonin reuptake		London Hospital
	inhibitor	**UHW**	University Hospital Wales
TENS	transcutaneous electrical	**VFM**	value for money
	nerve stimulation	**WHO**	World Health Organization

Introduction

The chapters in this book have been produced by people with considerable experience of health services in the United Kingdom, and in some cases abroad also. Clive Smee from the perspective of a senior official at the Department of Health introduces the chapters with a valuable overview, indicating both the scope for releasing resources in pursuit of more effective health care and some examples of how to achieve it.

Three sections follow, which draw out some of the themes. The first looks at what can be done to ensure that resources are tied more closely to outcomes. Richard Lilford sets the scene with a discussion of the nature of evidence for effectiveness. Graham Whitehouse and Vincent Marks look at the contribution of two vital clinical support services – diagnostic radiology and clinical pathology. Judy Clark and Michael Spencer discuss how effectiveness and efficiency in prescribing can be improved in general practice and the hospital. Two further chapters look at other aspects of the generation and use of evidence in general practice; David Lyon considers referrals to radiology and Jack Solomon asthma practice. Finally Harry Burns and colleagues and Chrissie Pickens consider the role of the commissioner in using evidence to secure access to services that are both appropriate and effective. They use the examples of gynaecology and services dealing with alcohol-related problems.

The second section approaches similar issues but from a different tack: what evidence is there that early interventions can help to reduce the occurrence of later poor health and avoidable complications? And that such services can make better use of available resources? Klim McPherson provides an overview drawing on a range of examples to suggest that a lot *can* be done. Andrew Dawson, Kevan Thorley and Trish Rouse describe new ways of providing care for mothers-to-be and Gaynor Bussell emphasizes the importance and potential of providing an appropriate diet. Jeremy Corson, Dominic Harrison and Wayne Richards look at a community-wide project to tackle heart disease; new ways of thinking about hospital's contribution and a re-orientation of individual practice – in this case in dentistry. Peter Donnelly argues the case for tertiary prevention, taking the examples of cardiac rehabilitation and osteoporosis. Sue Gardner summarizes the benefits of early treatment-interventions in psychology. Nick Gilbert and Tom Galloway describes a cost-effective alternative to surgery when tackling foot problems.

The final section opens with Morton Warner outlining some of the possible changes in health care in the next twenty years. He suggests that our imaginations should not be trapped by problems linked to the present pattern of resources. A number of examples from general practice build on this: Bill Holmes describes how single-handed practice even in a deprived area can work effectively; Denys Wells and Geoff Hackett offer case studies in the potential of taking on additional staff. Barry Robinson shows how general practice can form the basis for a new way of planning care for the whole community; while Neil Drummond and colleagues report on a major study on integrated care across the primary/secondary boundary. Michael Chapman and Nesta Williams emphasize the contribution of the pharmacist and the nursing profession to the primary care team, and how they can be used even more effectively. Janet Askham and Donald Pendlebury focus on older people. The former describes both the value of giving them special support to maintain and improve their health and how it might be done; the latter describes a particular scheme in Sussex that does it. Finally, Peter Brambleby describes a process of analysing existing services and resources, to help set the baseline for the development of imaginative alternatives.

Releasing resources overview

Clive Smee

Introduction

Now is a very appropriate time for looking at releasing resources. This is because the current period of fiscal retrenchment means health resources are unlikely to rise as fast as the public's expectations and as fast as those who work in the health service would like. Under the UK Government's published public expenditure plans we can expect an increase of no more than 1% a year in health resources over the next 2 or 3 years. So, if we are to move resources into the areas where there is scope for them to produce maximum benefit, we have to look very hard indeed at the areas where they may be producing few or no benefits.

This initial overview addresses four questions.

- Why is there still so much scope for releasing resources in a health service that is widely regarded as one of the most efficient in the world?

- Where is there greater scope for releasing those resources?

- What scale of resources might be released?

- What mechanisms will encourage release of those resources?

Why is there still so much scope for releasing resources?

It is in a sense a paradox that the National Health Service (NHS) is widely regarded as one of the most efficient health services in the world, yet there still remains much scope for releasing further resources. How is this possible? There are two important groups of reasons: inadequate information and inadequate incentives.

Inadequate information

There is a lack of understandable information on costs, on quality and outcomes and on cost-effectiveness. In some cases, perhaps many, there is too little information available. The health service is still very much like a cottage industry: people working in one part of it believe that what they are doing is done well and efficiently and do not have any way of comparing their performance with those working in another part. Few comparisons are possible on the important issues, few norms or standards exist. In consequence, there have been few opportunities for managers, purchasers or clinical peers to challenge existing behaviour.

This of course is changing. Royal Colleges are now carrying out surveys of clinical standards and outcomes from operations. Audit is expanding enormously. We have activities such as the Northern Regional Health Authority co-operating with the Maryland Quality Indicator Project on measures of outcomes and of adverse events in hospital care. Nevertheless, I think as a generalization it stands.

But, combined with too little information in some areas, there is, I think, a problem of too rapid medical advance producing too much indigestible information in other areas, particularly for doctors and clinicians dealing directly with patients. It is difficult to remember the indications, the complications and the costs and procedures of different drugs. There are just too many potential treatment strategies for medical practitioners to keep up with.

Inadequate incentives

Alongside these information problems, there are weaknesses in relation to incentives. First, it has long been pointed out that the health service is marked by separation of budget holding and decision making. Clinicians and doctors effectively allocate most health service resources but they usually do not see themselves as budget holders. General practitioner (GP) fundholding is one answer to that, clinical directorates in hospitals are another.

A second problem in relation to incentives is that medical ethics place emphasis traditionally on maximizing effectiveness of care for individual patients, with little attention to costs. Maximizing effectiveness is not equal to maximizing cost-effectiveness or health gain. Resources are scarce and all decisions have opportunity costs. However desirable it may be on moral or ethical grounds to give every possible treatment to an individual patient, particularly if the patient is a child or a baby, somebody in the system has to pay attention to what may be the costs in terms of lost health gains for other untreated children, other adults, or other members of society.

A third issue in relation to incentives is the limited pressures for innovation, for doing things differently from competition or from administrative interventions in the form of performance management. The health reforms were meant to strengthen these incentives but there is much further to go.

Where is the greatest scope for releasing resources?

There are no simple answers to this question, but several approaches are worth considering, particularly by those who actively have to make resource allocation decisions in purchasing authorities or GP fundholding practices.

Looking at costs

The approach of the industrial engineer to this question is to ask where are costs concentrated. In the health service, something like 70% of costs go on labour inputs, so an obvious starting point is to look at the scope for improvements in labour productivity.

There is rather good evidence from the USA and increasingly good English evidence that labour productivity is closely related to hospital performance[1]. We also know that there are very wide differences in labour productivity across the NHS.

Figure 1 shows an example of these differences. Even excluding the outliers there is something like a two-fold difference in the distribution of staff time per

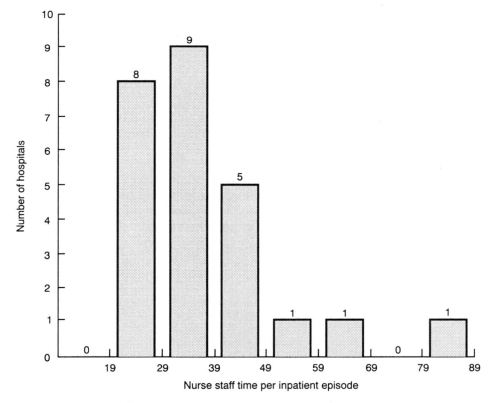

Figure 1   Nursing staff time (in hours) per inpatient episode for 25 hospitals. (Source: Jones J, Sanderson C and Black N (1993) Does labour substitution occur in district general hospitals? *Health Trends*. **25**: 68–72)

inpatient episode. This difference holds up after controlling for case mix and the types of hospitals. Similar differences were found in relation to consultant and junior medical staff and there was no obvious evidence of substitutability between nurses and these other categories. It may be that the differences are related in some way to quality of care, but that is not evident. Until it is, the Treasury and the public have every right to ask why all hospitals cannot move to the left-hand side of the diagram and reduce their numbers of nursing staff by up to a half.

Another way of looking at the distribution of costs is to note that costs are concentrated around hospital-bed stays and to examine the scope for reducing length of stay. There have been several studies in the UK, and more in the USA, which have suggested that in many hospitals something between 10% and 40% of days in hospitals are unnecessary or inappropriate[2]. The American studies conclude generally that the major cause is not the absence of community care, though that is important, but the way that the hospitals manage their discharge planning and test scheduling. Some idea of the resources that might be released in the UK through better management in these areas is provided by the difference between actual and expected average hospital stays in 200 or so acute hospitals in England after adjusting for Health Resource Groups, the new approach in the UK to diagnostic related groups. Figure 2 shows that after adjusting for case mix, hospitals

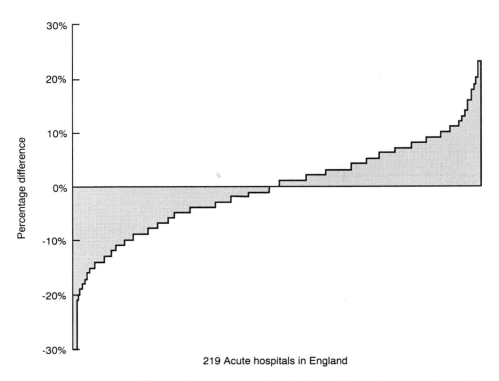

Figure 2   Percentage difference between actual and expected inpatient stay adjusted for case-mix in 219 acute hospitals in England. (Source: Department of Health)

Table 1   Burdens of disease: ten main causes of NHS expenditure (excluding community care) 1989–90

ICD 9 group (International Classification of Diseases)	% of total
Injury and poisoning	5.4
Schizophrenia	5.4
Mouth disease	4.6
Mental retardation	4.4
Symptoms	4.0
Stroke	4.0
Normal pregnancy and delivery	3.9
Ischaemic heart disease	3.6
Ulcers and stomach	2.8
Skin infection	2.6
Total top ten	**40.7**
All other causes	**59.3**

Source: Department of Health, England.

which have the shortest lengths of stay have average lengths of stay something like 40% shorter than those hospitals that have the longest lengths of stay.

There are other ways of looking at where costs are concentrated. For purchasers, a particularly fruitful approach may be to look at how health care costs are spread across disease groups. Table 1 is taken from recent work in the Department of Health on what is called the 'burdens of disease', an exercise that shows the contribution of major diseases to NHS expenditure, mortality and morbidity. This example shows that ten disease groups account for about 40% of health care expenditure. A question for each district purchaser is: 'Is my distribution of disease expenditures significantly different from the national picture and, if so, do I know why?'

Looking at uncertainty

Another way into the issue of where may there be scope for releasing resources is to look at where there is greatest uncertainty. Uncertainty can be exhibited by variations in intervention rates (after allowing for the obvious factors affecting need) and by doubts about appropriateness. There is a substantial international literature on variations in intervention rates, suggesting that large differences in rates primarily reflect differences in medical style in the face of uncertainty. For example, in England across district health authorities (DHAs) there are variations of two or more in intervention rates for hernias, prostectomies, hysterectomies, haemorrhoids and tonsillectomies[3]. Similar differences have been found in other countries. The problem, of course, is that we do not actually know what is the appropriate rate of intervention. If we did, then we could identify immediately where there was inappropriate or ineffective care and take steps to eliminate it.

Table 2   Appropriateness of cholecystectomies (%): North West Thames RHA 1989

Panelist agreement and views	Mixed panel	Surgical panel
Agreement:		
Appropriate	41	52
Equivocal	<1	3
Inappropriate	30	2
Partial agreement	14	23
Disagreement	15	21
Total	100	100

Source: Scott E, Black N (1992) Appropriateness of cholecystectomy: the public and private sectors compared. *Annals of the Royal College of Surgeons (England).* **74 (Suppl. 4)**: 97–101.

One rather interesting approach to identifying what is the right level of intervention or 'gold standard' is to ask doctors and their families what they do to themselves. A recent study of a large sample of Swiss doctors found that for ten common surgical areas intervention rates among the doctors and their own immediate families ran at about 30% below the rates for the general population[4]. The authors conclude, somewhat controversially, that as the public become as knowledgeable as doctors intervention rates will fall.

Alongside variations in intervention rates, and traceable to the same root causes, we also have increasing questions raised about appropriateness. Much of the early work in this area was in the USA, but there have been a number of studies in the UK. For example, there was a recent study of cholecystectomies in North West Thames Regional Health Authority (Table 2). What is interesting about this is not so much the finding that a surgical panel had a slightly different view of appropriateness than a mixed panel that included GPs and non-surgeons but that among the surgeons themselves there was disagreement, or only partial agreement, about the appropriateness of over 40% of the interventions. The implication is that in areas where there is known to be uncertainty, purchasers and providers should constantly be asking: how do our intervention rates compare with those of our neighbours and, if they are significantly higher, are there good reasons why that should be so?

Other approaches

There are other ways of identifying opportunities for releasing resources. As better information becomes available, one can look at variations in unit costs between providers and health authorities. One can also look at interventions where the outcomes or benefits are known often to be poor, or not significantly better than for lower cost alternatives. Commonly quoted examples include diagnostic D and Cs in young women, early treatment of 'glue ear', elective prostatectomies, and the use of SSRIs rather than tricyclics in the treatment of depression in primary care.

What scale of resources might be released?

To the economist there are two different approaches to this issue and I think both need to be pursued. One is to look at ways of doing things 'right', which economists call improving technical efficiency, and the other is to look at the scope for doing 'right things' or doing better things, commonly referred to as improving allocative efficiency.

'Doing things right'

In the recent past the concern about improving use of resources in the health service has concentrated on improving technical efficiency. There has been great progress in this direction through reduced lengths of stay and increases in day cases. Indeed, in annual discussions with the Treasury on the public expenditure round, the Department of Health can point with considerable pride to a record of improvements that goes back at least 10–15 years, a record showing that the NHS in England has been able to achieve a 1–2% reduction in unit costs year on year across the acute sector and in some sectors outside it. The Government believes these kinds of improvement in productivity or efficiency can not only continue but can be bettered. So for 1993–4 the NHS in England was set a 2% efficiency target, for 1994–5 it has been set a 2.25% efficiency target and for future years this figure might go even higher.

The advantage of going for technical efficiency is that it is often easier to identify. But can this continue? Have not the obvious opportunities already been exploited? It is often suggested that we must be approaching diminishing returns. However, no special reasons are apparent why there should be a greater tailing-off in productivity gains than in any other service industry which is subject to significant technical advance and rising overall resources.

'Doing right things'

Attention to allocative efficiency has been stimulated by the growing concern with appropriateness and with moving resources from secondary to community and primary care. The earlier cholecystectomies example illustrated that inappropriate interventions are not confined to extravagant health services such as the USA. If we look at another area, coronary procedures, we also see similar evidence of medical uncertainty and different views about appropriateness. Hampton and colleagues at Nottingham, working together with Brook and others from Rand, found that, in the view of a UK panel, around a fifth of interventions for angiographies and coronary artery bypass grafts (CABGs) in the Trent Region were inappropriate (Table 3)[6]. The figures were a little lower in the view of a USA panel but even the American doctors thought only two-thirds of the interventions were definitely appropriate.

All this seems to highlight the difficulty of identifying what care is appropriate. John Wennberg recently defined the appropriate rate of intervention as a 'rate of service that would occur if patients were fully and neutrally informed about the

Table 3   Appropriateness of coronary procedures (%): Trent RHA 1987–88

	UK panel	US panel
1 Coronary angiography:		
Appropriate	49	71
Equivocal	30	12
Inappropriate	21	17
2 CABG:		
Appropriate	57	67
Equivocal	27	26
Inappropriate	16	7

Source: Bernstin S, Ksecoff J, Gray D, Hampton J, Brook R (1993) The appropriateness of cardiovascular procedures – British versus US perspectives. *International Journal of Technology Assessment in Health Care.* **9 (1)**: 3–10.

state of medical progress, what works and what are the uncertainties and if they were free to choose the treatments they wanted'[7]. Any such world is a very long way off, as indeed is being able to identify precisely what interventions are inappropriate and what resources might be freed up if we could confine interventions to the appropriate rates.

The possibilities

The potential scale of savings from improving technical and allocative efficiencies is large but the exact size is highly uncertain. Also it will change through time. Americans are much bolder in making such estimates. At the end of the 1980s Dr Brook of Rand wrote: 'If one could extrapolate from the available literature, perhaps one fourth of hospital days, one fourth of procedures and two fifths of medications could be done without'[8]. No such bold statements are available for the UK. The Oxford Study of Perinatal Interventions found that of 284 interventions reviewed 35% were judged to be effective, 13% promising, 31% unknown and 21% useless or harmful[9]. That 21% were useless or harmful procedures does not necessarily imply that 21% of expenditure was wasted but it does suggest that a lot of money could have been better spent.

It is not known whether we can extrapolate from the perinatal figures to other parts of the health service. However, in the areas which are discussed later in this book there appears to be plenty of scope for releasing resources, for example:

- *on inappropriate clinical activity in interventions,* there is the advice from the Royal College of Radiologists about the scope for reducing x-ray examinations by a fifth or a quarter; a reduction by a quarter would have saved £60 million in 1991[10]; and there is the recent Audit Commission Report on drug prescribing in the health service suggesting very large sums of money might be saved[11].

- *on the unexploited scope for preventive care,* it is noteworthy that studies in the USA have suggested that perhaps 20% of admissions in some of their hospitals have been undesirably late and that such late admissions can be associated with the doubling of the length of stay and worse outcomes[12].

- *on the scope for doing things differently*, there are several relevant studies suggesting, for example, that the early discharge of hip fracture patients combined with good hospital at home care can save considerable amounts of money[13]; however, an economist must observe that some services are changing from hospitals to ambulatory settings in advance of hard evidence that the shift is cost-effective, or even to the patients' benefit.

What mechanisms will encourage the release of resources?

How can one achieve or free up the savings from these various areas of inefficient or inappropriate resource use? What mechanisms and incentives will encourage the release of resources? There are perhaps two broad approaches: general incentives for efficiency, and specific or micro-incentive mechanisms to encourage more appropriate care. Increasingly, the international trend is to pursue both. Historically, the USA has given little attention to general incentives for efficiency and particularly to budgetary mechanisms. It has tended to put much more emphasis on micro-incentives and micro-regulation. But the USA is now moving to give a greater role to general incentives.

In the UK we have tended to regard the wide application of general incentives – tight budgets, broad performance and efficiency targets, and competition – as a substitute for micro-regulation. But along with other countries there is now a growing belief that we need to follow both approaches.

General incentives are very effective at squeezing out technical inefficiency. But the weakness of these approaches is that they do not tackle medical uncertainty, and that I think is the driving force behind the more micro-measures that seem to be spreading all over the world. These measures include:

- the development and use of outcome measures

- health technology assessments

- the introduction of cost-effectiveness considerations (and, sometimes, hurdles) into the assessment of new drugs

- expansion of clinical audit, including the incorporation of cost and cost-effectiveness implications

- an upsurge of interest in service and clinical guidelines and protocols that can be linked to purchasing plans and contracts.

Some futurists see the way forward ultimately to lie through payments related to successful outcomes rather than to activities.

The problem is knowing which of these micro-approaches is most cost-effective, which is most efficient in changing clinical behaviour. The messages from the extensive American experience with micro-management are not clearcut. To change clinician behaviour you can use education, feedback, participation, administrative interventions and financial incentives. Surveys of the American literature tend to conclude that in certain circumstances all of these types of intervention can work but they work best if they are combined together in some way[14]. This is not very helpful. Nevertheless, more and more countries appear to be concluding that developing guidelines and protocols offers scope for improving effectiveness and/or for reducing expenditure growth. The French, for example, announced recently the introduction of 'références medicales' for 24 primary care clinical situations. In England, we are also putting particular emphasis on incorporating clinical guidelines and the results of health technology assessments into purchasing plans and contracts.

The success of these attempts at micro-management will depend on several factors.

1 How far the new guidelines and protocols are based on understanding the motivations underlying current practice – for example, does current practice reflect poor information, does it reflect lack of incentive to change, or what?

2 How far we obtain doctor and clinician involvement and support and allow for and indeed encourage local adaptation – it is essential to avoid undermining professionalism and self-esteem by appearing to promote what is called 'cookbook medicine'.

3 Acceptance that in the present state of knowledge there are implicit limitations on the role of protocols and guidelines because of the complexity of problems facing doctors – until we have much more and much better research, guidelines in most areas can only serve as an indicator and a source of encouragement of how things might be done.

4 There must be careful evaluation of the effects of guidelines and protocols, just as for any other diagnostic test or technology advance. The tendency to assume that management innovations and management changes do not need to be assessed and evaluated in the same way as changes in medical procedures cannot be defended. In particular, we need to look at the impact of clinical guidelines both on containing costs and on improving clinical effectiveness.

Learning points

To improve resource use, we must:

- Improve and use information.

- Improve our incentives.

- Look closely at our costs and others'.

- Compare practice with others'.

- Constantly review productivity.

- Review appropriateness.

- Use guidelines and protocols sensibly.

References

1   For USA evidence *see*: Prospective Payment Assessment Commission (1992) *Medicare and the American Health Care System – Report to The Congress*. Washington DC.

2   For USA evidence on inappropriate utilization *see*, for example: Payne S (1987) Identifying and managing inappropriate hospital utilization: a policy synthesis. *Health Service Research*. **22(5)**: 709–69.
    For UK *see*, for example Anderson P, Meara G, Broadhurst S *et al.* (1988) Use of hospital beds: a cohort study of admissions to a potential teaching hospital. *British Medical Journal*. **297**: 910–12.

3   McPherson K, Wennberg J, Hovind O *et al.* (1982). Small-area variations in the use of common surgical procedures: an international comparison of New England, England and Norway. *New England Journal of Medicine*. **307**: 1310–14.

4   Domenighetti G, Casabianca A, Gutzwiller F *et al.* (1993) Revisiting the most informed consumer of surgical services. *International Journal of Technology Assessment in Health Care*. **9(4)**: 505–13.

5   Scott E, Black N (1992) Appropriateness of Cholecystectomy: the public and private sectors compared. *Annals of the Royal College of Surgeons (England)*. **74(Suppl. 4)**: 97–101.

6   Bernstein S, Kosecoff J, Gray D *et al.* (1993) The appropriateness of cardiovascular procedures – British versus US perspectives. *International Journal of Technology Assessment in Health Care*. **9(1)**: 3–10.

7   Wennberg J (1993) Future directions for small area variations. *Medical Care*. **31(5)**: 7S75–80 Supplement.

8   Brook R (1989) Practice guidelines and practising medicine: are they compatible? *Journal of The American Medical Association*. **262**: 3027–30.

9   Enkin M, Kierse M and Chalmers I (1989) *A Guide to Effective Care in Pregnancy and Childbirth*. Oxford University Press, New York and Oxford.

10 Royal College of Radiologists Working Party (1991) A multicentre audit of hospital referral for radiological investigation in England and Wales. *British Medical Journal*. **303**: 809–12.

11 Audit Commission Report (1994) A Prescription for Improvement: towards more rational prescribing in general practice. HMSO, London.

12 Gonella J, Louis D, Zeleznik C *et al.* (1990) The problem of late hospitalization: a quality and cost issue. *Academic Medicine*. **65(5)**: 314–19.

13 Hollingworth W, Todd C, Parker M *et al.* (1993) Cost analysis of early discharge after hip fracture. *British Medical Journal*. **307**: 903–6.

14 Greco P and Eisenberg J (1993) Changing physicians' practices. *New England Journal of Medicine*. **329**: 1271–4.

Part One
Focusing Clinical Activity on Outcomes

1

Overview

Richard Lilford

Introduction

About five years ago, a structured review on the effectiveness of homeopathic treatment appeared in the *British Medical Journal*[1], apparently arousing very little interest. Releasing resources to achieve health gain must rely heavily on structured reviews, but the data assembled in a structured review require critical appraisal. That on homeopathy covered about 80 studies, over 60 of which were randomized clinical trials, mostly showing that the homeopathic medicine worked. At first sight, therefore, homeopathy has a proven effectiveness and henceforth people should purchase this inexpensive and effective treatment. This chapter will deal with how to sift and analyse clinical evidence and really make sense of it: it will show why people are right not to purchase homeopathy at this time.

The epistemology of clinical research

Clearly, using the most effective treatments enhances allocative efficiency, as discussed on pp. xxiii to xxxiii. How can knowledge be used to improve the cost-efficiency of the Health Service as a whole? The study of knowledge began in the time of Aristotle, but enthusiasm for good clinical evidence was given new impetus by Sir Austin Bradford Hill[2], probably the most deserving person never to get a Nobel prize. He was the first person to do a modern randomized trial, back in 1948, on the use of streptomycin for treatment of tuberculosis. His other famous contribution, with Richard Doll, was the discovery that smoking causes cancer.

Clinical trials, Bradford Hill pointed out in the 1940s, are only required where the effects of treatment are not obvious. Some treatments introduced in his day had quite obvious beneficial effects. Then people with untreated meningococcal meningitis died almost invariably. With the advent of penicillin, they hardly ever died. Here Bradford Hill would be the first to say that a clinical trial would not be needed, but most modern treatments have much smaller, less obvious gains, detectable most reliably by clinical trials. The results of laboratory experiments alone are insufficient to show the effects of clinical interventions on humans. For example, prophylactic drugs to stop a disturbance in the heart rhythm are not effective after heart attack, while blood thinners are. Yet cardiologists, before trials were conducted, favoured drugs for rhythm and eschewed blood thinners.

The idea of randomized trials started from using clinical studies as a source of evidence, then the notion of control groups was added and finally with Bradford Hill randomized assignment to control and treatment groups was introduced to overcome any bias from allocating people with a different prognosis to each group. The concept of the appropriateness of randomization has been backed up by empirical studies. For example, one showed that randomized studies, as a general rule, show smaller gains than alternative designs[3].

In the early days of the health reforms, the author argued that health commissioners should have a role in purchasing and commissioning the right kind of research[4]. Health-care purchasers in Yorkshire pay money into a central fund, under the control of the Regional Research Director, who is then able to purchase access to important clinical studies. In this way the NHS can make its contribution to the international research effort, to help clarify what is effective care. It is appropriate that such studies should be of high quality and this will often involve randomization. It is also important that they are ethically sound.

Ethics of clinical trials

Ethics of principle is about whether one should do it in the first place. Here the issue is ethics of procedure – how one should do something, perhaps the more substantive issue.

The basic tenet for the ethical conduct of a clinical trial is captured in the word 'equipoise'. Equipoise means that observers are completely unsure as to which of two treatments is better[5]. It is sometimes referred to rather loosely, for example by Richard Peto, as the 'uncertainty principle'. But 'certain' is rather a vague word in this context because it leaves the degree of certainty undefined. The word 'equipoise' means that it is thought equally likely that treatment A and treatment B will bring most benefit. The relative odds or relative risk of the two treatments having different effects is perceived as one in two, or one to one. A clinician should be at or very close to this point of equivalence before entering a patient in a trial in clear conscience, assuming that the two treatments under comparison are generally freely available.

Equipoise may be represented as a curve, the peak of which is the most likely result. Thus, as a potential (hypothetical) result becomes more extreme, so the likelihood of that result occurring declines. These likelihoods are reflected on the 'equipoise curve'.

Of course the situation is more complicated than this, because treatments are not simply better or worse. In some cases, a treatment has known and obvious side-effects. In this case, equipoise is not that there is no absolute difference between the treatments, but rather that there is a difference sufficient, but only just sufficient, to make up for the known side-effect of the treatment with greater known side-effects. Imagine a clinician who thinks that it is more likely than not that treatment B is better than A, but B has a known severe side-effect. Imagine, then, a patient who would demand a 20% improvement of survival to make the side-effects worthwhile. A clinical trial would then be ethical if a 20% gain in survival was perceived by the clinician to be the most likely result *and* if the patient would be indifferent between the two treatments at this gain in survival. Equipoise around 'no difference' between treatments is called 'absolute equipoise' and 'no difference' around the effect which precisely compensates for the more invasive treatment is called 'effective equipoise' (Figure 1.1).

While the main obligation of a purchaser is to maximize the health – broadly defined – of a community, the primary obligation of the clinician is to the individual patient. To understand the ethics of clinical trials, it is necessary to draw the distinction between the obligations of clinicians to individual patients and those of purchasers to patients in general. The individual clinician–patient pair should be in effective equipoise for trial entry, while a purchasing authority (or funding agency) need ensure only that clinicians as a whole are equipoised – 'collective equipoise'. The requirement for patient–clinician couples to have effective equipoise places a constraint on clinical trials because the physician must think that

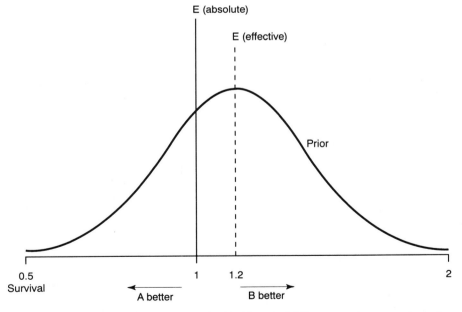

Figure 1.1   Equipoise curve. This shows the likelihood of different results as seen by a doctor or group of clinicians before a trial. E (effective) is the magnitude of effect that would make the side-effects of a treatment with greater side-effect worthwhile, in this case treatment B. E (absolute) would represent equipoise around a most likely effect of no difference either way

the most likely treatment effect coincides with that which the patient would require. That surely must be a fairly unusual clinical scenario. Many completed clinical trials, if judged by this criterion, would be declared unethical. The famous trial of folic acid for the prevention of neural tube defects may be difficult to defend on this basis.

However, a distinction should be drawn between treatments like folic acid which are freely available and treatments such as ECMO (extra corporeal membrane oxygenation – an artificial lung), which is not in routine use. A group of physicians in Harvard decided they would like to do a trial of this very expensive and invasive treatment. The randomized trial started in effective equipoise; they thought the benefits the equipment might offer were about equivalent to what their patients might demand of them. However, the first patients studied did much better with ECMO, and they stopped the study. They have been criticized for this, because the questions provided had not been answered in the usual scientific sense, but they were right to stop the trial when they did; they had access to the equipment and to enter patients further would violate the principle of equipoise, because they believed that ECMO was effective.

A more extensive trial of ECMO is taking place in the UK, with four designated treatment centres. The doctors will offer the parents of babies with lung failure a choice between conventional treatment or entry into the randomized trial. They are right to offer randomization, even if they perceive benefits greater than those required for effective equipoise. This is because access to ECMO is only available through the trial. The people who are funding that trial are also right to restrict access in this way and the Government is quite right to restrict ECMO in this country until a clinical trial can show whether the amount of benefit that it gives is sufficient to justify the cost. There is enough uncertainty to make the trial ethical from the perspective of those providing care – they must help clinicians and society at large to glean evidence about new treatment ethically by evaluating new technology in trials.

Combining trial results

How do these ethical considerations affect our interpretation of data? The first question is how do we know the effects of treatments? Interpretation of clinical evidence depends on three things: prior perceptions of clinicians of the likely effects, precision of studies and their likely accuracy. Obviously, when a large study has produced a precise answer with safeguards against bias (inaccuracy), then it is likely to influence purchasing decisions strongly. As far as the precision is concerned, it was Archie Cochrane who emphasized the importance of assembling systematically all the evidence on particular subjects[6]. Iain Chalmers and colleagues have done precisely that and have led the way in producing structured reviews of clinical evidence[7].

Meta-analysis is the powerful statistical tool for combining studies. The most famous meta-analysis ever conducted dealt with medicines to thin the blood in case of heart attack. The meta-analysis shows that the chances of survival are improved by giving this blood thinning medicine. There are some interesting lessons to be learnt from this exercise. Perhaps the most interesting famous clinical trial ever, ISIS 2, began *after* meta-analysis including the famous Italian GISSI trial had reported clear benefit. It is surprising that clinical judgement and hence equipoise had not shifted at an earlier stage since the precision of the estimate of benefit was already considerable. This can be contrasted with another group of studies of surgical treatments for breast cancer (*see* below) where the opposite happened. In that case a handful of small trials yielded findings that could not answer the question to the required precision, but were nevertheless associated with changes in surgical practice. The lack of association between evidence and behaviour is emerging as a subject for study.

A criticism often heard of meta-analysis is that it combines different studies, in different places and different times. There clearly must be some differences between them – in the patients and way the medicine is given – and this could influence the results of each study. How can we just 'lump' all these trials together?

One way of answering this objective is to argue that heterogeneity increases *generalizability*. It is obvious that each locality cannot undertake its own local study on every issue. So a locality, say Cardiff, must look at the literature. If we had access to one massive study only, the generalizability of the results to Cardiff would be suspect. However, studies grouped together from many places are more likely to be generalizable to Cardiff. Thus if the study had been repeated in America, Australia and Europe, with broadly similar results, then it becomes very difficult to say that the Welsh, unique as they are, would be different in their response to the medicine. Thus, heterogeneity of patients and procedures is actually a strength when combining trial results.

A second issue in meta-analysis is *quality*. I do not think that one should bundle together in meta-analysis different trials of completely different quality without qualification. The Leeds Institute of Epidemiology and Health Services Research are Cochrane collaborators in the review of treatments for subfertility and indicate the quality of evidence in presenting results. The first meta-analysis, M1, is restricted to the best quality studies, then those of intermediate quality studies are added to M1 to create M2 and so on. Taking the example of clomiphene citrate for unexplained subfertility, the better studies indicate that 'the jury is still out', while inclusion of the poorer quality studies produces a 'significant' result. So it is likely that most clinicians are still in equipoise about this treatment and it might be ethical to do further clinical studies.

Design of trials

Decision analysis could help in the design of clinical trials[8]. Take as an example cancer of the breast. There are two types of physical treatment for early cancer of the breast: lumpectomy (taking out the lump, or a segment of the breast), versus a much more mutilating operation, mastectomy. Either of these possibilities may save the person's life. The small operation is less mutilating but it may have a lower chance of cure; 60% of people with palpable tumour will die of their disease.

Trialists would need to consider that following lumpectomy, 60% plus an unknown increment which can be called delta, might die of their disease. The trial then, should be large enough to measure the increase in death rate, delta, which women would trade off against avoidance of mutilation. Given delta, the risk women would run to avoid mutilation, it is possible to calculate sample size. Delta, in turn, can be calculated by decision analysis; from a knowledge of the specific trade-offs women would make between mutilation and death. For a woman prepared to run a 10% risk of death to avoid mastectomy, the improvement required of surgery delta is 4%. If, more plausibly, a woman was prepared to run only a 5% risk of death to avoid mastectomy, she would demand a 2% improvement in mortality to make surgery worthwhile. If, perhaps most plausibly, a woman would run only a 2% increased risk of death, then the trial would have to be able to measure an improvement overall in mortality of 1%. The existing trials on this subject have a few hundred patients in each group; not enough to measure even the 4% change in mortality demanded by a woman who would trade a 10% risk of death to avoid mutilation. Yet despite the small numbers the shift in practice from mastectomy to lumpectomy is claimed to be based upon the evidence of clinical trials, which is certainly insufficient in itself to justify such a change.

It has become very fashionable to add quality of life measurement to trials. In the case of breast cancer such studies show very little difference in quality of life, according to whether a more or less mutilating operation was performed. However, if quality of life measures move in a different direction to the major benefit, one must decide how to balance the two. To do this one must examine the trade-offs people are prepared to make between one outcome and another. So, quality of life measures which are not converted to specific trade-offs are of very limited value in clinical decision making.

One last point on the construction of trials is a strange anomaly that has arisen in statistical thought. It is now common to set at a much greater level the chance of accepting on the basis of the trial evidence the hypothesis that a treatment is better than the alternative, even when it is not actually so (a false-negative result) than the chance of getting a false-positive result, where the hypothesis is rejected on the trial data, again incorrectly. This means that trialists in effect do more to avoid a false-positive result than a false-negative result. An analysis looking at all the trials for two years in the three big weekly medical journals where the authors specified the chance of getting a false-negative trial result[9] found that in virtually every case, the chance of getting a false-positive result was set at 5% (the traditional *P* value) while the chance of a false-negative result was 20% or more. It is totally and utterly illogical to set these values differently if delta is correct. In other words, once the magnitude of treatment effect is sufficient to offset the differential costs of treatment, there is no further premium on positive or negative false results.

Thoughts on interpretation

A revolution in the interpretation of clinical trials is imminent. Clinical trials do not exist in a data and belief vacuum as sometimes believed. In fact probabilistic information cannot be derived from conventional statistics. If a trial has shown a halving of the risk of death with one of the treatments, and the *P* value was exactly 0.05, the author previously thought that this meant that we could be 50% certain that the intervention in question reduces the mortality by half.

To give another example, imagine two treatments, A and B, for blood pressure control. Say we thought that B might drop blood pressure by 10 mm Hg more than A and the measured mean blood pressure with B was then measured as exactly 10 mm Hg lower than with treatment A in a trial. Again, the *P* value was 0.05. Now, most non-statisticians would tell you the probability that B is better than A by 10 mm Hg or more is 50%; the probability that B is better than A is 97.5% (two tailed); the probability that A is actually better than B is only 2.5%. However, this is only true under one rather extraordinary condition – namely, that one starts from equipoise, with no idea about the possible magnitude of the results, believing that a result of no difference was as likely as a doubling or halving or quartering of the mortality rate or whatever. That is implausible; one never starts a study with a prior belief that all outcomes are equally likely. The more the result varies from our point of greatest likelihood – equipoise in many trials – the less likely it is to happen. What we start out with is a prior set of beliefs. This is what statisticians refer to as the 'prior' and without the 'prior' it is impossible to calculate the probability that the treatment has an effect of given size or the most probable size of effect. Small trials impress us less than equal quality large trials with the same level of statistical significance; their confidence limits are wider and they therefore have less influence on our 'prior' distribution of beliefs. The narrower the confidence limits of the data relative to our 'prior', the more they pull belief across towards the data mean. So if we start with a fairly sceptical prior and get a bizarre result (i.e. showing much greater than expected reduction in risk) we are not strongly influenced. The results of hormone therapy to stop recurrent miscarriage were good examples, showing ten times reduction in risk. We did not all convert to this medicine because our 'prior' was relatively tight. That is why a small trial, even if it has a statistically significant result, has less legitimate claim on our belief than a large trial of the same quality showing similar results. The statistical technique for combining a prior belief curve with the data is called Bayesian analysis.

Conclusion

This chapter began with reference to trials of homeopathy, and purchasers are quite right not to include homeopathy on a list of effective treatments. People have a very sceptical prior set of beliefs ('prior') and those few trials in homeopathy are not nearly enough to move them across into sufficient certainty to contract for their use. On the other hand, purchasers should contract for blood thinning medicine in heart attack because the precision of the data must overcome all but the most extreme 'prior'. Lastly, purchasers should leave choice of breast cancer surgery to patient and physician and should be prepared to buy into further trials of surgical therapies for this disease. However, only patients whose value system places them in absolute equipoise should enter the study.

Learning points

- Resources should be focused on care supported by evidence.

- All involved in health care should understand the principles of evidence-based care.

- Where possible, research should be supported.

- Good decisions on priorities can only be based on good science, well digested.

References

1   Kleijner J, Knipschild P and Ter Riet G (1991) Clinical trials of homeopathy. *British Medical Journal.* **302**: 316–23.

2   Silverman W A and Chalmers I (1992) *Controlled clinical trials.* **13**: 100–5.

3   Sacks H, Chalmers T C and Smith H (1982) Randomized versus historical controls for clinical trials. *The American Journal of Medicine.* **72**: 233–40.

4   Lilford R J (1991) Medical education and research after the Health Service Reforms. *Journal of Management in Medicine.* **5(1)**: 49–53.

5   Lilford R J (1992) The substantive ethics of clinical trials. In Chervanak and McCullough (eds) *Clinical Obstetrics and Gynaecology,* pp. 827–45. Lippincott.

6   Cochrane A L (1972) Efficiency and Effectiveness: Random Reflections on the Health Service. Nuffield Provincial Hospitals Trust, London.

7   Enkin M, Keirse Marc J N C and Chalmers I (1989) A Guide to Effective Care in Pregnancy and Childbirth. Oxford University Press, Oxford.

8   Lilford R J and Thornton J (1992) Decision logic in medical practice. *Journal of The Royal College of Physicians.* **26(4)**: 1–20.

9   Lilford R J and Johnson N (1992) The alpha and beta errors in randomised trials (correspondance section). *The New England Journal of Medicine.* **322(11)**: 780–1.

2

Use of diagnostic imaging resources

Graham Whitehouse

Introduction

Diagnostic imaging nowadays demonstrates the presence and extent of disease with a high degree of accuracy. Modern imaging techniques are generally also faster, safer and produce less discomfort to the patient than methods that they have replaced, such as exploratory surgery and earlier imaging procedures. Inevitably, imaging equipment is becoming more complex and more expensive. In recent years we have seen increasing sophistication in ultrasound, radionuclide imaging, computed tomography (CT) and the development of magnetic resonance imaging (MRI). Film technology has also improved while developments in digital radiography have brought us to the brink of the filmless x-ray department. Radiographic contrast media have become safer and more versatile in the last two decades. In the field of interventional radiology, diagnostic methods have been extended into therapeutic procedures. Several issues arising around these technical developments, some of which are caused by increasing demands on imaging resources, will be considered in this chapter.

Communication with clinical users

This is essential in promoting the most effective use of imaging resources. In any hospital, the x-ray department should be 'open house' for clinicians of all specialties and grades. One of the most important functions of the x-ray department is the clinicoradiological meeting, which provides an interface between clinicians and radiologists and gives a forum for reviewing images and defining diagnostic strategies. It is important that radiologists educate their clinical colleagues in the appropriate use of imaging modalities, the strengths and limitations of the various modalities, the hazards of ionizing radiation and the importance of providing the radiologist with clinical details.

Education in diagnostic imaging should begin at undergraduate level. The new medical undergraduate syllabus will offer a different perception of learning and teaching. It is based on a closer integration between specialties, allows some choice of subject and depends on self-motivation. Imaging should play an important part in this new climate of medical education, where we are trying to stimulate and not stultify our students.

Diagnostic pathways defined by audited guidelines

The appropriate diagnostic pathway for various clinical situations should be defined by audited guidelines wherever possible.

One of the most important recent developments in the NHS is the emphasis given to audit. Within the x-ray department, audit should be on several levels: evaluating not only the effectiveness, safety and cost of investigations, but also the efficiency of the department and its lines of communication with the rest of the hospital and the primary care sector. Its remit should include patient throughput, patient comfort, the process of patient referral and the transmitting of diagnostic information to the referring clinician. Determining the best application of radiological resources requires coordination with clinical colleagues.

At least 20% of radiological examinations carried out in the UK are clinically unhelpful[1], in the sense that there is an extremely low probability of obtaining information which would be useful in patient management. This figure dates from the late 1980s. The situation is now compounded by the wider range of investigations available.

General practitioner referrals may constitute up to 50% of the work-load of x-ray departments in general hospitals. As within the hospital, lines of communication have to be established with GPs to ensure that an efficient and effective service is given to their patients. Early studies reviewing the effects of open-access x-ray facilities for GPs, such as the one published by Wright *et al.* in 1979[2], found that GP referrals produced fewer repeat and follow-up requests, fewer multiple requests and a greater proportion of abnormal reports than referrals from outpatient clinics. Referrals from GPs were usually preceded by appropriate clinical examinations. A recent audit of GP use of hospital x-ray services[3] showed that, if open radiological access had not been available, 78% of the patients would have been referred to specialist clinics. The effect of a normal initial radiological examination was that only 12% would require referral to a specialist department. Radiological access for GPs therefore has a tremendous impact on hospital services.

A multi-centre audit, undertaken by the Royal College of Radiologists in the late 1980s[4], found that referral rates for all x-ray examinations in hospitals varied considerably between firms in the same clinical specialty by a factor of eight for inpatients and by a factor of 13 for outpatients. These disparities indicate that a considerable number of radiological investigations are likely to be inappropriate, supporting the earlier suggestion that at least one-fifth of x-ray examinations may be clinically unhelpful.

In 1990, The Royal College of Radiologists published guidelines for the effective use of the radiological examinations used most frequently. The second edition became available in 1993[5]. These guidelines have been distributed widely among hospital doctors and GPs. After the first edition was made available, the College assessed the influence of the guidelines on radiological referrals from GPs, and found that the referral rate had fallen from 88.4 per 1000 to 77.2 per 1000.

The commonest reasons for referral were for examinations of the chest, spine and limbs. Referral rates for these parts fell by 9.4%, 17.57% and 13.5% respectively. The sharp decline in requests for spinal radiology reflects the strong emphasis in the guidelines concerning the limited use of spinal x-rays in clinical management. Referrals for skull x-rays fell by 30%, indicating the realization that skull radiography has a very limited role in the assessment of patients with headaches, epilepsy and strokes.

The College has also assessed the influence of the guidelines in hospital practice[6]. Inpatient referrals were reduced by 7.7% and outpatients by 9%, falling well short of the estimated 20% level of inappropriate radiological investigations. Nevertheless, within the 300 000 inpatients and over a million outpatients in this study, this decline in referrals resulted in a potential saving of £180 000. The main reason for the disappointing outcome was that the adoption of the guidelines was voluntary. There was no pressure from purchasers or providers, and peer review was arbitrary. The problem of how to ensure compliance with an agreed standard of practice remains.

One element of unnecessary radiology is the duplication of investigations following the referral from primary care to a secondary centre, or from secondary to tertiary referral centres. This is largely due to ineffective communication or radiographs sometimes being mislaid or lost. An example of unnecessary usage is the tendency in some neurological centres to repeat routinely CT scans of satisfactory quality from referring general hospitals.

Cost-effectiveness and priorities for use

Scarce imaging resources have to be used in the most cost-effective manner and priorities have to be established for their use.

Magnetic resonance imaging is an expensive and limited resource, despite a significant increase in the installation of machines over the last two years. It is now the method of choice for diagnosing several common conditions. For instance, the excellent soft-tissue contrast and clarity of detail are qualities that are particularly helpful in evaluating soft-tissue injuries by MRI. Meniscal and ligamentous injuries in the knee are diagnosed with an accuracy of 95–97%. Importantly, MRI is a non-invasive method. The only technique that can diagnose internal derangements of the knee with comparable accuracy is arthroscopy, which requires general anaesthesia as well as having inherent hazards and limitations. The safety and accuracy of MRI means that it should be performed as an initial screening test in all patients with suspected internal derangements of the knee. Arthroscopy is not appropriate in those with negative MRI scans. If there is a remediable lesion, then the site of injury is accurately delineated for the arthroscopist. There are also cost implications. Although MRI is an expensive test, arthroscopy is also costly. In the Nuffield Orthopaedic Hospital in Oxford, the cost of arthroscopy has been calculated as £600 while an MRI scan costs £185[7].

The other prime uses of MRI are the investigation of the brain and spine. There have been some audit exercises looking at the usage of MRI in these areas. A study from Cambridge[8] showed that performing an MRI scan altered the clinician's leading diagnosis in 21% of cases and the clinician became more confident about his prime diagnosis in 54% of cases. The MRI scan resulted in a change of management in two-thirds of cases while, overall, MRI made important contributions to management in almost three-quarters of patients. Another study from the same centre[9] showed that MRI could replace two or three other investigations, giving more information for the same cost.

Another example of the cost-effectiveness of MRI is illustrated in the diagnosis of acoustic neuroma[10]. Although these are rare tumours, screening for them generates a large work-load in Ear, Nose and Throat (ENT) departments. Various routine tests have only a 70% accuracy, while MRI is 100% accurate in diagnosing acoustic neuroma. The cost of an audiovestibular protocol is only £3.50 less than the cost of an MRI scan per patient.

Given that MRI is a limited but valuable resource, it is important to maximize its use. Aggregating MRI scans of the same body area within the same session improves throughput by avoiding the need to change coils and scanning protocols as would happen with a mix of cases. Preplanned protocols – especially for commonly scanned regions such as the brain, knee and spine – are aimed at decreasing scanning times and improving throughput further. A recent study showed that preplanning could increase throughput by 80–125% for commonly scanned regions, resulting in 90% of a variety of clinical problems being successfully solved[11].

Interventional radiology, which is the extension of diagnostic imaging methods into therapeutic and biopsy techniques, has expanded considerably over the last 20 years. The commonest therapeutic method is percutaneous transluminal angioplasty (PTA), which is used to treat narrowed and blocked arteries, especially in the lower limbs. Case selection is important, requiring discussion between radiologists and vascular surgeons as to whether open surgery or PTA is the appropriate method of treatment in individual cases. Patients undergoing PTA usually stay in hospital overnight, but are sometimes treated as day cases. A longer hospital bed occupancy, a large number of staff and the need for general anaesthesia all contribute to the costs of a surgical procedure. A comparison of the costs of vascular surgery and PTA in lower limb ischaemic disease showed that PTA by a radiologist costs £300 compared with £1500 for a surgical operation[12]. However, introducing PTA into vascular practice causes patients to be investigated earlier in the progress of their disease and enables more patients to be treated effectively with greater cost-efficiency, but does not reduce the overall cost of investigation and treatment of ischaemic disease in the lower limb[13].

Delays in treatment negate the efficiency of imaging service

An efficient, fast diagnostic imaging service is undermined if there is a long delay before subsequent outpatient attendance and inpatient admission.

This is a pertinent issue in view of the current interest in league tables for hospital attendances and admissions. It is particularly important when dealing with what might be cancer. Rapid diagnosis clinics provide fast-track imaging and tissue diagnosis, together with subsequent treatment, for certain presenting symptoms – for instance, breast lumps, haematuria and the passage of blood *per rectum*.

Non-malignant conditions can also deteriorate rapidly. An isolated narrowing of a lower limb artery represents an ideal situation for treatment by PTA. If the narrowing develops into a long segment of blocked artery, as it is likely to do in time, then PTA will become considerably more difficult or impossible. Approximately one in five patients with an angiographically confirmed narrowing in the femoropopliteal artery progress to total arterial blockage within six weeks[14]. There is therefore a need to expedite decision making and treatment as soon as possible after the diagnosis of an abnormality which is treated by PTA.

Pre-existing expertise and facilities

Screening tests including imaging are best performed where the facilities and expertise already exists.

This is already well shown in the national breast screening programme. As a general principle, training and quality assurance are best organized in centres of excellence. Screening in any form especially requires a scrupulous technique as sub-clinical abnormalities are being sought. The expertise in a breast screening unit should not only be used for the assessment of cases referred from basic screening, but also for the evaluation of patients with symptoms because the specialist mammographic resources, ultrasound, biopsy and cytopathological techniques are on site. Nowadays there is little justification for isolated mammographic units dealing only with cases where symptoms are present.

There has been some recent interest in screening for abdominal aortic aneurysms by ultrasound in general practice. Bearing in mind the high cost of appropriate ultrasound equipment and the need for trained personnel to perform the scans, it is preferable to use the established resources which will exist within most hospital imaging departments for this purpose.

Technological advance is complementary

The latest technological advance does not usually supplant other 'high-tech' modalities but tends to be complementary to them.

This is a vast subject which can only be considered briefly. Looking back over the development of ultrasound, CT and more recently MRI, each method clearly has its own diagnostic niche. In the case of MRI, some situations which are optimally shown by this technique have already been described above. Magnetic resonance imaging has certainly not supplanted CT, which at present gives better detail in, for instance, the lungs, abdomen and bone. Magnetic resonance imaging, CT and ultrasound would all be capable of diagnosing accurately some conditions, for instance gallbladder disease. However, ultrasound gives a quick and usually very precise delineation of the gallbladder, with no hazards or contraindications. All three modalities are capable of diagnosing accurately liver metastases. Computed tomography and MRI are slightly more accurate than ultrasound, but if metastases are shown on an initial ultrasound scan then there is usually no need to proceed to another technique.

High costs

Imaging technology has high running costs, updating costs and eventually replacement costs.

A large modern hospital will contain imaging equipment whose total cost is likely to be in the region of £6 million. The annual capital expenditure would be in the order of £400 000 and annual revenue costs would approximate to £2.7 million with staff accounting for 70% of revenue. An MRI scanner costs about £700 000–£750 000 and often requires building costs of about £300 000. A screening set or CT scanner costs £250 000–£300 000. Maintenance costs are also high: approximately £50 000 for a CT scanner and £80 000 for an MRI scanner each year. Doppler ultrasound costs £100 000–£120 000, with maintenance costs of £5000 per annum.

Costs of updating equipment are also high. For instance a high-field MRI scanner purchased in 1988 required an updating cost of over £200 000 three years later.

For smaller items, such as standard ultrasound machines which cost £20 000–£30 000, bulk purchasing on a regional or even supra-regional basis should reduce costs. Bulk purchase of consumable items, such as x-ray film and contrast media, is a well-established practice.

Implications of expansion

Expansion of clinical services has resource and staffing implications for imaging departments.

The development of specialist clinical services within a hospital, for instance vascular surgery, demands not only the availability of radiological expertise, but also high-quality angiographic equipment.

The work done by radiologists in England increased by 322% between 1968 and 1991. In the same period, the number of radiologists in NHS posts in England and Wales increased by 213%[15]. There are 0.34 radiologists per million of the population in the UK. This is well below the level in all countries in Western Europe and North America. The Royal College of Radiologists, following an audit exercise, concluded that full-time consultant radiologists should undertake an average mix of general and specialized radiology which amounts to no more than 12 500 cases per annum, without prejudicing professional studies. In England the annual work-load for radiologists is 20 000 cases, and in Wales it is 22 000 cases. The additional number of consultants required to deal with the recommended 12 500 cases per annum would be 823 in England and Wales. This figure does not allow for the fact that we are trying to eliminate the 20% of unnecessary investigations.

There is still a remorselessly increasing demand for radiology. Radiologists spend an average of 38 hours per week on clinical work, which is more than any other clinical specialty. Half of the time spent by radiologists on continuing medical education comes from annual leave, and 40% of radiologists do not take all of their annual leave; 25% of audit work is done by radiologists outside normal working hours. The pressures from insufficient radiological staffing are also reflected by the fact that the percentage of radiological work-load reported in two working days is only 60–65%. The aim should be to report all investigations in the same session as they are performed.

On average, each surgeon and each physician in a hospital needs the support of one-third of a radiologist. Unfortunately the radiological staffing requirements are rarely taken into consideration when making an appointment to a new consultant clinical post. It is now the trend for district hospitals to have physicians and surgeons based locally in specialties which have high demands on radiology departments, for instance, gastroenterology, urology and vascular surgery. Again, there is often little consideration given to the increased use of imaging resources. Skill mix, in which radiographers undertake some of the tasks previously done by radiologists, has a limited application and little effect on easing radiological staffing deficiencies.

Conclusion

Attention has been drawn to some of the key issues and problems in clinical imaging. In 1995 we celebrate the centenary of Röntgen's discovery of x-rays. The subsequent development of imaging has been one of the most extraordinary medical achievements of this century. However, there is a danger that technical developments, as well as clinical demands and expectations, are in danger of outstripping financial and manpower resources.

Learning points

- Communication with clinical users is essential in promoting the most effective use of imaging resources.

- The appropriate diagnostic pathway for various clinical situations should be defined by audited guidelines wherever possible.

- Scarce imaging resources have to be used in the most cost-effective manner and priorities have to be established for their use.

- The establishment of an efficient, fast diagnostic imaging service is negated if there is a long delay before subsequent outpatient attendance and inpatient admission.

- Screening tests including imaging are best performed where the facilities and expertise already exist.

- The latest technological advance does not usually supplant other 'high-tech' modalities but tends to be complementary to them.

- Imaging technology has high running costs, updating costs and eventually replacement costs.

- Expansion of clinical services has resource and staffing implications for imaging departments.

References

1   National Radiation Protection Board and Royal College of Radiologists (1990) Patient dose reduction in diagnostic radiology. *Documents of the NRPB.* **1(3)**.

2   Wright H J, Swinburne K and Inch J (1979) The general practitioner's use of diagnostic radiology. *Journal of the Royal Society of Medicine.* **72**: 88–94.

3   Barton E, Gallagher S, Flower C D R *et al.* (1987) Influence on patient management of general practitioner direct access to radiological services. *British Journal of Radiology.* **60**: 893–6.

4   Royal College of Radiologists Working Party (1991) A multicentre audit of hospital referral for radiological investigation in England and Wales. *British Medical Journal.* **303**: 809–12.

5   Royal College of Radiologists (1993) *Making the Best Use of a Department of Clinical Radiology,* 2nd edn. RCR, London.

6   Royal College of Radiologists Working Party (1992) Influence of the Royal College of Radiologists' guidelines on hospital practice: a multicentre study. *British Medical Journal.* **304**: 740–3.

7   Spiers A S D, Meagher T, Oslere S J *et al.* (1993) Can MRI of the knee affect arthroscopic practice? *Journal of Bone and Joint Surgery.* **75B**: 49–52.

8   Dizon A K, Southern J P, Teale A *et al*. (1991) Magnetic resonance imaging of the head and spine: effective for the clinician or the patient? *British Medical Journal*. **302**: 78–82.

9   Southern P, Teale A, Dixon A *et al*. (1991) An audit of the clinical use of magnetic resonance imaging of the head and spine. *Health Trends*. **23**: 75–9.

10 Robson A K, Leighton S E J, Anslow P *et al*. (1993) MRI as a single screening procedure for acoustic neuroma: a cost effective protocol. *Journal of the Royal Society of Medicine*. **86**: 455–7.

11 Moore N R and Golding S J (1992) Increasing patient throughput in magnetic resonance imaging: a practical approach. *British Journal of Radiology*. **65**: 70–5.

12 Jeans W D, Danton R M, Baird R N *et al*. (1986). A comparison of the costs of vascular surgery and balloon dilatation in lower limb ischaemic disease. *British Journal of Radiology*. **59**: 452–6.

13 Jeans W D, Danton R M, Baird R N *et al*. (1986) The effects of introducing balloon dilatation into vascular surgical practice. *British Journal of Radiology*. **59**: 457–9.

14 Gallino A, Mahler F and Probst P (1983) Progression to total occlusion of lower limb artery stenoses selected for percutaneous transluminal angioplasty. *Lancet*. **i**: 8314–5.

15 Royal College of Radiologists (1993) *Medical staffing and workload in Clinical Radiology in the United Kingdom National Health Service*. RCR, London.

3

Audit of x-ray referrals from a general practice

David Lyon

Introduction

This chapter describes an audit into the use of x-rays and ultrasound carried out in a GP practice. The practice has six doctors, two of them job-sharing and 12 500 patients. The doctors have individual lists, so that the doctor who has a patient registered with them will see that patient every time, if present in the health centre.

A GP spends a great deal of NHS money, through signing prescriptions, requesting investigations and referring people to a specialist. On becoming fundholders the partners decided that it was time to look at how this money was spent. The review covered a number of areas, starting with consultations and how the doctors communicated with the patient. This showed that sometimes what the patient wanted was an explanation, rather than a drug or an investigation or an operation. Looking at prescribing proved quite easy because prescribing details are provided by the Prescribing Pricing Authority. Investigations were more difficult to look into because of the volume.

The process and the findings

A start was made on x-rays and ultrasound, because there were a manageable number – only a few hundred per quarter. They are also the most expensive investigation ordered: items like blood tests are relatively cheap. There are, in addition, other reasons to keep x-rays to a minimum:

- to reduce waiting times
- to speed issuing of reports
- to avoid unnecessary exposure to radiation

- to reduce costs

- to reduce demands on the radiology service.

Requests for x-rays ought to be confined to those cases where the results are relevant to clinical management.

To supplement the reports from radiology departments, additional details were recorded manually, such as the patient, the investigation and the result. After three months the data were reviewed. The investigations were grouped as follows (Table 3.1):

- chest x-rays

- any view of the spinal column, from the neck down

- limbs, including hips and pelvis, and shoulders

- ultrasound

- other, including skull x-rays, enemas and barium meals.

Table 3.1   X-ray and ultrasound activity (February – April 1992), by doctor

Investigation	Doctor						Total
	A	B	C	D	E	F	
Chest x-ray	8	25	20	15	9	4	81
Spines	21	4	9	8	7	3	52
Limbs	15	11	12	8	12	9	67
Ultrasound	1	1	2	0	0	0	4
Other	4	9	4	2	0	4	23
All	49	50	47	33	28	20	227

Analysis threw up a number of issues. For example, compared with anybody else, one doctor requested more spinal views. It was discovered that spinal views are virtually useless to help manage patients, and so this highlighted a learning need for that particular doctor. The number of chest and limb x-rays were also closely examined. The latter were mainly used to look for fractures, but this was often many days or even weeks after the event that caused the injury and from 67 requests only one fracture was found. Though a number of cases of arthritis in joints and spine were found, they were not counted as positive results, as arthritis is an expected finding. (Of the 227 investigations, there were 22 positive results – only 10%, of which ten were chest x-rays, mainly infections, with a couple of cancers.)

Learning the lessons

These various findings were discussed by the doctors together, who agreed some recommendations and a target as follow.

1 *Have confidence in clinical acumen.* The first audit cycle had displayed the doctors' clinical acumen, and prompted them that they ought to have confidence in their own abilities. In fact, there was no abnormality on this cycle that was not predicted by the doctor in advance.

2 *Be specific about the part to be x-rayed.* Sometimes a doctor ordered two views, for the same injury, for instance one view of the neck and one view of the shoulder, or an ankle and foot together. It was agreed that the doctors ought to be more specific about the part to be x-rayed, so that it was cheaper and used less radiation.

3 *Spinal views should be reduced.* They rarely help with the management of back pain.

4 *With chest infection, treat and review to consider x-ray.* It emerged that frequently the report came back, confirming the chest infection and advising treatment and a repeat of the view in two weeks time, so that the patient was exposed to radiation twice for the same condition. This was unsatisfactory. In future it was agreed that, if the diagnosis was made, the patient should be treated and asked to come back in a fortnight. At that point a decision would be made on whether an x-ray was necessary.

5 *Limb x-rays could be reduced.* It was highly unusual for a genuine fracture to be brought to general practice some weeks after it occurred. A lot of the time it did not really matter because by then nothing much could be done. It was agreed that here too there was scope for a reduction in requests.

6 *Reassurance is not a valid reason for blasting people with radiation.* It was evident that the use of investigations for reassurance was an issue that needed to be recognized explicitly. Doctors feel under pressure a lot of the time to do something when face to face with patients. A lot of the time investigations are initiated to reassure the doctor or the patient or both. Often, the patients did not want an x-ray but a good explanation.

7 *Royal College Guidelines should be followed.* It was discovered during the exercise that none of the GPs had read the guidelines of the Royal College of Radiologists on the use of x-ray, and so a copy was acquired for each of the partners. A lot of the points that they had discovered for themselves were set out in the guidelines, and that was very reassuring[1].

The effect on practice

Looking at the results of the review, a *target* reduction of 10% in requests seemed desirable and feasible. There was in fact a drop at one stage of nearly a half. The numbers crept up after several months and a further review was made a year on. This time, data collection was easier because the practice was fundholding, and the hospital trust did the accounting. Table 3.2 shows the shifts identified as a result of the second audit a year on. The total number fell by 28%, far exceeding the target

Table 3.2   Changes in numbers of investigations identified at second audit

	February – April 1992	January – March 1993	Total
Chest x-rays	81	44	–37
Spines	52	15	–37
Limb	67	51	–16
Ultrasound	4	22	+18
Other	23	30	+7
All	227	162	–65

of 10%. The proportion of positive results stayed the same at 10%, the first year there were 22 positive and the second 16.

The number of chest x-rays almost halved. In the first audit there were 13 with positive findings, ten of which were infections, two were cancers and one a pulmonary embolism. In the second there were only four chest x-rays with positive findings, two of which are infections, one was a cancer and one asbestosis.

Spinal views fell even further, by more than 70%. This is an impressive response to the recommendations. However, requests for views of various bits of limbs remained 30% of the total, even though this was a reduction in numbers. This time two fractures were discovered, as against only one in the first round.

Ultrasound increased. It became open access in that year and because this high technology equipment was available, it was used. This group now boasts the highest proportion of positive results 33%, three gallstones, one kidney stone, one viable pregnancy, one non-viable pregnancy, and one polycystic ovary. Last time there were two kidney stones found.

The 'other' group was disappointing. There was an increase in numbers without much return. Much of the rise was because of mammograms. A mobile service was due to start in April but some could not wait because they were too worried. There were six extra mammograms and all were normal. There was one positive result, a plain abdomen demonstrating a perforation! There were five intravenous peritograms (IVPs), as previously, and again all were negative. The four barium studies were normal as opposed to two before. Ten were investigations of the kidney, ureter and bladder, most of which were combined with ultrasound, whereas there were only two previously. However, skull and sinus x-rays were reduced, with only one ordered compared with eight before.

There are a number of points of interest here. The chest x-rays flattened out. Only one doctor ordered many, and even his numbers fell. One of the doctors who job-shares did not order any at all. Spinal views also dropped dramatically and evened out. One doctor ordered 21 in the first quarter and only two the following year, a remarkable reduction. Limbs also were more even. In fact, the pick-up rate of fractures in that second cycle was higher – there were two! The ultrasound actually came out quite well for positive results, because things like kidney stones and gallstones were detected that had not been found previously. But there was some concern about gynaecological ultrasounds, looking for things like ovarian cysts or pelvic inflammatory disease. Most of the time a rather vague report came back which did little to help clinical management. Following discussions with the gynaecologists, there has been a slight reduction since then. The 'other' group changed slightly in that procedures like IVPs had fallen, replaced by ultrasound.

An increase in the use of ultrasound demonstrated an ability to respond to changes in the availability of new technology and expertise, and a willingness to use less invasive but potentially more expensive methods to provide the best for patients. Nevertheless, one must be sure that this resource is being used appropriately, and it was agreed that protocols should be drawn up with the hospital consultants.

The number of limb x-rays remained disappointingly high, but here the reassurance factor played a part. At least, the proportion of positive results increased. The biggest disappointment was the rise in numbers of the 'other' group. It was agreed that careful assessment would be needed before ordering IVPs, barium studies and mammograms.

Conclusion

There has been an impressive reduction in total numbers and the practice can be especially proud of the reduction in chest x-rays and spinal views. The changes have had little effect on the GP fund since the practice had a block contract with the hospital, but undoubtedly there has been a release of resources overall. As for patients, a lot fewer are having their time wasted or being frustrated going to a department for five hours in an afternoon. In addition, there is less uncertainty for them because the doctors' clinical acumen improved so that they are able to deliver a clearer message about the patient's condition and about how things are going to progress. That is something that patients value a great deal. They are also subjected less to unnecessary radiation. Overall, the exercise had offered considerable benefits all round.

Learning points

- Systematic audit can improve performance and release resources.

- With changing technology frequent reviews will be necessary.

Reference

1   The Royal College of Radiologists (1993) *Making the best use of a Department of Clinical Radiology: Guidelines for Doctors.* 2nd Edition. London.

4

Pathology services

Vincent Marks

Introduction

This chapter explores the role of clinical pathology services. Clinical pathology is formed from the disciplines of clinical biochemistry, haematology, microbiology and histopathology.

It is an understanding of the nature and causes of disease that distinguishes modern medicine from alternative or complementary medicine. Great advances in treatment have come about because there has been an increased understanding of the nature of disease[1]. Clinical pathology is a discipline involved both with the treatment of individual patients and also the search to increase understanding of disease[2]. Patients are the material upon which clinical pathology bases its understanding of disease processes and since diagnosis is at the root of treatment, if the diagnosis is not right, treatment is unlikely to be successful. Most minor illnesses are self-limiting so whatever is done the patients will get better and this explains why alternatives to licensed medicines are successful – because, regardless of what is done, the patients get better. More serious illnesses require an understanding of their pathology, and that is where clinical pathology becomes essential for diagnosis and treatment.

Growth of laboratory services

Results of several surveys have shown that the number of laboratory tests performed has been rising exponentially since clinical pathology was established as a discipline in 1922. For example, at that time it took several hours to do a single assay for blood glucose in diabetic patients. Now it can be done within a minute either in the laboratory or at the bed-side, at comparatively little cost.

The geometric increase in the number of tests is partly because technology has made it possible to do far larger numbers for remarkably little extra total cost[3,4] and partly because of the larger variety of tests due to greater knowledge.

Is NHS clinical pathology too costly?

International comparisons

How competent are British hospitals compared with other developed countries? A study published a few years ago compared three teaching hospitals in Britain, two from Scotland and one from central London, with three Canadian teaching hospitals. It showed that for most analyses between 10 and 20 times as many tests per patient per week were carried out in Canada as in Britain. There is little evidence that the Canadians were providing better care. On these criteria, British laboratories were many times more efficient than their Canadian counterparts.

Clinical pathology can be considered inefficient because modern management techniques have not kept up with some of the developments that have occurred in the subject and pathologists themselves are innately conservative. At a conference in 1953 looking at the scientific basis of medicine Lord Adrian, a Nobel Laureate in Medicine, argued that:

> 'the pathologists and biochemists will find their time is taken up with measurement of uncertain values in which they are not especially interested, and the final result may well be that the work is turned over to specially trained experts who are the last people to give a dispassionate judgement on the value of what they are doing. The point surely is that if such data are to be valuable there must be the right people to consider them.'

This philosophy conflicts with the view that laboratory testing is simply about producing analytical data[5]. Apart from the enormous increase in the number of laboratory data produced, it is as possible to misinterpret the result and treat the patient wrongly, as to get it right. Clinical pathology is the specialty that is concerned with interpretation of laboratory data.

Clinical pathology practised throughout the whole of the developed world is very similar. Interestingly, the British have been able to produce first-class clinical pathology up until now at up to one-fifth of the cost of some other countries.

A study carried out in Australia compared the laboratory costs incurred in a large teaching hospital by each of its 18 consultants in general medicine[6]. The two who asked for the most specimens per patients per day incurred ten times the expense of those who asked for the least: the average cost per patient per day was somewhere near the middle. It is very easy to compare this type of information, but it lacks significance with the incomplete information available.

Are clinical pathologists necessary?

In determining whether laboratory tests are being abused an assumption is made that those asking for the very most are overusing it. It is the responsibility of clinical pathologists to evaluate the clinical value of the procedures that they carry out, as it is likely that clinicians are ignorant of the value and limitations of the various test procedures they request. Unless they have researched the subject thoroughly, it constitutes no more than a small part of their professional knowledge[7].

It is the job of the clinical pathologist to evaluate the value to individual patients of the procedures carried out in their laboratories and this involves the production of data and the outcome of using them. This may be called research or it may be medical audit; it has always, however, been the stock-in-trade of the clinical pathologist.

Sir John Nabarro, one of the most distinguished physicians in the UK, said in 1967 that ideally every report (and he referred to the pathology report) should be scrutinized by a medically qualified person who had before him the patient's provisional diagnosis and the results of previous tests.

The wisdom of his words was recently highlighted by the tragic events that took place in Grantham Hospital, where there was no consultant chemical pathologist to scrutinize the results and discuss them with the clinicians looking after the patients who were being poisoned by a malevolent nurse. The clinicians were doing their job – caring for the patients – extremely well; indeed saving them from almost certain death by their expertise in treatment. They could not also be expected to be experts in chemical pathology, nor to see all of the results coming out of the laboratory which would have pointed to a surprisingly high incidence of unexplained hyperkalaemia in the paediatric wards. One might also have expected a chemical pathologist to take a different attitude to unexplained hypo-glycaemia occurring in an inpatient, compared with that adopted by a clinician whose primary job was to prevent it from killing the patient.

Medicine has come on a long way since the day when one man could encompass every bit of medical knowledge, even one of Osler's stature. In my view, he would be lucky if he could write a chapter on it today. Therefore, the job of the pathologist is to determine the significance of the analytical data compared with the role of the technician in generating them.

Automation and mass-produced results

There have been changes in how laboratory work is done – in the time taken, in the numbers done and the economies of scale – in the development of today's big laboratories. Analytical quality has improved since about 1965 and there is now a national quality control scheme, which has improved quality enormously. A generation ago it would be quite common for there to be a two-to-threefold difference (200–300%) between analytical results from different laboratories. Now we expect to get results within 10–15% of each other. This provides better opportunities for experts to interpret data[8].

There is a more comprehensive and wider menu and, whereas once upon a time there would be 10 or 20 routine tests, there are now at least 500 tests for which clinical indications exist. In fact there are about 500–600 tests in clinical chemistry alone, with a similar number in haematology and bacteriology. Consequently it is no longer possible for any single laboratory anywhere in the world to provide a really comprehensive menu. One way to reduce costs is to reduce quality. By doing so, quality of interpretation is lost and the clinician buys analytical data of uncertain value. If doctors who asked for tests knew exactly how to interpret them, pathologists would not be needed, but in practice, this does not happen. Some people believe that all a laboratory has to do is to ensure that it provides analytically accurate results, and that whether they are appropriate and interpretable is the responsibility of the purchaser. In this situation the purchaser – the hospital in which the specimens originate, or general practitioner from whom they came – is the 'care-provider'. In future, clinicians who have contracted for an analysis-only service may need to renegotiate the contract for advice from those who have specialized in interpretation[1]. The true comparison of clinical pathology is with real specialties, like cardiology or neurosurgery, where there is a concerted, integrated reaction to ensure that each patient gets the right investigation and treatment and not, as some would have it, with the laundry and other support services.

Location of pathology services in the UK

Laboratory services

There are several characteristic features of provision of the *in vitro* diagnostics in the current health care service in Britain. For example, the country has a highly concentrated central laboratory network (there are only about 600 in the UK) providing a consultative service; and (very important) all pathologists exercise, or used to exercise, a gatekeeper role, that is, a budget is adhered to and the laboratory advises on what are the most appropriate investigations, both in general and in individual patients. Selling and marketing assays is completely different exercise from consultative clinical pathology[9].

The geographic organization of laboratories was, and still is, dictated by the need to provide emergency cover. Emergency services were required, on site, in every major hospital that undertook any surgery, intensive care or any accident and emergency work, because there are life-saving procedures that were required occasionally throughout the 24-hour period[10].

Near-patient testing

Since about 1980, advances in technology have enabled clinical biochemistry to be carried out much nearer to the patient, particularly for many of the more simple procedures that are required on a daily basis[11–15]. The clinical benefits of near-patient testing are that:

- it saves patients' and doctors' time

- there is an immediacy; the results are available there and then

- it is part of the physical examination; the patient can be dealt with in doctor's surgery (office) and this facilitates clinical interpretation.

Table 4.1   Hierarchy of clinical testing

1	In patient's home
2	In pharmacy
3	In doctor's office
4	Satellite laboratory in special unit within hospital (e.g. A & E, Intensive Care)
5	Central laboratory of hospital
6	Regional laboratory (or Consortium)
7	National laboratory (or Supraregional Assay and Advisory Service)

At home

Self-testing has become possible, as with pregnancy tests and blood glucose tests for diabetics. Patients get a result which is accurate enough for them to regulate their treatment at home by the use of a small piece of apparatus and a reagent-impregnated stick. It is easy to teach them how to do this.

Walk-in laboratories

Walk-in laboratories[14] are a developing trend in the USA and may occur here in the UK. Patients are persuaded to have tests and the results written on a form without interpretation. They are then told to see their doctor or go to the hospital to find out what they mean. In my view, this trend should be discouraged.

In pharmacy

I undertook a survey of pharmacy testing in which 60 questionnaires were sent to shops; 28 were returned. In 25 cases they were doing urine tests; only three, at that time, were doing blood tests.

In some cases the person performing the test also reported it (Table 4.2). Manufacturers trained the staff to use their equipment. Sometimes the pharmacist or the manager trained the staff. Pharmacists are seeing this provision as a

Table 4.2   Results of survey of pharmacy testing

	Conducting the test	Reporting the test
Pharmacist alone	11	22
Pharmacist/technician	7	1
Pharmacist/dispenser	3	–
State registered nurse	1	1
Sales staff	3	1

commercial opportunity[15,16]. A sensible role more specific to their special expertise would be the measurement of drugs in blood to ensure that the patient is getting the right amount. There are many medicines that are ineffective or harmful unless they are administered properly in the right dose. The right dose depends on the individual and means getting the blood level right; and that is where pharmacists can make a valuable contribution to patient care[17].

In the doctor's office

Comprehensive laboratories are no longer needed in every district general hospital or every acute hospital. Pathology services do need reorganization. In-office tests become possible when the economics are worked out properly but they do require space, equipment, adequate training, equipment maintenance, good quality assurance and specialist advice[18]. Near-patient testing does, therefore, need to be linked, in some way or another, to a laboratory where there are professionals who are competent to help. Whether they should be run by that laboratory or pay for the services they receive are matters that are going to have to be worked out between individuals.

Clinical pathologists' concerns about near-patient testing are:

- results may not be recorded accurately; this is essential both for the proper treatment of patients and also, should the matter ever assume medico-legal significance, for the doctors themselves

- the analytical work may not be of a very high quality

- interpretation of the results is critical and may require specialist knowledge

- the safety of patients and operatives with particular reference to human immunodeficiency virus (HIV) or hepatitis B

- the cost to patients and NHS; near-patient tests are likely to be more expensive per unit cost than when they are done in a central laboratory

- loss of income to the laboratory.

Coordinated clinical pathology service

I believe that the optimum sized laboratory is one serving a population of about 900 000 to 1 000 000 people (Figure 4.1). This could be managed independently on behalf of participating hospital trusts; it could be a trust in its own right selling services to doctors, hospitals and clinics; or it could be a joint venture between the NHS and private investors.

However, not all tests need to be centralized. Provided an efficient courier service and electronic reporting existed, each existing laboratory could be a centre of expertise for outposts. Each outpost could be a reference centre for GPs, with the facilities for near-patient testing.

It is not necessary for a clinician to order a bank of tests when a patient is admitted to hospital, to establish a profile. This concept was popular in the 1960s, but there has been a return to discretionary testing rather than profiling except in a few very well-defined situations[19].

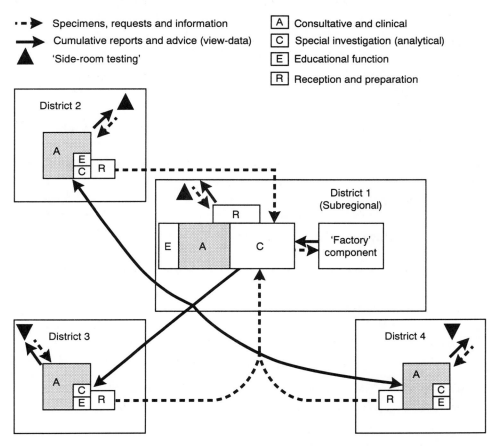

Figure 4.1   Scheme for an integrated Clinical Pathology Service for a sub-region serving appoximately 1 000 000 people through four district or general hospitals. Only the three lower tiers are shown; the supraregional or national tier is omitted. Each district laboratory would be staffed by at least two consultants – a clinician and a chemist (analytical) who would serve on the board of directors of the integrated laboratory

Learning points

- A centrally coordinated network of clinical pathology services expands the expertise available.

- An integrated service offers economies of scale.

- The service could be provided as an NHS Trust, thus not prone to the necessity of generating commercial profit.

References

1 Marks V (1972) The role of Clinical Biochemistry in community health. *Royal Society of Health Journal.* **93**: 131–4.

2 Labib M, Marks V, Smith MJ (1988) The role of a clinical investigation unit in a district general hospital. *Hospital Services Management.* 126–8.

3 Morgan DB (1985) The appropriate use of diagnostic services: ii: The case for fewer measurements of the plasma sodium concentration: costs and gains. *Health Trends.* **17**: 1–3.

4 Fleming PR, Zilva JF (1981) Work-loads in chemical pathology: too many tests? *Health Trends.* **13**: 46–9.

5 Holland WW, Whitehead TP (1974) Value of new laboratory tests in diagnosis and treatment. *Lancet.* **ii**: 391–4.

6 Grivell AR, Forgie HJ, Fraser CG, Berry MN (1982) League tables of biochemical laboratory costs: an attempt to modify requesting patterns. *Med J Aust.* **2**: 326–8.

7 Brod J (1977) The rational basis of diagnosis in internal medicine. *J Roy Coll Phycns.* **11**: 323–34.

8 Editorial (1977) Quality control of laboratories – or of pathologists. *BMJ.* **(1)** 1180.

9 Marks V (1978) Clinical biochemistry: trade or profession? (revised version of inaugural lecture). *Biologist.* **25**: 15–21.

10 Marks V (1988a) The economics of near-patient testing. In: *Laboratory Data and Patient Care,* Edited by Kerkhof PLM and van Dieijen-Visser MP; pp. 17–23.

11 Marks V (1983) Clinical Biochemistry nearer the patient. *BMJ.* **286**: 1166–7.

12 Marks V (1988b) The Clinical Laboratory: Nearer the Patient. *Adv Pathol.* **1:** 1–30.

13 Manek N, Wise R (1986) Bedside and rapid bacteriology. *BMJ.* **292**: 573–4.

14 Editorial (1987) Blood tests to go. *Medical World News.* **13**: 23.

15 Maguire TA, McElnay, JC (1990) Performance of 'bench top' cholesterol analysers. *Pharmaceutical Journal.* **May 12**: 566–8.

16 Marks (Editorial): (1990) TDM for community pharmacists? *Pharmaceutical Journal.* **(Sept)**: 357.

17 Mould G, Marks V (1988) The use of solid-phase chemistry in therapeutic drug monitoring. *Clinical Pharmacokinetics.* **14**: 65–70.

18 Marks V (1988c) Essential considerations in the provision of near-patient testing facilities. *Ann Clin Biochem.* **25**: 220–5.

19 Marks V (1980) The choice between discretionary and profile testing. In: *Centrifugal Analysers in Clinical Chemistry*; pp. 259–70; Price CP, Spencer K (eds) Praeger, Eastbourne, UK.

5

Rational prescribing in primary health care
Judy Clark

Introduction

This chapter examines some of the ways in which a systematic evaluation of practice can help release resources in the area of prescribing in primary care. Several examples from Derbyshire Family Health Services Authority (FHSA) are introduced to indicate how this might be achieved.

There is an increasing interest in GP prescribing and ways to influence prescribing trends due to the ever expanding primary care drug budget. The net ingredient cost (NIC) of all prescriptions dispensed by GPs in England during 1993 amounted to £3.159 million. This represented a 10.5% increase over the spend for 1992. This increase in prescribing costs resulted from an increase in both prescription items (4.4% increase over 1992 figures) and average NIC per item (5.5% increase over 1992 figures)[1].

This increase in prescribing costs has taken place despite several Government initiatives[2], including:

- the introduction and expansion of the Limited List

- the development of PACT data

- the introduction of target budgets (previously termed 'indicative prescribing amounts') and of fundholding drug budgets

- downward pressure on FHSAs through challenging annual increases in drug budgets and corporate contracts with Regional Health Authorities.

The problem of increasing primary care drug expenditure is compounded by issues including a lack of prescriber accountability, limited incentives for change, increasing patient demand, prescription charge exemption, extensive repeat prescribing, new technological advances, cost shifting from secondary care, price differentials across the primary/secondary care interface and the influence of the pharmaceutical industry. Furthermore, international comparisons of drug expenditure per person for the year 1990 found that Britain was 23% below the West European average which may serve as a disincentive for prescribing change in this country[3].

To try and control the increase in prescribing costs there is a greater emphasis on the need for 'rational prescribing'. This term is being used widely, appearing in literature ranging from Department of Health Circulars to drug industry promotional material. However, it is important to define what it means. A frequent misconception is that rational prescribing is just cheap prescribing. A more suitable definition is that rational prescribing is *effective, appropriate, safe and economic* prescribing[4]. A move towards rational prescribing is likely to result overall in a release of resources, though not necessarily in a decrease in costs.

Release of resources

Although rational prescribing could be used to release resources, it is important to ensure that any decision-making processes adopt a holistic approach. It is necessary to look beyond the NIC of a drug and consider any associated costs such as those relating to administration, therapeutic monitoring and side-effects, and the effects on secondary care, community care and indeed the patient. Difficulties in considering cost in this wide context include the way prescribing budgets are set on an annual basis and the existence of separate primary and secondary care budgets.

A further question that must be asked if we are going to look at potential release of resources is whether current levels of prescribing are appropriate.

Releasing financial resources through prescribing

This question of appropriate prescribing is being addressed by Prescribing Advisers within FHSAs or Health Commissions and, more recently, by the Audit Commission. It is important that this work focuses on all prescribers, targeting potential under-spenders as well as over-spenders, to maximize quality of patient care. When analysing increasing primary care prescribing levels it is important that factors such as increased primary care management, a growing elderly population and increased screening activities are taken into consideration.

The Audit Commission report *A Prescription for Improvement* identifies a number of key areas where appropriate changes in prescribing behaviour could result in significant cost savings[3]. The analytical method used by the Audit Commission was to identify 50 practices with prescribing patterns that conformed to specific quality markers. Calculations were then performed to identify potential savings which could be realized if all practices changed their prescribing patterns to conform to those of the selected practices. Overall the Audit Commission identified £425 million of savings that could be made with time. These savings were linked to specific changes in behaviour:

- reduced over-prescribing   £275 million
- less prescribing of drugs of limited clinical value   £45 million
- use of comparable but cheaper drugs   £25 million
- increased use of generic drugs   £50 million
- less prescribing of expensive format preparations   £30 million.

On the other hand, the Audit Commission identified that improved asthma pre-scribing, in line with British Thoracic Society Guidelines, would increase GP prescribing costs by £75 million, and this is not unexpected. FHSA prescribing advisers are already seeing significant increases in prescribing costs in areas of disease management that are being actively encouraged in primary care. Table 5.1 shows prescribing trends relating to some of these areas for Derbyshire FHSA.

A large proportion of the increase in prescribing costs for these therapeutic areas is to be expected due to increased screening activities, health promotion and appropriate management. This may mean that resources are saved elsewhere. For example, the increase in prescribing costs relating to hormone replacement ther-apy has positive implications for the release of future resources, especially as osteoporotic fractures cost the UK £800 million per year for hospital costs alone. Thus, when looking at appropriate levels of prescribing, consideration must be given to areas where prescribing levels should be encouraged to increase, as well as where they might be reduced.

The role for new drugs needs to be considered to ensure rational prescribing. Table 5.2 shows examples of relatively new drugs where Derbyshire FHSA has seen large prescribing increases.

Table 5.1   Derbyshire FHSA prescribing costs (for quarters ending)

Therapeutic area	October 1991 (£000)	April 1992 (£000)	October 1992 (£000)	April 1993 (£000)	October 1993 (£000)	Percentage increase (%)
Inhaled corticosteroids	610	666	752	844	958	57
Diabetic agents	261	294	364	386	423	62
Hormone replacement therapy	236	254	295	302	336	42

Table 5.2   Derbyshire FHSA prescribing costs (for quarters ending)

Therapeutic area	October 1991 (£000)	April 1992 (£000)	October 1992 (£000)	April 1993 (£000)	October 1993 (£000)	Percentage increase (%)
ACEIs	425	454	506	581	640	51
Omeprazole	120	213	312	441	588	390
SSRIs	81	122	195	250	279	244
Sumatriptan	3	22	55	76	95	3066

Although some of these increases in costs appear dramatic consideration must be given to improvements in patient care and potential release of resources in other areas. These include the better side-effect profile and reduction in risk of overdose for the new antidepressant drugs (the selective serotonin reuptake inhibitors – SSRIs), the beneficial effects of angiotensin-converting enzyme inhibitors (ACEIs) in diabetic hypertensive patients and in heart failure, the ability to control peptic ulcer disease and reflux oesophagitis in primary care with the proton pump inhibitor omeprazole and the improved quality of life and early return to work relating to use of sumatriptan in patients with migraine. It is important to recognize that there is a role for new drugs, but that they should not be used indiscriminately.

Repeat prescribing accounts for two-thirds of prescriptions and so it is vital that appropriate mechanisms are in place to ensure regular review. A recent national Audit Office report has highlighted the need to address this issue[5]. A pilot study of polypharmacy in 200 Derbyshire patients (patients taking more than one kind of medicine) found that review by a pharmacist resulted in an agreed action plan with the prescriber for prescribing changes for almost 60% of patients reviewed. Review of repeat prescribing systems is of particular concern owing to the quantities of waste drugs being returned in FHSA DUMP campaigns. Derbyshire FHSA currently collects over 1.5 tonnes per quarter of patient-returned medicines from community pharmacies across the county.

Initiatives to facilitate the necessary rationalization of prescribing include the development of prescribing guidelines and protocols. Such processes must involve appropriate representatives from both primary and secondary care. Any document produced must not be seen as prescriptive but should serve as a framework around which prescribers can develop their own prescribing protocols. Practice-based formulary development is a particularly useful educational method to facilitate rational prescribing change and has been a focus of rational prescribing activity in Derbyshire FHSA over the past three years. The production of a practice-based formulary by all the prescribers involved facilitates ownership, local sensitivity and allows for individual preferences and experiences. Fundholding and the development of incentive schemes are useful methods to encourage prescribers to address rationalization of prescribing habits. However, any such developments need to be accompanied by efforts to educate patients. For example, Trent Regional Health Authority has coordinated campaigns to educate patients about generic prescribing and a 'Help Us To Help You' initiative targeted better use of medicines and self-treatment of minor ailments.

Releasing resources in secondary care

Increased prescribing in primary care and the introduction of new drugs have the potential to release resources in secondary care. Increased patient management in primary care, shorter hospital stays and a greater emphasis on preventive work in general practice all contribute to this. Examples include primary care management of asthma, diabetes, peptic ulcer disease and increased management of palliative care in the community. New drugs can reduce the need for patients to be referred or managed by secondary care. For example, the introduction of a relatively new drug for psoriasis (calcipotriol) has been shown potentially to reduce a hospital dermatology inpatient budget for this disease area by more than £85 000[6]. However, one of the problems faced by managers of primary care budgets is that there is no flow of resources from secondary care to fund the increased costs associated with this activity in primary care. Fundholding does at least address this issue partially by enabling virement of moneys across budgets.

Releasing resources in general practice and community care

It is tempting only to look at financial factors when contemplating release of resources through rational prescribing. However, it is necessary to look further and consider the effect of prescribing decisions on the primary health care team. Some older drugs may be cheap, such as mianserin used for the management of depression, but there may be considerable associated costs, in this case relating to the need to perform regular blood monitoring. The costs to the practice of patient recall, testing procedures, interpretation of results and outcome activity may be so great that an alternative, more expensive drug may be more cost-effective. Appropriate simplification of drug regimens and a reduction in polypharmacy may reduce problems relating to drug side-effects and release precious GP time.

As practice nurses are becoming increasingly involved in management of patients with chronic diseases, prescribing decisions must take into consideration the effect on practice-nurse time. Similarly, drug therapy can have a substantial effect on resources in community care. The use of simplified regimens and less frequent dosing intervals for drugs being administered by district nurses will release resources in terms of time. Community pharmacists have an important role to play through the provision of prescribing advice, compliance aids and monitored dosage systems to facilitate this community care.

Releasing resources and the patient

It is important not to forget the patient when making prescribing decisions. The most expensive drug is one that is not taken, so issues relating to compliance and quality of life must be considered. The need for therapeutic drug monitoring, inpatient stay and outpatient consultations has an effect upon patient time. Time off work will have resource implications for business and the economy. Finally, the effect of patient management and prescribing decisions on the family unit, both in terms of social factors and finances, must also be considered.

Conclusion

Rationalization of prescribing in primary care should provide an opportunity to release resources, both financial and other. However, it is vital that this process of rationalization is based on a holistic approach and includes consideration of the effects on secondary care, the primary health care team and the patient.

> ## Learning points
>
> - Plenty of material is available to further rational prescribing and improve resource focusing.
>
> - Rational prescribing may include increased prescribing costs in selected areas.
>
> - The resource consequences of practice changes across all sectors should be considered.
>
> - Practice changes to be effective require collaboration of all those likely to be affected.

References

1   Government Statistical Service (1994) *Statistical Bulletin 1994/6*.

2   Department of Health (1989) Indicative Prescribing Budgets for General Medical Practitioners. Working Paper No. 4 Working for Patients, HMSO, London.

3   Audit Commission (1994) *A Prescription for Improvement*. HMSO, London.

4   Parish P A (1974) Sociology of prescribing. *British Medical Bulletin*. **30**: 214–17.

5   National Audit Office (1993) *Repeat Prescribing by General Medical Practitioners in England*, HMSO, London.

6   Cork M (1993) Economic considerations in the treatment of psoriasis. *Dermatology in Practice*. **Jan/Feb**: 16–20.

Further reading

Bloor K and Maynard A K (1993) Cost effective prescribing of pharmaceuticals: the search for the Holy Grail? In: Drummond M F and Maynard A K (eds) *Purchasing and Providing Cost Effective Health Care*. 198–216. Churchill Livingstone, London.

Wells F O (ed.) (1992) *Medicines: Responsible Prescribing*. Greystone Book, Antrim.

6

Asthma: an outcome-focused audit

Jack Solomon

Introduction

This chapter looks at an audit of asthma, focusing on outcomes for patients. It follows a systematic planned approach which can be adopted more widely, using the infrastructure of a practice-based asthma clinic.

'Outcome' has been defined as the changes in the patient's current and future health status that can be attributed to antecedent health care[1]. It is therefore a measure of effectiveness of treatment and directly tackles patients' interests – a reduction in morbidity. This may be expressed differently depending on the knowledge patients have of their disease and its management. In most cases, medical input can result in behavioural change, generating better health for patients. Outcome measures are an essential tool for quality assessment in general practice. The benefits to patients are:

- prevention or amelioration of disease
- prevention of death
- improvement of quality of life
- shortening of disability due to disease.

One way of measuring outcomes is through the use of medical or clinical audit. This is the method used by health professionals to assess, evaluate and improve the care of patients systematically to enhance their health, well-being and quality of life.

Achieving improved outcomes through audit

The start of the audit cycle is to define standards and criteria. Data can then be collected which provide information on current performance. This can then be compared with the standards set, and areas requiring change are identified (Figure 6.1).

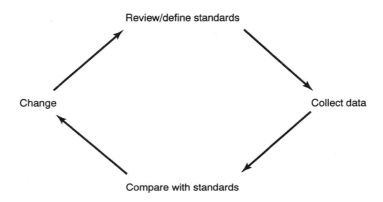

Figure 6.1   The audit cycle

The size of the asthma problem

In this chapter asthma is used as an example. Asthma is a very common illness; it is estimated that between 5% and 10% of the adult population has asthma and that this figure is even higher in children[2]. There is significant morbidity and mortality with asthma (some 2000 deaths per year in England and Wales[3]) and it has been estimated that 40% of asthmatics have sub-optimal control[4]. Under-diagnosis is also a problem. In the UK the prevalence of asthma is rising (by 20–60% over the past 25 years) and it appears that the disease itself is becoming more aggressive. It is thought that atmospheric pollution is partly to blame.

Around 100 000 asthmatics are admitted to hospital each year, usually with acute emergencies requiring emergency treatment. Asthma also causes a disruption of life-style due to sleep disturbance.

Asthma management: good practice

There is general consensus that care can be improved, as can patient education[4]. It is relatively easy to measure outcomes in asthma e.g. peak flow, days lost from work or school. Asthma management may be deficient in both hospital and primary care settings. While numbers of nearly all other causes of 'avoidable death' have decreased in the past ten years, the number of deaths caused by asthma has remained unchanged. More aggressive intervention should reduce the number of deaths that occur.

An asthma clinic is one way in which data can be collected on patients, their disease and its management, together with outcome measures to indicate the success of treatment e.g. peak flow, days lost from work or school. It is therefore a good setting in which to conduct audit. Some outcome measures in asthma are:

- symptoms (e.g. during the day, night, or exercise)

- peak expiratory flow rate (PEFR) (start and end)

- compliance with therapy

- inhaler technique

- days off work or school

- acute attacks (needing nebulization, or a course of oral steroids, or hospital admission).

The clinic also provides a suitable setting to help patients understand their condition and their treatment. For example, they may be taught that bronchodilator therapy should be intermittent when necessary and inhaled corticosteroids or other prophylactics should be regular. The place of systemic steroids and antibiotics may also be discussed and patients taught how to use their inhaler devices and peak flow meters effectively.

Good practice in asthma management requires standards to be set against which current practice can be measured. There are a number of sources which can be used to define standards. The British Thoracic Society (BTS) has set down clear guidelines on the management of asthma (Figure 6.2)[5]. These guidelines look at the stage of treatment and asthma control and can be used by clinicians to decide whether to step up or step down therapy depending on the severity of disease.

Data collection and monitoring the success of management have become more widespread through payments for Chronic Disease Management Clinics and the requirements for audit to take place for payment to be made[6].

The aims of an asthma clinic are:

- to recognize asthma and abolish symptoms

- to reduce morbidity and mortality

- to enable normal growth in children

- to reduce school and work absence

- to educate patients

- to treat asthma in a stepwise manner.

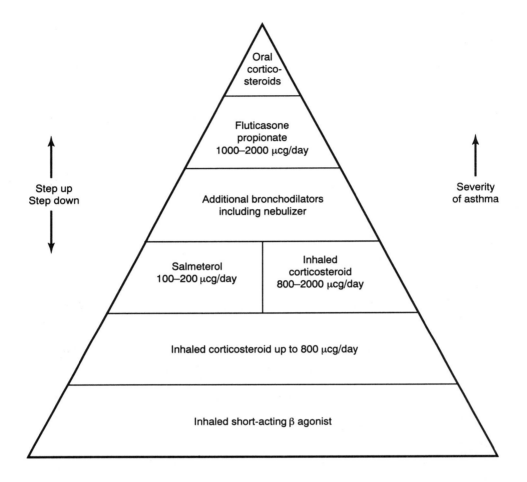

Figure 6.2 British Thoracic Society guidelines on chronic asthma management (Source: British Thoracic Society)

Asthma audit in practice

In the practice described in this chapter, only about 5% of patients were on the asthma register. This meant a probable under-diagnosis of asthma. About 50% of those registered were children.

Forty-eight patients took part in the audit exercise. A number of outcome-based measures were recorded, using the Tayside Asthma Stamp (Figure 6.3). Patients were asked specific questions because many patients felt the need to please the practice by saying they were well whereas a more detailed line of questioning revealed symptoms e.g. at night and on exertion. Results were compared at the beginning and end of six months clinic attendance. Drug compliance was also

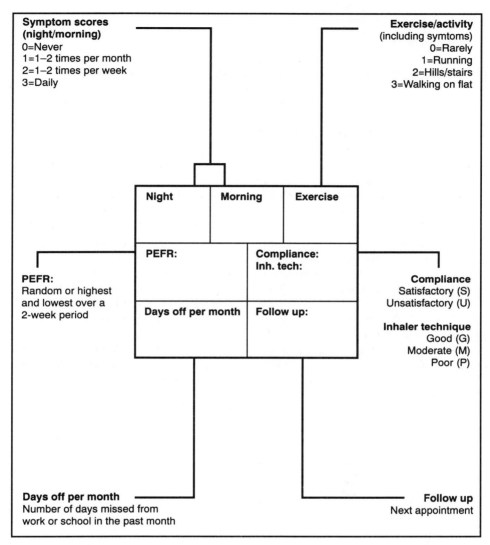

Figure 6.3 The Tayside Asthma Stamp. (©The Tayside Asthma Group)

looked at. Compliance was monitored through patients' subjective reports (for metered dose inhalers) or in those using disk devices, from examination of remaining and spent 'disks'. Inhaler technique was also checked. There are five different processes in using a metered dose inhaler correctly:

• taking the cap off the inhaler

• shaking it

• breathing out

- actuating the device while breathing in; and

- holding the breath for five seconds afterwards.

Good technique was classed as performing all these processes correctly.

Outcomes from the asthma audit

The results obtained showed overall improvements. Symptoms during the day and at night and on exercise were all reduced (Figure 6.4).

Peak flow measurements improved by around 25%. Compliance with therapy improved as did inhaler technique. Days lost from work and school also fell as did the number of acute attacks requiring hospitalization or nebulization (Figure 6.5). Other practices in the area performed the same asthma audit and all noticed similar improvements in the outcome measures.

The results indicated the effectiveness of the asthma clinics and that the time spent running the clinics and educating the patients was very worthwhile.

In parallel with these positive results, the practice saw a rise in prescribing costs, as asthmatics received medication, some for the first time, to prevent as well as relieve asthma attacks. It is generally considered that prophylactic therapy in line with the BTS guidelines is part of good asthma management. These data were obtained from PACT level 3 reports. Balanced against this increase in costs is the increased quality of life for an asthma patient when the disease is under control – a worthwhile investment.

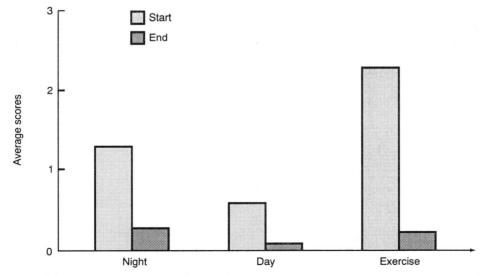

Figure 6.4   Symptom scores in asthma audit

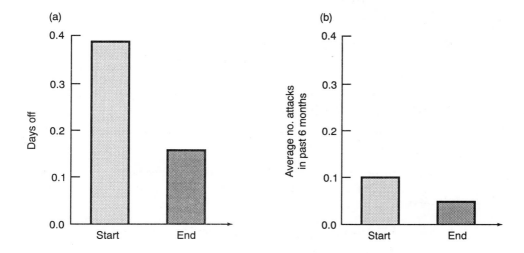

Figure 6.5   (a) Days off work or school in 6 months and (b) number of acute attacks needing nebulization or hospital admission during asthma audit

The practice identified a 50% increase in spend on respiratory medicines compared with a similar period in the previous year. This was largely accounted for by an increase in the number of inhaled corticosteroids. Prescribing costs of β2 agonist also rose by approximately 50%. However, the practice prescribed fewer antibiotics and fewer antitussives, a pattern seen by others[7].

It is therefore possible to measure the costs of asthma prescribing and good asthma management. There are costs associated with poor asthma control which are more difficult to measure[8] – more consultations, hospital admissions, absence from work or school and a reduction in quality of life.

The costs of poor asthma management are:

• increased casualty attendance   (£30–80 per visit)

• increased outpatient costs   (£50 per visit)

• increased hospital admissions   (up to £300 per night)

• increased GP attendance and out of hours calls

• increased ambulance call-out   (£90–100)

• increased absence from work and school.

By treating asthma effectively in the community, using regular inhaled corticosteroids where appropriate, it becomes less of a problem, reducing treatment in hospital, requiring fewer ambulance call-outs and less time lost from work or school.

Learning points

- Audit is a powerful tool which enables care of patients to be examined and identifies areas of management which can be improved to achieve health gain.

- Asthma lends itself to audit and the study of (and purchasing for) health gain, with quantifiable interventions and outcomes.

- The information obtained can be educational and constructive and assists planning for the future.

References

1   Donabedian A (1966) Evaluating the quality of medical care. *Millbank Memorial Fund Quarterly.* **44**: 166–204.

2   Gellert A R, Gellert S L and Iliffe S R (1990) Prevalence and management of asthma in a London inner city general practice. *British Journal of General Practice.* **40**: 197–201.

3   Swinburn C R (1993) Asthma mortality, can it be reduced? *Care of the Critically Ill.* **8(5)**: 198–200.

4   Evans D (1993) To help patients control asthma the clinician must be a good listener and teacher. *Thorax.* **48**: 685–7.

5   British Thoracic Society (1993) Guidelines on the management of asthma. *Thorax.* **48(2)**: 1–24.

6   General Medical Services Council (1993) *Chronic Disease Management – Asthma Audit.* In *The New Health Promotion Package.* BMA, London.

7   McCarthy P (1993) Analysing the cost of inhaled asthma therapies. *Prescriber.* **5 Jan**: 55–6.

8   Solomon J (1994) Making audit happen. In *Effective Asthma Audit.* Colwood House Medical Publications, pp. 10–11.

7

Appropriate prescribing in hospitals

Michael Spencer

Introduction

This chapter looks at the mechanism of more appropriate hospital prescribing as a method of releasing resources in secondary care.

The rise in hospital drug expenditure in Wales between 1987 and 1992 is larger than the rise in hospital sector price index (HSPI). However, an appropriate drug budget for a given hospital is unknown – despite existing information on allocation and expenditure. Within a typical teaching hospital with around 900 beds and 35 000 inpatients per year the annual expenditure on drugs may be in the order of £5 million. In round figures this equates to £125 per inpatient or £10 spent on drugs every minute of every day.

There are a number of pressures on medicines spend, some causing spend to rise and others designed to reduce costs. The balance between these pressures determines the rate and extent of rise in drug expenditure in a particular hospital. The upward pressures on medicines spend are:

- therapeutic improvements over existing agents e.g. enflurane or isoflurane replacing halothane as an inhalational anaesthetic

- medicines for previously untreated conditions e.g. artificial surfactant for preventing and treating respiratory distress syndrome in pre-term babies

- new indications e.g. for interferons, growth factors

- changes in clinical practice e.g. increased use of propofol linked to the rise in day surgery

- the arrival of new clinical staff

- price increases.

The downward pressures on medicines spend are:

- effective drug purchasing e.g. regional drug contracts, locally negotiated deals and the use of 'shortline stores'
- drug and therapeutics committees
- formularies
- clinical pharmacy services.

Other factors influencing the use of medicines include case mix (e.g. increased numbers of patients for: cystic fibrosis, HIV, transplantation), patient throughput (although a reduction in throughput may not always create a reduction in medicines spend) and clinical research interests. In some cases this may mean that the new budget does not cover what has been spent in the previous year.

The amount spent on medicines will be the result of all of these factors. The allocation, however, is likely to be one rolled forward from the previous year with a little added for 'inflation'.

How can more appropriate prescribing assist in releasing resources?

In devising a strategy to release resources the incentives to do so, where to target activity and the resources available to be released, should be considered.

Incentives to release resources

Devolution of up to 70% of their overall budget to Clinical Directorates provides an incentive for savings in one area to be used in another. The budget may cover staff, medical and surgical equipment as well as medicines. The effects of case mix and patient throughput on drug expenditure are not well understood. This can have significant consequences on the patient contracting process especially when relatively simple methods are used for costing patient treatment and determining case cost. The pharmacy computer system can identify patterns of resource use and then investigation can identify savings which may accrue from more appropriate medicine use.

Most resources can be released by targeting specific areas of medicine use. Drug costs vary widely, usually dependent on date of introduction and the technology used in development. Suitable areas to target may be improving the prescribing of potentially toxic drugs, or those whose expenditure is high due to high inherent cost, long-term treatment or high use of low- to medium-cost items.

Staff time can also be released by changing drug choice. If two antibiotics have the same daily drug cost for intravenous administration and one is given once daily rather than three times a day, there will be potential savings in staff time and consumables (e.g. syringes, diluents, needles etc.). The time saved can be used elsewhere, as can the cash saved by reduced use of consumables. A change from intravenous to oral administration may release more resources. However, when the overall daily drug cost of the once-daily oral agent is higher than that of the three times a day oral agent or when a three times a day agent is compared with that of a once-daily intravenous agent, the calculations are more complex.

Optional medicine use may reduce the length of stay or prevent the need for admission through day case surgery. This can then increase patient throughput, which should be accompanied by more contract income.

There are additional benefits which may accrue to patients through being discharged earlier, although these are benefits not accrued to the health service.

Areas suitable to target activity

Resources can be released through a number of strategies:

- development of drug use policies

- development of policies or protocols

- drug-use evaluation studies

- clinical and medical audit

- cost benefit studies

- medical staff induction and training.

Firstly the introduction and implementation of drug use policies can lead to significant savings e.g. the routine use of sodium chloride 0.9% in patients with short-term indwelling catheters, rather than heparin flusher saved around £10 000 per year at the University Hospital of Wales (UHW).

Secondly, the use of treatment protocols (or guidelines) offers a means of optimizing patient treatment and using drugs cost-effectively, e.g. preferential use of streptokinase as a thrombolytic agent following heart attack (list price £85 per case) compared with alteplase (£816) and anistreplase (£495). Strict adherence to the protocol would save £700 each time streptokinase is used in preference to alteplase. For a unit with 30 heart attacks per month, a 10% 'failure' rate (alteplase administration rather than streptokinase) may cost an additional £2000 per month.

Thirdly – drug use evaluation (DUE) the formal review and evaluation of the use of pharmaceutical and related items (e.g. dressings) – may enhance drug therapy quality and help promote cost-effective prescribing. The objectives of DUE are to ensure the appropriate, safe and effective use of drugs and to focus on treatment outcomes. Drug use evaluation may also provide cost justification if a new agent introduction adds significantly to drug expenditure, but releases resources in other areas e.g. staff time and shorter length of stay. A DUE of propofol carried out at UHW identified potential savings of £14 000 annually if all propofol use in the hospital was in accordance with criteria produced by the anaesthetists.

Drug use evaluation also considers drug cost, ease of use, effectiveness, benefits over existing products, cost of consumables (e.g. administration sets, diluents etc.), staff time to prepare and administer the product and storage implications, incidence of adverse effects and achievement of optimal treatment levels. Drug use evaluation may also be used to help determine treatment guidelines between the hospital and GPs, particularly where there is a significant cost differential of the agent between hospital and community sectors e.g. β blockers and ulcer healing agents.

The DUE process comprises the following steps:

- choose drug/drug group

- develop standards based on appropriateness, safety and effectiveness

- collect data

- review data

- action plan

- assess effects.

Fourthly, clinical audit may indicate areas for releasing resources e.g. an audit of oral anticoagulation in hospital can identify areas of duplication of effort, potential for adverse events to occur, communication problems between hospital and primary care and even under-dosing, leading to lack of anticoagulation. Efforts to overcome these problems can lead to optimum therapy for the patient and the release of resources.

Fifthly, the greater use of health economics, through the use of cost-benefit and cost-effectiveness analysis, can be used to identify which treatments or interventions offer the best value for money. Increasingly, published health economics evaluations are providing evidence to aid local decision making.

Finally, the economic use of medicines could form part of medical staff induction and training. This has started in some medical schools and could be followed by induction programmes to top up existing knowledge and explain the local situation.

Resources available to be released

The types of resources which can be released are cash, staff time, consumables and length of stay. If a cheaper medicine can be used with a similar outcome to a more expensive one, then cash will be released. In practice it is often difficult to compare outcomes of different medicines and some clinical value judgement has to be applied e.g. there are now four different artificial surfactants licensed in the UK for the prevention and treatment of RDS for neonates. The price per case various significantly. Change from one agent to another can release cash. However, this should be done only if the clinician has confidence that the outcome will be as good with the cheaper agents as with the more expensive ones.

Learning points

- Prescribing policies in hospital can assist in releasing resources.

- With devolved budgets clinical directorates have the incentive to make savings on drug expenditure.

- Clinical pharmacists can identify target areas.

- Ensuring optimal drug use can release resources with no reduction in treatment outcome.

8

Achieving change by stealth

Harry Burns, Gillian McIlwaine and Sarah Twaddle

Introduction

The conventional approach to purchasing health care begins with an assessment of need. Arguably, conventional needs assessment is a pointless exercise. It is doomed to failure for two reasons. Firstly, it attempts to describe what services should be purchased in isolation from any appreciation of the resources that are needed to deliver those services. Needs assessment will produce a 'wish list' of services but will not allow sensible prioritization since the costs of meeting identified needs remain uncalculated. Secondly, needs assessment ignores the fact that the present pattern of service delivery has developed in an incremental fashion over decades. Typically, powerful professional interests have determined how services have developed. Often the advice received from professionals over the past few decades has been influenced by research needs as much as by genuine clinical considerations. Technologically complex services have often been developed at the expense of services for mentally ill, the elderly and primary care. Although needs assessment can indicate where change in service pattern is required, it gives no clue as to how that change might be achieved. Stagnation is the result.

Programme budgeting and marginal analysis

Programme budgeting and marginal analysis (PBMA) seems to fit our requirements for a technique which allows services to be matched more closely to needs yet recognizes the difficulties purchasers and providers face in moving resources from one area to another. Basically, programme budgeting identifies all current spending on a service or group of patients and hence determines the total budget available for reallocation. This information is then considered alongside activity and outcome measures. The process of marginal analysis involves identifying components of the programme which might be changed. The costs and benefits of the proposed changes are calculated.

This approach has many attractions. It requires purchasers to be clear about the potential health gain and cost of service developments. In addition, developments can be made on an incremental basis. The way in which clinicians work can be changed slowly without causing undue turbulence. Furthermore, the benefit of knowing precisely how much money is spent on a particular programme aids financial management and improves the quality of contracting decisions.

The Glasgow experience

In 1993, Greater Glasgow Health Board set out to examine the effectiveness of PBMA as a means of improving the way in which services are purchased. We identified gynaecology as a suitable service in which to pilot the approach since it is a specialty which is clinically quite circumscribed yet covers services which range from screening and primary prevention through to terminal care. The first step in the process was to draw together a project team which consisted of representatives of each of the five main providers of gynaecology services within Glasgow. A Consultant in Public Health Medicine and a Health Economist ran the project.

To construct the programme budget, information on work-load was collected from a variety of routine data sources. Within Scotland, all admissions to acute hospitals are recorded on a standard form known as the SMR1. As well as containing demographic and specialty data it includes diagnosis and treatment information. The SMR0 is the form which records outpatient activity. No diagnostic information is included on this form. General practitioner prescribing data relevant to gynaecology patients were provided by the Chief Administrative Pharmaceutical Officer and information on the cervical screening programme was obtained through an analysis of payments to GPs. Information on terminal care within hospices was obtained from local sources. Family planning and well-women services were not considered by this project team.

An activity matrix was constructed (Table 8.1). This shows the number of operations or admissions split by whether they receive elective, emergency or day case care. Obviously detailed information on the type of operation is available and was necessary in constructing the financial profile of the programme.

The costed budget

Average costs based on GP fundholder prices issued by each of the units involved were calculated. Where appropriate total prescribing costs from general practice were used. This information allowed a costed matrix to be constructed (Table 8.2). The programme budget identified a total expenditure of £14 942 686. Of this, 73% (just under £11 million) is spent in the secondary sector. This information was then used as the basis for discussion with the clinicians.

Table 8.1 1992 activity

Group	Unable to group	Bleeds	Cancer (+CIS)	Inflammatory disease	Benign tumours	Menopausal symptoms	Incontinence	Prolapse	TOP	Sterilization	Infertility	Others
Prevention			86 531 smears									
Primary care	9136 prescriptions					114 212 prescriptions	10 536 prescriptions				1176 prescriptions	35 072 prescriptions
Outpatient clinics	58 738 attendances		13 784 attendances									
Outpatient procedures			1746 COLP									
Day case surgery		518	73	85	18	225	123	5	1619	411	182	1087
Inpatient surgery		1072 EL 55 EM	459 EL 52 EM	372 EL 148 EM	267 EL 19 EM	510 EL 17 EM	262 EL 10 EM	562 EL 11 EM	798 EL 1101 EM	938 EL 18 EM	515 EL 10 EM	1110 EL 44 EM
Inpatient no surgery		29 EL 155 EM 14 DC	50 EL 39 EM 1 DC	13 EL 129 EM 3 DC	6 EL 1 EM	23 EL 6 EM 4 DC	75 EL 35 EM 3 DC	22 EL 5 EM 4 DC	16 EL 91 EM 14 DC		11 EL 1 EM 5 DC	212 EL 1565 EM 247 DC
Inpatient terminal care			5 EL 13 EM									1 EL 2 EM

EL = elective admission, EM = emergency admission, DC = day case, COLP = colposcopy treatment, CIS = carcinoma in situ, TOP = termination of pregnancy.

Table 8.2 Programme budget for gynaecology services (1992 costs)

Group	Unable to group £000	Bleeds £000	Cancer (+CIS) £000	Inflammatory disease £000	Benign tumours £000	Menopausal symptoms £000	Incontinence £000	Prolapse £000	TOP £000	Sterilization £000	Infertility £000	Others £000
Prevention			1972									
Primary care	207					1358	162				173	154
Outpatient clinics	2295		461									
Outpatient procedures			201									
Day case surgery		120	19	20	4	52	28	1	374	95	42	251
Inpatient surgery		783	432	405	313	251	208	798	818	447	281	1119
Inpatient no surgery		63	111	66	2	8	57	26	26		4	699
Inpatient terminal care			32									4

CIS = carcinoma in situ, TOP = termination of pregnancy.

Marginal analysis

We asked the clinicians to identify objectives for their service. The key points they identified were very similar to those we would expect to see identified by clinicians in other specialties. These were:

- to provide an effective and efficient gynaecology service

- to eliminate unnecessary investigations

- to maximize the appropriate use of new technology

- to promote guidelines for best clinical practice for a variety of conditions.

Clinicians were then asked to identify a series of service changes which would meet these objectives. A large number were discussed but four key changes in service provision were identified. Some of these changes, in addition to improving care, would release resources which could then be channelled into other areas of service development. The four service changes identified were:

- increase the use of day surgery for surgical termination of pregnancy and laparoscopic investigation

- increase the use of outpatient endometrial sampling, and as a consequence, reduce the number of dilatation and curettage procedures

- implement city wide guidelines for the management of urinary incontinence

- implement a city wide policy for the management of gynaecological cancer.

The costs and benefits of the marginal changes in service were then calculated.

Areas suitable for a change to day case

Increase the use of day surgery for termination of pregnancy and laparoscopy

In 1992 there were a total of 3518 medical and surgical terminations of pregnancy carried out on Glasgow residents in local hospitals. Of these, 1890 were carried out as inpatients and 1619 as day cases. In discussion with gynaecologists, they agreed that 90% of terminations could be carried out on a day case basis with the remainder having an inpatient stay of one night. They agreed that day surgery is as safe as inpatient surgery for the vast majority of women and therefore the outcome of the two approaches was similar. Table 8.3 shows the financial effect of moving towards a 90% day case termination rate. It can be seen that a change in clinical practice which results in 90% of terminations being carried out as day cases implies a saving to the purchaser of £309 400. This target of 90% of terminations as day cases is rather in excess of that suggested by the Audit Commission Report on Day Surgery in England and Wales. A crucial factor here is that the 90%

Table 8.3   Cost of moving 90% of terminations to day case

	Number (1992)	Cost (1992) (£)	Number with 90% day case	Cost with 90% day case (£)
Inpatient	1899	818 469	352	151 712
Day case	1619	373 989	3166	731 346
Total	3518	1 192 458	3518	883 058

Table 8.4   Cost of moving D & C to 65% endometrial sampling

	Number (1992)	Cost (1992) (£)	65% Endometrial sampling number	65% Endometrial sampling cost (£)
Inpatient	1039	419 756	362	146 248
Day case	773	178 563	272	62 832
Outpatient	–	–	1178	103 099
Total	1812	598 319	1812	312 179

day case rate was suggested by the clinicians themselves and they, therefore, have a vested interest in ensuring that this high day case rate is delivered.

Laparoscopy/laparoscopic sterilization

A similar approach was taken when dealing with laparoscopy. Rather fewer than a third of all laparoscopies were undertaken as day cases and the clinicians again felt that 60% of patients could be treated on a day case basis. A saving of £108 646 was identified if the change in clinical practice was delivered. Increased day case surgery, therefore, results in savings to the purchaser in excess of £418 000.

Replacing dilatation and curettage with endometrial sampling and ultrasound

Gynaecologists felt that 65% of D&C procedures could be replaced by endometrial sampling and ultrasound with the remaining 35% split between day case surgery (15%) and inpatient surgery (20%). Table 8.4 shows the cost benefits of carrying out 65% as outpatient endometrial sampling. It can be seen that using endometrial sampling under ultrasound control to replace a high proportion of D&C procedures could save potentially £286 140. The changes in practice proposed by clinicians that could lead to savings in excess of £700 000 have been identified.

Areas for investment

Incontinence

Clinicians felt they needed to improve care of women with urinary incontinence. They agreed that the components of an improved gynaecological incontinence service were:

- an education programme for GPs and the provision of physiotherapists with an interest in the treatment of urinary incontinence to work in primary care
- the provision of basic urodynamic equipment in each unit with training in its use for junior medical and nursing staff
- development of a tertiary referral centre in an appropriate unit.

As a first stage, therefore, it can be seen that the major revenue cost of an improved incontinence service is the provision of a physiotherapist for each gynaecology unit. For Glasgow as a whole this would mean the employment of five additional physiotherapists. The cost of this would be £105 000.

Gynaecological cancer

Guidelines for the management of gynaecological cancer were prepared and the aim of those guidelines is ultimately an appropriately staffed tertiary referral service. In the short-term, the guidelines advocate:

- access to a named consultant radiation oncologist and medical oncologist
- specialist referral for surgical treatment of cancer of the cervix, vagina and vulva
- specialist referral for ovarian cancer cases
- each unit to have access to other appropriate specialities such as surgery, urology and plastic surgery
- an additional five sessions of consultant time in one centre to support the increased work-load resulting from the identification of that centre as the tertiary referral centre for gynaecological cancer surgery
- a gynaecology/oncology liaison assistant to assist in the efficient running of the chemotherapy service.

The immediate resource implications of these guidelines were, therefore, an additional five sessions of consultant time together with the appointment of a whole-time nurse specialist. The total cost of these two new appointments was £54 000.

Implications for the purchaser

The programme budget identified an annual expenditure on gynaecology services in Glasgow of approximately £15 million. Four areas were considered as areas of potential change for the service. In two cases large potential savings were identified by service changes which were also recognized as representing an explicit move towards more appropriate care. In other areas expansion of important services has been supported. The whole process is self-funding and importantly the clinicians themselves have identified the areas for change. The approach has the built-in incentive that increasing day case practice is linked closely to service developments which have been identified by all clinicians as having a high priority. Failure to deliver the change in clinical practice will lead to a lack of funding for the service developments. The clinicians are aware of this and in terms of managing clinical practice, it appears that programme budgeting provides managers with a mechanism for achieving change in a controlled and incremental fashion.

The approach is not without its problems. The savings identified require to be realized. Many trusts do not yet have a costing system of sufficient sensitivity to allow day case and outpatient procedures to be costed in the detail necessary. It is difficult, therefore, for Health Authorities purchasing from those trusts to be certain of the robustness of financial calculations.

The main difficulty faced by users of this technique is the translation of notional savings into real money which can be moved between services. Realistically, in this example we did not expect to disinvest the entire £700 000 identified as potentially saveable by a switch to day case surgery.

Learning points

- We have succeeded in developing new services at no additional cost while delivering care in more appropriate settings.

- We have formed good working relationships with clinicians.

- Those clinicians now have a firmer understanding of concepts such as opportunity cost and the necessity to work within existing resources.

- The technique of programme budgeting and marginal analysis offers a useful tool for identifying how resources can be released to improve services.

Further reading

Donaldson C and Mooney G H (1991) Needs assessment, priority setting and contracts for health care; an economic view. *British Medical Journal.* **303**: 1529–30.

Donaldson C and Farrar S (1993) Needs assessment: developing an economic approach. *Health Policy.* **25**: 95–108.

Mooney G, Russell E M and Weir R D (1986) *Choices for Health Care: a Practical Introduction to the Economics of Health Provision*, 2nd edn. Macmillan, London.

Mooney G, Gerard K, Donaldson C *et al.* (1992) *Priority Setting in Purchasing: Some Practical Guidelines.* National Association of Health Authorities and Trusts, Birmingham.

9
Commissioning appropriate alcohol services

Chrissie Pickin

Introduction

This chapter argues that to achieve health gain effectiveness is not the only criterion for commissioners. Appropriateness or relevance to social need cannot be ignored. Health needs assessment is an important process in deciding whether services are likely to achieve health gain and therefore in determining disinvestment and reinvestment. Drawing on experience of health commissioning in Salford, I shall try to show this using the example of alcohol services.

Identifying possible aims

Salford currently spends nearly £500 000 on specialist alcohol services. Of this, 70% is from health authority resources and 30% from social services. The key question for the commissioners is, 'Is this money spent in the right way, i.e. in the way most likely to achieve the most health gain?' To answer this they need to know whether current services are effective – but effective at what? Clarifying exactly what commissioners are trying to acheive in health outcome terms is something that has until recently been neglected. The health gain agenda forces commissioners to make it explicit. While there are always a number of possible aims, the most health gain will be achieved if the aim is appropriate to population need; that is, relevant to social need.

If appropriateness is ignored at this stage, then there is a danger of commissioning effective but inappropriate services. Articles have been published that say a service hasn't been found to be effective at delivering A but is effective at delivering B, therefore the aim should be B. This is a clear case of the tail wagging the dog. So what might a purchasing authority be trying to achieve with its £500 000 of resources?

Possible aims might be:

1   to discourage alcohol use altogether

2   to reduce the weekly per capita consumption to 'sensible' or 'safe' limits

3   to reduce the harm from intoxication, rather than concentrating on weekly amounts drunk

4   to focus on dependent drinkers and to get and keep them sober

5   to keep drunks off the street.

There are other options, but for the present purpose these five highlight the key point, that the health gain strategy put forward will be very different depending on which of these outcomes it aims to achieve. To suggest that one pattern of services can address all of these aims makes no sense and there is a real danger of achieving none of them in an attempt to address all of them. So how does one decide which of these aims is the most appropriate?

Using health needs assessment

Health needs assessment is the tool. It requires three perspectives to inform decision making: the epidemiological; the clinical or professional; and the lay or public.

The epidemiological perspective provides information on the effect that alcohol has on the population of Salford as a whole. Using this perspective in Salford it is estimated that within the local population about 40 000 people drink above 'sensible' limits, although this whole concept of sensible limits has been challenged recently by the Royal College of Physicians[1]. At least 4000 drink above 'safe' limits, that is 50 units for a man and 35 units for a woman. The epidemiological perspective also makes it clear that moderate amounts of alcohol are health promoting in certain circumstances. It is now indisputable that alcohol use has a cardio-protective effect and commissioners need to balance the positive effects of alcohol with the harmful effects and try to optimize that balance at a population level.

What are the harmful effects of alcohol? The estimated number of incidents of alcohol-related harm each year in Salford are:

- children injured on the road – 17

- deaths from cancer – 25

- people admitted to psychiatric hospital – 350

- convictions for drink-driving – 500

- assaults – 575

- offences of criminal damage – 3700

- cases where work suffers – 4700.

In addition there are other issues where we know alcohol plays a large but unquantified role, for example in marriage breakdown and in child abuse. The epidemiological perspective thus shows that the chief health problems of alcohol use are mental health and accidents. However, at a population level the major effects are social and in particular are associated with crime and with relationships. Many of these are not as a result of regular dependent drinking but are as a result of occasional or binge drinking and of the relationship between the pattern of drinking and the situation in which it occurs.

To obtain the *professional* perspective, 20 agencies who currently respond to alcohol problems in Salford were asked what they thought the problems associated with alcohol use were[2]. The most frequently mentioned problems were impact on families, crime, road traffic accidents and under-age drinking. Social problems were mentioned twice as often as health problems.

In our research we also interviewed 100 local people in order to get the *lay* perspective on how alcohol effects the lives of local Salford people[3]. For them, the major concerns were drunkenness, particularly in young people, and the public order offences that occur as a result of it, or at least the fear of the public order offences. For example, people talked about young people hanging around street corners drinking. They also identified the positive aspects of social use, from 'having a good night out'.

So the lay perspective is:

- drunkenness
  - public violence
  - crime
  - threat of crime

- young people
  - gangs

- positive effects of alcohol
  - 'a good night out'.

Any needs identification process needs to combine these three perspectives, and there are evidently many areas of commonality between them, so that a prediction can be made as to what a service that was appropriate to need might look like. The key point from the needs assessment work is that most of the harm caused by alcohol in the community is caused by the occasional binge drinkers, rather than regular dependent drinkers. An appropriate alcohol service would reduce the harm caused by intoxication and therefore would concentrate on the pattern of drinking and the situation in which it occurred, rather than concentrate on a weekly 'safe' limit. An appropriate service would address social problems, especially crime, and it would address the fear of crime. It would address the health consequences that occur as a result of intoxication such as accidents. This would mean it would identify problem binge drinkers and occasional drinkers as well as regular dependent drinkers. It would address under-age drinking and also target harm reduction at young people.

Choosing the appropriate aim

Having determined an appropriate service, the question now is: which of the aims mentioned earlier is most appropriate to need, drawing into the discussion information from effectiveness reviews? Of the five aims mentioned earlier, two are easy to exclude at this stage: (1) stopping people drinking altogether, as this is now clearly inappropriate on public health grounds alone; and (5) getting drunks off the street. Although the latter may be an implicit aim for some, there are probably much cheaper ways of doing it. So which of the remaining three are appropriate to need and what evidence exists that there are interventions that achieve these aims?

Firstly, should the aim be (2): to maintain the weekly per capita consumption to below a weekly 'safe' or 'sensible' limit? The epidemiological perspective suggests that this is a very difficult message now because it is unclear what 'safe' or 'sensible' is. The balance between the potential harm and the potential good that alcohol use confers may mean that a different message has to be promoted for different individuals, so that for a middle-aged man the cardio-protective effects may outweigh the potential harm but for a young person, particularly a woman, the message may be different. At a population level it is going to be very difficult to predict the overall effect on health. Also, most harm from alcohol is caused by binge drinking in people who may well not drink above weekly recommended limits but whose pattern of drinking is harmful to themselves and others. From the lay and professional perspectives too, reducing weekly consumption was not the key issue; it was harm due to drunkenness or intoxication.

If this was the aim would it be achievable, that is do effective interventions exist? Helpful evidence comes from the Nuffield Institute's effectiveness bulletin on alcohol interventions[4]. This shows that there are effective interventions in reducing per capita consumption of alcohol. Simple screening instruments with very brief interventions of often only one interview, offering advice and counselling, have been shown to reduce some people's consumption and they are as effective in primary and community settings as in specialist units. This would appear to be an effective and potentially very cheap intervention. But however much we reduced the weekly consumption of heavy drinkers, this would not address the harm caused by occasional binge drinking.

So maybe the aim should be (3): to prevent the harm caused by intoxication. The pattern of drinking would have to change and the context in which it occurred, to try to reduce crime, accidents, unwanted pregnancies, relationship problems and so on. On the basis of health needs assessment this would be a very appropriate aim. Those judging from all three perspectives agreed that this is the key issue. Is there evidence for effective interventions to achieve this aim?

Possibilities include public education to drink less, together with increased availability of soft drinks in pubs; education to behave differently after drinking e.g. drink-driving campaigns; or encouragement of a different pattern of drinking. Other interventions include ones to reduce public order offences e.g. extending licensing hours, making public transport freely available (particularly taxis), having more police or making street drinking illegal. Other interventions again may be aimed at reducing the health consequences of binge drinking e.g. availability of emergency contraception.

The effectiveness of public education is not well supported. Topic-based alcohol education, particularly in schools, has been shown to be often ineffective and sometimes to be actually counter-productive[5]. So what about the other suggestions people have put forward about reducing the harm caused by intoxication? There is some evidence that the increased availability of soft drinks together with public campaigns centred around drink-driving has led to an improvement in attitudes and that young people appear to have been particularly receptive to that message, which is a good sign. The question is: how does the change in attitude convert into changed behaviour, and more importantly how much more can be achieved through more of the same?

On interventions to reduce street violence, such as making cheap public transport available, and extending the licensing hours so that everybody does not leave at the same time, either the literature is lacking or of poor quality or the evidence is conflicting. The evidence about the type of drinking comes from France, where although the per capita consumption is higher, the pattern of drinking is different, with most consumption occurring within the home and with family members, and drinking being spaced out during the day, rather than concentrated on a Friday night. This pattern of drinking is said to be associated with much less social harm, but at the expense of increased medical harm with increased standardized mortality rates (SMRs) for cirrhosis of the liver and carcinoma of the oesophagus. So although making this the aim of commissioners would be very appropriate to need, most of the proposed interventions are of unproven effectiveness. This is generally because the research has not been done. Clearly there is an agenda here for the NHS Research and Development directorate.

So maybe there should be a concentration on (4): dependent drinkers, trying to get and keep them sober. Is this appropriate to need? Epidemiology suggests that the dependent drinkers are very few and that most of the harm is not caused by them but by the occasional drinkers. This aim was not seen as a priority by local people and even the professionals who were working predominantly with dependent drinkers, identified under-age drinking and reducing alcohol-associated crime as much higher priorities.

What about the evidence on effectiveness? Some factors have been shown to increase the likelihood of dependent drinkers becoming sober e.g. a supportive spouse, involvement in an aftercare programme and an involvement with Alcoholics Anonymous[5]. In view of the fact that the literature suggests that for most people, non-specialist interventions are as effective as specialist and inpatient care, attention has focused on how to match the patient to the most effective intervention, i.e. identifying those who require the more specialist interventions. Unfortunately the evidence seems to suggest that this cannot be done and that although, for some, specialist interventions may help, for most, in the long-term, treatment plays a very minor role in influencing outcome[7,8]. So it appears that this would be an inappropriate aim and that there is very little evidence of any effective intervention.

Moving the resources

How is the £450 000 currently spent in Salford? The bulk of it, £250 000, is spent by the DHA in contracts with two alcohol treatment units (ATUs) offering specialist inpatient programmes to dependent drinkers, about 70 finished consultant episodes (FCEs) per annum. There is a community alcohol team, joint between DHA and social services, 70% of whose time is spent on direct patient work, mainly with dependent drinkers, and 30% carrying out educational programmes with health and social care professionals. This service costs approximately £100 000. Also social services run half-way hostels and after-care support for dependent drinkers costing approximately £105 000. So the current service is focused clearly on dependent drinkers, which on the evidence is not the most appropriate service and has not been found to be very effective. So how does one move to a more appropriate and a more effective service?

If the alcohol treatment units are inappropriate and ineffective, the need is to disinvest from them. Just reducing the contracted numbers of FCEs would require success in influencing the referral patterns of GPs; otherwise there would be a large expenditure on extra-contractual referrals (ECRs). It may be that for the time being there is a need to maintain a small residential unit for the very small number of dependent drinkers until other services take over.

The proposed strategy in Salford is to reduce the cost of the 70 FCEs and release resources in this way. This could be done by:

- encouraging the demedicalization of the service; certainly in Salford, there is a very expensive medical-led alcohol service

- insisting on shorter lengths of stay; the current service has a 4-week intervention programme – why not reduce this to two weeks?

- stopping residential care altogether, and shifting the focus on to outpatient attendances

- transferring the contract to a cheaper provider unit; the price range in the locality for these ATUs varies from £135 a day to £45 a day.

After reducing the cost and agreeing a disinvestment plan with the ATU, there will still be a contract with the local ATU, and therefore part of the health gain agenda must be about making what remains more relevant to need. The aim is to ensure that they provide much more of a community resource with an outreach focus and do much more of their work with the occasional drinkers, rather than just the regular drinkers. This would mean they may have outreach workers within casualty departments, within the courts, within domestic violence units, on medical wards and so on.

Another contract that ought to change is that for health promotion to commission skills based education for young people and to discourage topic-based education. This includes stopping Drink Wise campaigns that rely on the concept of 'sensible' drinking limits. Young people are going to get drunk and education needs to be about ensuring that they stay alive and out of prison while they are drunk.

So having released resources through disinvestment and ensured that the remaining specialist service is more appropriate to need, where should the released resources be spent? Of course, they could be removed from alcohol services altogether. However, some could be used within the service to make it more appropriate and more effective. What Salford is proposing is to expand the community alcohol team to offer assessment and short-term interventions in primary care, perhaps to carry a case load, but more importantly to support GPs and primary health care team members in increasing their competence and more importantly their confidence in offering the brief interventions that have been shown to be effective[9]. It is also intended to develop counselling in primary care and in the community (e.g. through RELATE and Alcoholics Anonymous) to reduce some of the harm and impact of alcohol on families. There must be easy access to emergency contraception and condoms to reduce unwanted pregnancies. Probably the most appropriate thing, but its feasibility is unclear, would be to facilitate a free late night taxi service to reduce assaults and other street violence. The development of health alliance groups to encourage social changes such as this is an important element of the health gain agenda.

In conclusion, in the case of alcohol services, questions remain. There appears to be a choice between investing in effective but inappropriate services, or in appropriate services that are of unproven effectiveness and lobbying for research to ensure high quality in valuative studies in this area. Another option is to disinvest altogether from specialist services, and instead support community non-specialist responses. What is clear, however, is that if health gain is to be achieved, effectiveness cannot be looked at in a vacuum. Health needs assessment and agreement on appropriate aims are important prerequisites.

Learning points

- Commissioners have a variety of tools to help focus resources, but health needs assessment will help them decide whether what they are doing is appropriate to need.

- Health needs assessment should include several perspectives: epidemiological, professional and lay.

- The assessment should be used to guide commissioners in choosing what is an appropriate aim for their resource distribution.

- Effectiveness information should be used to identify the practical actions in support of the appropriate aim.

References

1   Day C P (1994) Alcohol – risks and mechanisms of damage. *Journal of the Royal College of Physicians*. **28**: 254–9.

2   Chrysanthou M and Murphy J (1994) *The Provider Perspective on Alcohol Consumption and its Impact on Services and the People of Salford*. Unpublished report, Salford and Trafford Health Authority.

3   Chrysanthou M (1994) *Community Perceptions of Alcohol Consumption and its Impact on Peoples' Lives in Higher Broughton and Eccles*. Unpublished report, Salford and Trafford Health Authority.

4   Nuffield Institute (1993) Brief interventions and alcohol use. *University of Leeds. Effective Health Care Bulletin no. 7*. University of Leeds.

5   Bagnall G and Plant M (1987) Education on drugs and alcohol: past disappointments and future challenges. *Health Education Research*. **2(4)**: 417–22.

6   The Centre for Research on Drugs and Health Behaviour (1994) *Alcohol treatment since 1983 – a review of the research literature*. Report to the Alcohol Education and Research Council.

7   Vaillant G E, Clark W, Cyms C *et al.* (1983) Prospective study of alcoholism treatment. Eight year follow up. *The American Journal of Medicine*. **75**: 455–63.

8   Edwards G, Brown D, Oppenheimer E *et al.* (1988) Long term outcome for patients with drinking problems: the search for predictors. *British Journal of Addictions*. **83**: 917–27.

9   Drummond D C, Thom B, Brown C *et al.* (1990) Specialist versus general practitioner treatment of problem drinkers. *Lancet*. **336**: 915–18.

Acknowledgements

The alcohol strategy for Salford was developed with Ian Williamson, supported by Jim Murphy and Mark Chrysanthou.

Part Two
Acting Now to Prevent Later Problems

10
Overview
Klim McPherson

Introduction – the general debate

The idea exists that there is some kind of conflict between curative health services and preventive services, in the relevant campaigns for resources for each of these aspects of health provision. The great bulk of expenditure that goes into health care in this country and elsewhere is for curative services; and the reasons for this are that it is essentially complicated, concerns specialists with anxieties about relatively short-term outcomes and is largely demand led. But appropriate prevention services are also complicated. However, they are much more likely to be multi-sectorial, multi-disciplinary and they have much more long-term and more diffuse outcomes. They tend to cost a lot of money and happen largely as a matter of public policy rather than as a matter of individual clinical decision making. There lies the difference in terms of policy with respect to the two, and this presents one of the major uncertainties associated with health care provision in contemporary developed countries.

The business of allocating resources is not at all clear. The provision of curative services is enormously variable and the extent of the variation is quite extraordinary. Table 10.1 shows some data for different kinds of surgical procedures. A coronary bypass surgery in the USA is ten times as common as in the UK and in Norway is half as common. For hysterectomy rates in the USA are maybe three times as common as in the UK, and in Norway about a third as common. These kind of variations in the use of curative (so-called) services are of course ubiquitous and could, in principle, once we knew about outcomes and appropriateness of these services, give rise to enormous savings which could be spent on other aspects of care.

Part of what goes on in this kind of variation in the use of so-called curative services is, in fact, justified under the rubric of preventive care – preventing a later problem. Cholecystectomy rates are high in some countries because people

Table 10.1   Admission rates per 100 000 per annum

	USA	UK	The Netherlands	Norway
Hysterectomy	557	250	381	150
Appendicectomy	130	131	149	120
Coronary bypass graft	61	6	5	13
Prostatectomy	308	144	116	238

Source: McPherson K (1989) International differences in medical care practice. *Health Care Financing Review. Annual Supplement.*

believe that having acute cholecystitis is a lethal condition which could be prevented by having the gallbladder removed. Others, in the past, have argued that it is a good idea to use hysterectomy as a prophylactic against cancer of the uterus, ovary and cervix. These arguments have been well made and well believed by clinicians over the years. Their actual formal justification in terms of cost benefit is very hard to make but nevertheless these uncertainties give rise to different kinds of behaviours in different countries (Figure 10.1) which could, if reduced, result in substantial saving in some countries.

If the UK, which is already low, performed hysterectomies at the rate they are performed in Ireland or Norway, a lot of money could be saved. The same would be true of the USA, if it started doing hysterectomies at the same rate as the UK. In fact, the USA is beginning to do so, and the rate of hysterectomies in the USA is falling quite fast. All this is to say really that the money that goes to curative services is not in any sense fixed or indeed *necessarily* appropriate. So, there is a major policy issue to do with the organization of health care and how money is devolved to cure and/or prevention.

The other part of this general argument has to do with what effects curative service have had on one aspect of health gain – death rates. If we look at amenable deaths (that is those deaths deemed to be amenable to treatment) Figure 10.2 shows dramatic reductions in all countries through recent decades[2]. For non-amenable deaths there is little change. However, the scale for non-amenable deaths is 400 per 100 000, indicating that the bulk of mortality is essentially not amenable to treatment and, moreover, is not improving very much. Those aspects of treatment that have an effect on mortality have essentially had most of their effect due to advances in medical care.

The challenges therefore facing the providers of health care, and most particularly the purchasers of health care are:

• the ability to assess routinely the effect of treatment or prevention on the quality of life and functioning from a patient's point of view

• the creation of a decision-making process which is capable of using data about patient outcomes effectively and efficiently.

There is a lack of data about patient outcomes and there is an urgent requirement to create a system where patient outcomes can be measured much more effectively than is now the case.

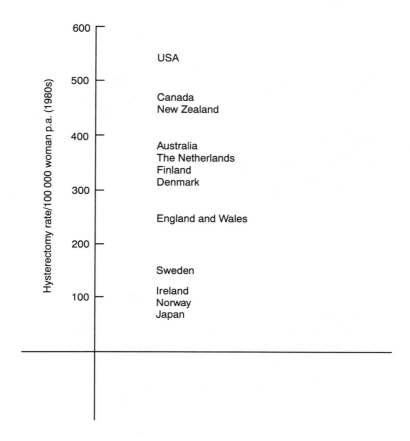

Figure 10.1   Hysterectomy rate in the mid-1980s. (Source: McPherson K (1993) Diversity and similarity of health organization practice and assessment. In: *Europe Without Frontiers* (Normand C and Vaughan P, eds). John Wiley & Sons, Chichester)

To take the matter further (Table 10.2), if premature mortality is defined as all deaths under the age of 65[3], 13% are due to female breast cancer and 37% to deaths from circulatory disease in males. These are the big killers. For working years of life lost, again breast cancer for women and circulatory disease for men feature strongly.

The policy implications of practice variations

Table 10.3 indicates the percentage of population attributable risks, associated with certain exposures or lifestyle factors[4]. For example, mostly lung cancer is caused

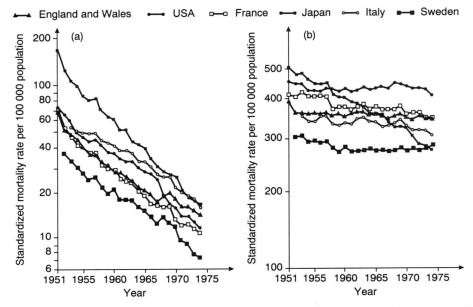

Figure 10.2 International comparison of standardized death rates per 10 000 aged 5–64. (a) Amenable deaths: hypertensive disease, cervical cancer, pneumonia or bronchitis, tuberculosis, asthma, chronic rheumatic heart disease, acute respiratory infections and influenza, bacterial infections, Hodgkin's disease, hernia, cholecystitis, appendicitis and deficiency anaemias. (b) Non-amenable deaths: coronary heart disease, cerebrovascular disease, chronic obstructive lung disease, lung cancer, breast cancer, colon cancer and cirrhosis. (Source: Charlton J R H (1987) Avoidable deaths and diseases as monitors of health promotion. In: Measurement in Health Promotion and Protection. *WHO Regional Publications European Series.* **22**: 19)

Table 10.2   England and Wales OPCS mortality statistics 1990

Cause of death	Percentage of deaths from all causes age under 65		Working years of life lost between 15 and 64 (thousands)	
	Males	Females	Males	Females
All cancers	29	45	179	196
digestive organs	8	8	46	29
breast	–	13	–	59
Liver disease including cirrhosis	1	1	?	?
Circulatory	37	24	212	76
CHD	28	14	152	35
CVD	7	6	27	23
Accidents	8	4	159	46
road traffic accidents	4	2	97	26
Suicide	5	2	65	15
Total	100	100	984	575

CVD = cerebrovascular disease; CHD = coronary heart disease.

Table 10.3   Chronic diseases and their risk factors

Disease	Major modifiable risk factor	Population attributable risk (%)
Lung cancer	Smoking	87
Cervical cancer	Sexual partners	38
	Smoking	32
Breast cancer	Obesity	12
	Late pregnancy	7
CHD	Cholesterol	43
	Exercise	35
	Blood pressure	25
	Smoking	22
	Obesity	17
Stroke	Blood pressure	26
Cirrhosis	Heavy alcohol	65
Hip fracture (F)	HRT	19
	Thin body build	18
	Smoking	10

Source: Reference 4. CHD = coronary heart; HRT = hormone replacement therapy.

by smoking. By contrast, a relatively small proportion of the incidence of breast cancer is explainable by known risk factors. This gives rise to problems with respect to prevention policies. Indeed, it is not even clear what is known about the effect of obesity on breast cancer; or whether if a woman were to lose weight the mortality from breast cancer would change. The major issue is the big proportion of known mortality caused by smoking, and the very small proportion attributable to other risk factors. The exception is for coronary heart disease, where several lifestyle factors are implicated. However, some of the studies which implicate cholesterol and exercise change suggest that these factors may not be quite as strong as represented here.

Another way of looking at this is to examine five common non-amenable causes of death and see the extent to which they can be attributed to different kinds of activity[5]. Table 10.4 shows well-known risk factors which, in principle, if subject to lifestyle changes, could give rise to changes in coronary heart disease, stroke, and cirrhosis. For mammography, a public policy associated with screening for breast cancer can be expected to produce, and does produce, probably only a 1% reduction in these five non-amenable causes of death. Why? Because breast cancer is not the only cause of death for women; screening only works among women of a certain age group; and of that certain age group, screening only reduces the mortality by 30%. So one large and expensive public policy for prevention will not have a big effect on overall mortality.

In terms of policy formulation, the size of uncertainties associated with epidemiology, the medical condition and the extent to which behavioural changes can give rise to changes in disease outcome are important. Let us take two targets from *The Health of the Nation*[6], for example. One is to reduce by at least 50% the rate of

Table 10.4   Prevention of deaths from five common non-amenable causes of death: lung cancer, CHD, CVD, cirrhosis and breast cancer

	Percentage of deaths attributable	Cause of death
Smoking	33%	including 86% of lung cancer
Cholesterol	23%	including 43% of CHD
Hypertension	20%	including 25% of CVD
Obesity	24%	including 17% of CHD
No exercise	23%	including 35% CHD
Alcohol	1%	including 65% of cirrhosis
No mammography	1%	including 19% of breast cancer

Source: Reference 5. CHD = coronary heart disease; CVD = cerebrovascular disease.

conceptions amongst girls under 15 by the year 2000. The other is to reduce the death rate from breast cancer in the population eligible for screening between 50 and 64 years by 25%, again by the year 2000.

What is known about the interaction of these? First, we know that breast cancer mortality is rising in the UK and is higher than for most other countries although it is rising in them too. It is not a disease on which any kind of preventive measures at the moment are having any effect whatsoever. Nor, for that matter, are therapeutic measures having a dramatic effect on mortality.

Second, the incidental consequences of oral contraceptives are:

- Benefits
  - anaemia
  - benign breast disease (BBD)
  - pelvic inflammatory disease (PID)
  - ovarian cysts
  - ovarian cancer
  - endometrial cancer

- Risks
  - myocardial infarction
  - stroke
  - thromboembolism
  - liver cancer
  - cervical cancer?
  - breast cancer?

Use of oral contraceptives is an efficient way of achieving the first target. Their incidental consequences are – to reduce anaemia, benign breast disease (BBD), pelvic inflammatory disease (PID), ovarian cysts, ovarian cancer and endometrial cancer quite dramatically. Long-term use of oral contraceptives reduces the incidence of these two cancers by about a half. What it also does is increase the risk of heart attack, and possibly of stroke and almost certainly increases the risk of liver cancer. It might increase the risk of cervical cancer. The important uncertainty is 'What effect do oral contraceptives have on breast cancer?'

This is an important question because it could give rise to fairly massive public health consequences. If we think of oral contraceptives used before first-term pregnancy – which is a plausible risk factor for breast cancer because age at first-term pregnancy is itself a risk factor of breast cancer – there are very cogent biological arguments for believing that what happens to a woman's hormonal milieu before her first-term pregnancy might have an effect on subsequent breast cancer risk. Table 10.5 shows that amongst sexually active women in the UK[7], the number of young, mostly nulliparous, women sometime using oral contraceptives, went from 11% in the 1970s to 46% in the 1980s to something like 95% (1995). What, then, is believed about the use of oral contraceptives and breast cancer? Mostly that there is no causative effect, but if there is some it happens only amongst small sub-groups. Largely it is believed there is bias and artefact in the epidemiology and that if there is an effect on breast cancer it is justified or compensated by potential reduction in endometrial and ovarian cancer. The one point to be made is about epidemiological uncertainties and the relevance of these uncertainties when associated with a requirement to understand the role of epidemiology.

Understanding complicated epidemiology

Oral contraceptives and breast cancer

The point is very well illustrated in Figure 10.3 which looks at the effect that diethylstilboestrol (DES) has on breast cancer risk when taken by women who were at risk of miscarriage[8]. Here the incidence of breast cancer amongst a cohort of 3000 women who took the drug is compared with the incidence amongst a cohort of women who did not. This presents lessons for us in terms of the understanding of epidemiology, because what can be seen is that there is no effect for something like 25 years. If you take 1975 or 1980 as being the time at which women started using oral contraceptives very commonly when they were young, the elapsed time is only 20 or 15 years ago. The reason perhaps that we do not understand the epidemiology of oral contraceptives and breast cancer is it is

Table 10.5 Exposure of sexually active women in the UK to oral contraceptives. Results are given as percentages

Age (years)	Single women		Married
	1970	1975	1975
16–17	4	29	61
18–19	11	46	
20–24	22	67	64
25–35	23	45	33

Source: Reference 4.

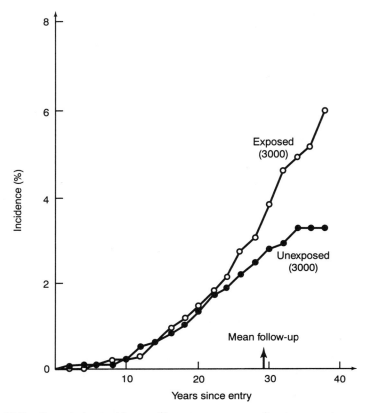

Figure 10.3 Cumulative incidence of breast cancer according to years since exposure to DES. (Source: Reference 8)

much too early to see any possible effect. This is a normal epidemiological finding in breast cancer which is a common disease which we might want to try to prevent.

Yet the epidemiology is insecure precisely for these kinds of reasons. The disease may have a long pre-cancerous stage in its induction before it gets to a point where it is diagnosable by mammography or anything else. So if under-standing the epidemiology is problematic, the relationship between oral contra-ceptives and breast cancer is equally problematic. Table 10.6 shows in summary[9] the relative risk associated with 'ever use' of oral contraceptives before first-term pregnancy, showing the relative risk to be about 1.6 and about 1.3 for over 4 years use. If that kind of risk is real we will be faced with another epidemic of breast cancer in 5 or 10 years unless acting appropriately in time to stop it. What could happen to the risk of breast cancer attributable to current oral contraceptive use could possibly be quite dramatic by the end of this century amongst women born in 1950 or later. The trends need to be carefully monitored[10].

Table 10.6   Meta-analysis. Use of oral contraceptives before first-term pregnancy and relative risk of breast cancer before menopause

Duration of oral contraceptive use (months)	Relative risk
Never	1.00
1–24	1.04 (0.9–1.2)
25–48	1.21 (1.0–1.5)
49–96	1.34 (1.1–1.6)
96+	1.61 (1.2–2.2)

Source: Reference 9.

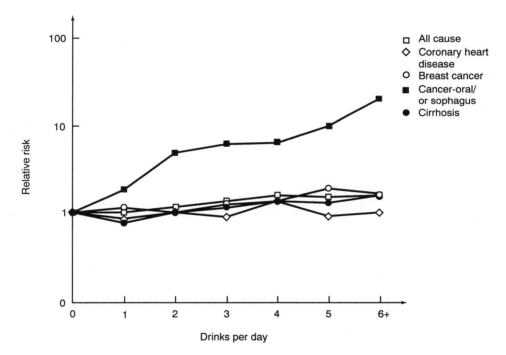

Figure 10.4   Mortality relative risks by daily intake of alcohol in females. (Source: Garfinkel L *et al.* (1988) Alcohol and breast cancer: A cohort study. *Preventive Medicine.* **17**: 686–93)

Alcohol and disease

One can be more optimistic regarding the association of alcohol and disease. There are about 11 or 12 big cohort studies in which proper adjustment for confounding has been made and mortality attributable to different causes has been plotted against numbers of drinks per day. Figure 10.4 shows there is a reduction of risk in CHD for even two to six drinks per day. But, for all causes of mortality, there is a U-shape curve associated with alcohol consumption. This is adjusted for the selection effects related to abstainers from alcohol, people who do not drink, and those who have given up drinking for health reasons. In these studies this has been accounted for and the possibility remains of an important protective effect associated with alcohol consumption.

And so we move from risk factors to the possibility of a fairly potent protective factor. Figure 10.5 shows that drinking is associated with a reduction in all cause mortality amongst men of about 7% under the age of 65 and 11% over the age of 65. For women there is an increase associated with alcohol under the age of 65 and a slight reduction over 65. This is because quite a few studies show an increased risk of breast cancer associated with alcohol. I do not believe that interpretation of the epidemiology, and believe that this is an artefact of confounding. The dietary associates of drinking are more likely to be the causative agent in this increase in breast cancer. There might actually be a reduction in overall mortality from drinking amongst women as compared with amongst men. Also there is the well-known association with cirrhosis, a big attributable risk, and cancer of the oral cavity and associations with accidents and suicide. On the other hand alcohol may and probably does have an effect in reducing CHD. This would give rise, therefore, to quite important reductions in mortality associated with normal use patterns; and if people who drink to excess could drink less then this might even have a bigger effect on overall mortality as a consequence of alcohol consumption.

Health policy and prevention – some conclusions

The dominant issues with respect to policy and prevention are:

* it is important to recognize the extent of the uncertainties and where these might lead us

* the quality of the provision of preventive services and their costs

* the nature of supplier-induced demand with respect to therapeutic services and the effect that that might have on policy itself

* the need to pay much more attention to consumer preferences in health care provision.

Table 10.7 looks at the standardized rates for total mortality, amenable mortality and non-amenable mortality excluding coronary heart disease, and these data appear to show there is a major potential for reducing mortality from non-amenable causes of death. With Hungary and the former East Germany showing high figures, and former West Germany, England and Wales and the USA low figures, there must be some connection to lifestyle and prevention policy issues.

Changes over time are marked also (Table 10.8). In Hungary these mortality rates are going up, and those in the UK are coming down though not quite as fast as they are in the USA.

Another important issue has to do with getting away from the business of measuring mortality. We must measure health status more routinely and more sensitively so we can track intelligently improvements in population health status

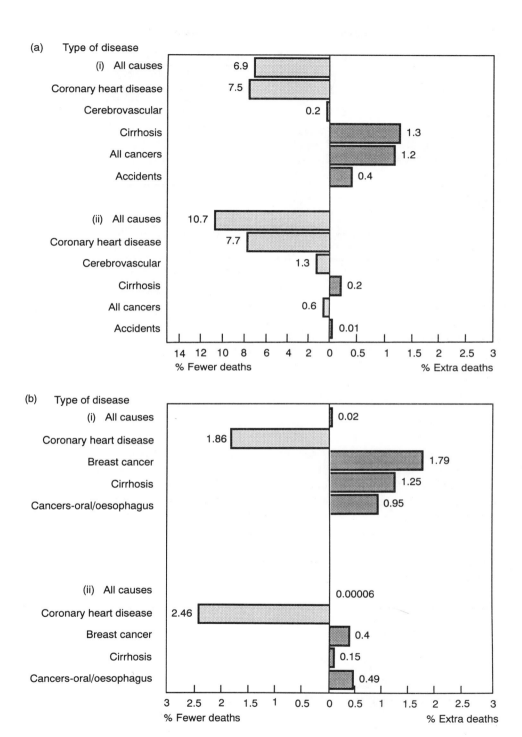

Figure 10.5 Percentage of all cause mortality attributable to alcohol consumption in England and Wales. (a) Males, (i) aged under 65 and (ii) aged over 65. (b) In females, (i) aged under 65 and (ii) aged over 65. Applying ACS relative risks to E & W consumption patterns

Table 10.7   Standardized rates per 100 000 for mortality 1985–87, for people aged 0–64

Country	Total	Amenable	Non-amenable (excluding CHD)	CHD
Hungary	520	104	295	142
East Germany	338	57	217	65
West Germany	282	29	188	71
England and Wales	287	35	159	123
USA	330	33	215	93

Source: Reference 11. CHD = coronary heart disease.

Table 10.8   Change in standardized mortality rates (as percentages) between 1970–74 to 1985–87

Country	Total	Amenable	Non-amenable	IHD
Hungary	+17	−15	+29	+26
West Germany	−4	−27	+3	+1
East Germany	−27	−62	−19	−20
England and Wales	−22	−50	−15	−16
USA	−26	−51	−22	−10

Source: Reference 11. CHD = coronary heart disease.

over time, and so we can compare the health status of populations and inform purchasing activity about issues which have much more relevance to quality and life-styles and populations. This is developing quite rapidly and quite well.

So what is needed is to concentrate the policy issues on knowledge of outcomes, and on informing patients, clients, customers and communities. The incentives for these kind of changes must come from the increasing costs associated with curative services, from increasing pressure for empowerment of populations and a desire on the part of governments to get value for money.

Geoffrey Rose[12] has summed the dilemma of preventive medicine up in the following way: 'Low attributable risk for an individual may be ignored. But a burden for society may not be ignored.'

Learning points

- Curative services can be largely preventive – and are in some cases.
- Non-amenable death rates have changed little over recent decades – known risk factors are difficult to define and to alter.
- Quality of life is the most important element.
- The emphasis must be on outcomes, and informing patients and communities of those, which are attributable to intervention.

References

1   Coulter A, Klassen, A, MacKenzie I Z *et al*. (1993) Diagnostic dilatation and currettage: is it used appropriately? *British Medical Journal*. **306**: 236–306.

2   Charlton J R H (1987) Avoidable deaths and diseases as monitors of health promotion. In: T. Abelin, Z J Brzezinski and V D L Carstairs (eds) *Measurement in Health Promotion and Protection*. WHO Regional Office for Europe, pp. 467–79.

3   OPCS Series DH5 No. 19 (1992) *Mortality Statistics. Review of the Registrar General on Deaths by Area of Usual Residence in England and Wales*. HMSO, London.

4   American Public Health Association (1993) *Chronic Disease Epidemiology and Control*. In: R C Brownson, P L Remington and J R Davis (eds) American Public Health Association.

5   Hahn R A *et al*. (1990) Excess deaths from non chronic diseases in the United States 1986. *Journal of the American Medical Association*. **264(20)**: 2654–9.

6   HMSO (1991) *Health of the Nation*. HMSO, London

7   Bonne M (1979) *The Family Planning Services: Changes and Effects*. Office of Population Census and Surveys. HMSO, London.

8   Greenberg *et al*. (1984). Breast cancer in mother given DES in pregnancy. *New England Journal of Medicine*. **311**: 1393–8.

9   Delgado Rodriguez, M. (1992) Does early oral contraceptive use increase the risk of pre-menopausal breast tumors? A meta-analytical answer. *Fertility Control Reviews*. **1:(1)**: 22–7.

10 McPherson, K. (1991) Latent effects in the interpretation of any association between oral contraceptives and breast cancer. In: Mansel R E (ed.) *Benign Breast Disease*. Parthenon, London.

11 Boys R J *et al*. (1991) Mortality from causes amenable and non-amenable to medical care: The experience of Eastern Europe. *British Medical Journal*. **303**: 879–83.

12 Rose G (1993) *Preventing Disease*. Oxford University Press, Oxford.

11

Antenatal care patterns: horses for courses

Andrew Dawson

Introduction

Patterns of antenatal care in many ways still owe their origins to clinics set up during World War I, chiefly from 1915, although there were clinics in Scotland before that. It is perhaps surprising that we have not wandered very much from this approach over the years. One medical model of care, put forward by Warren Hern in 1975[1], identified 25 complications of pregnancy. Many pregnant women can be fitted into one medical category or another and are therefore treated as patients.

However, many of the dangers which the original antenatal clinics were set up to deal with are now quite remote. Maternal, as well as perinatal, mortality could be measured as percentages, and yet now maternal mortality is measured against a denominator of a hundred thousand maternities. In the triennial Report on Confidential Enquiries into Maternal Deaths in the UK[2], 145 direct maternal deaths are analysed out of 2.36 million maternities; and perinatal mortality in most areas, certainly in the valleys of South Wales, is in the region of 7 per 1000 births. Pregnancy is not as dangerous as it used to be, and antenatal care is not entirely responsible for improved outcomes[3,4].

During the last 25 years many reports[5-7] have addressed the difficulties in providing effective and acceptable antenatal care. The Short Report[6] had 16 pages of summary recommendations. These were based chiefly on a model of hospital care provided by doctors, with rather less emphasis on the work of midwives or GPs.

The Maternity Services Advisory Committee[7] produced a series of reports in the 1980s which recognized that other health professionals were not being utilized to their full extent and could provide antenatal care for pregnant women. There clearly should be a tailoring of antenatal care patterns to suit women according to their needs.

Innovations in South Wales

Innovation one

Studies in South Wales have been conducted mainly in the hospitals at Merthyr Tydfil and Abergavenny, with catchment areas serving large numbers of women in the Valleys areas. The Home Antenatal Care in the Valleys (HACV) studies were funded by the Welsh Office to whom the results will be presented over the next two years. This chapter deals with one of the original pilot activities and was carried out by a research fellow, Dr Claire Candelier[8].

The provision of antenatal care for women with higher risk pregnancies in their own homes was the central issue, and risk had to be quantified. The scoring system suggested by Hobel et al.[9] was modified to determine any changes in risk factors or adverse events throughout pregnancies. The study was carried out in January 1990, with 156 mothers attending for their first appointment over the four-week period. The consultant was asked to mark the women's notes at booking according to a subjective risk category. In this chapter the data are divided simply into *high risk* or *not at high risk*. Dr Candelier scored the notes independently. The consultant's assessment of risk of these women correlated well with the modified Hobel Score. This is indicated in Table 11.1. The patterns of care for all these women after they had delivered, irrespective of the risk category was of the type that would be expected for women with higher risk pregnancies.

Table 11.1   Risk scoring outcome (%)

	Consultant	Modified Hobel
High risk	34.8	47.4
Low risk	65.2	52.6

For simplicity the results are divided into a four-cell diagram. The consultant found about 35% of women to be at high risk against 47% by the Hobel Score. For low risk there was a higher proportion identified by the consultant than by scoring. The first difference is probably accounted for by the weighting of social factors in the risk scoring system, and this sample was undoubtedly from a deprived population of women. The main conclusion that can be drawn is that care tended still towards the medical model for most mothers-to-be. This was deemed unsatisfactory and care modifications proposed to ensure a better match with consultant skills.

Innovation two

The Friday afternoon antenatal clinic at the University Hospital of Wales in 1989 tended to follow an unsatisfactory pattern, often finishing at 6.00 or 6.30 in the evening with much frustration for mothers and staff alike. An audit was, therefore, carried out over nine weeks, with nearly two hours spent each Friday morning examining the notes prepared for mothers attending the hospital antenatal clinic which provided for high and low risk mothers. The consultant examined the notes of women attending for apparently routine appointments. 'Routine' was used when no risk factors were identifiable, and there were no other reasons recorded by medical or midwifery staff. At that time the schedule for routine visits was:

- 16 weeks: alphafetoprotein (AFP) (spina bifida) screening

- 18 weeks: ultrasound scan

- 28, 34, 38, 40 and 41 weeks, as recommended by the Royal College of Obstetricians and Gynaecologists (RCOG)[10].

About 42% of 186 visits made by women during this period were off this schedule. There were two reasons for this: first, the junior medical staff seemed to feel that they were being more thorough if they asked women to attend the clinics more often; and also there was a problem with block appointments.

An attempt was made to introduce an appointment system, but the timings of the local buses, and other social constraints, such as afternoon school hours, made it difficult for this to succeed. A printed schedule was agreed with clinic staff. The number of scheduled visits was also reduced because nearly all the women were booked for shared care where GPs and midwives were involved already. The printed schedule asked women to attend the clinic at booking, 16 and 18 weeks for screening, 28, 36 and 41 weeks. There was a wait of many months before the full effect of this policy came into being, because of the length of pregnancies. Ultimately, nine clinics were re-audited in a similar manner. About 40% of 172 visits were off schedule. This marked a slight improvement taking into account a 10% increase in the number of women being referred to the antenatal clinic. The best evidence of success, however, was that the clinics were finishing at 4.30 pm. Women were taking the trouble to remark on the differences. Resources were probably being released but not in a way that would allow cash value or savings to be attributed. It was clear that resources were being used a great deal better. This, then, was an example of an attempt to improve care in the hospital for low risk mothers with a greater use of community care programmes already in existence.

Innovation three

If consultants are going to be well used, it is preferable for hospital clinics to give greater emphasis to higher risk mothers. In 1985, prior to the introduction of the Cardiff Integrated Antenatal Care Scheme (CIACS), 726 antenatal admissions to the professional unit at the University Hospital of Wales were reviewed. The results are shown in Table 11.2

About a third might have been in labour, and for some there were mandatory reasons such as a major bleed or serious concern about the fetal condition. There were a further 299 admissions for other reasons. Of the total, 22% were assessed to be eligible for suitably designed domiciliary care.

Table 11.2 Number (%) of professional unit antenatal admissions, University Hospital of Wales, January to October

Number (%)	Reason
242 (33)	Labour
185 (26)	'Mandatory'
299 (41)	Other
726 (100)	Total
162 (22)	Suitable for domiciliary care

As a result the CIAC Scheme was proposed for those mothers with identified higher risk pregnancies. The main approaches were based on midwifery skills with support and communication, provided by direct and telephonic surveillance. The CIAC Scheme transferred from being a research activity to normal NHS provision in 1989 with one G grade midwife working 20 hours a week.

Over three years the midwife had 225 referrals, from South Glamorgan consultants, of which 204 were accepted. Some could not be taken for clinical reasons and others because of limits to the volume of her activity. Continuity is virtually 100% and the midwife reports directly to the consultant or deputy. Most of the support is by telephone, but the midwife does make home visits for assessments and to help with any technology that is involved. The main technical surveillance is:

- blood pressure monitoring, which remains an important risk factor in pregnancy (up to 25% of women in their first pregnancies will develop significant blood pressure problems by term)

- telephonic monitoring where there is a genuine risk of fetal compromise.

The use of telephonic monitoring has reduced somewhat over the last couple of years despite much initial media interest. The service is comprehensive, integrated into hospital practice, and appears to be very popular with mothers. Initially it saved admissions, although changes in current practice reduce the strength of that claim, perhaps partly stimulated by the scheme itself.

In a 1989 study[3] 40 women were randomized to domiciliary care and 17 to conventional care where hospital admission was intended (2 : 1 randomization). Table 11.3 shows that all the women in the conventional care groups were admitted to hospital. For the domiciliary group the admission of many women was avoided completely.

Where admission did occur the number and duration were reduced.

Turning to the activity of the CIAC Scheme, Table 11.4 shows referral levels for three years to October 1993. Mostly referrals are for blood pressure problems, rather than for risk of fetal compromise. But in total the 204 cases represent otherwise uncommon admission problems. Release of resources occurs with appropriate referral. However, it is important that the work carried out by the midwife is not being used for filling linen cupboards, preparing off-duty rotas,

Table 11.3 Domiciliary care versus conventional inpatient care, University Hospital of Wales, 1989

	Domiciliary	Conventional
Number	40	17
Women admitted	19 (47%)	17 (100%)
Total admissions	23	26
Admissions per woman:		
mean (SD)	0.58 (0.68)	1.53 (0.80)*
range	0–2	1–4
Proportion of study period spent as inpatient:		
mean (SD)	16% (27)	50% (34)[†]
range	0–96%	7–100%

* Mann-Whitney $P<0.01$. [†] $t=4.02$, $P<0.001$.

Table 11.4 CIAC scheme referrals by cause, 1991–93

Year	Raised blood pressure	Reduced fetal movement	Rhesus haemolytic disease	Reduced growth	Poor history	Ante-partum heritage	Total
1991[1]	24	5	2	22	14	4	71
1992[2]	38	3	0	12	16	4	73
1993[3]	26	3	6	14	10	1	60
Total	88	11	8	48	40	9	204

Number of women assessed but surveillance ceased before labour: [1] = 15, [2] = 9, [3] = 6.

answering routine telephone calls, or many of the other distractions faced by hospital midwives. Her time must be used to support women at home and to help them with their own pregnancies.

Innovation four

Finally, in the Home Antenatal Care in the Valleys (HACV) project, an attempt has been made to quantify the costs of antenatal care for higher risk women. Preliminary analyses suggest it is at least revenue neutral and possibly gives true savings. Most important, better quality of care can be provided for women with higher risk pregnancies.

By way of example, an examination of a sample from the CIAC scheme of 57 women with hypertensive pregnancies showed there was a mean of three-and-a-half admission days saved when compared with women on the ward who were assumed to remain admitted until delivery (Table 11.5).

Table 11.5 Duration analysis for 57 hypertensive women on CIAC scheme, 1993

	Mean	SD	Range
Duration on CIAC scheme	4 weeks, 0 days	3 weeks, 2 days	2 days–15 weeks
Antenatal admission durations	1.2 days	2.54 days	0–12 days
Pre-delivery admission durations	2.86 days	3.68 days	0–14 days
Minimum admission days	3.49 days	4.49 days	0–17 days
Gestation at delivery	38 weeks, 4 days	2.16 weeks	32–42 weeks

It is not surprising that these women were all delivered slightly early at a little over 38 weeks, and that a high proportion received obstetric interventions, because they were selected for being at high risk. In the longer term it is possible that interventions might be reduced as confidence in surveillance methods increases. Many obstetric interventions take place in advance of potential problems.

Conclusions

This chapter has given examples at both ends of the obstetric risk spectrum. For those lower risk mothers who will continue to require some hospital-based antenatal care, it can be provided in a much more acceptable way, with relatively little effort. For high risk mothers there is domiciliary surveillance, which either supplements the care provided by frequent antenatal clinic attendances or perhaps reduces the number of antenatal clinic attendances, as well as inpatient admissions. It is horses for courses, but a better use of resources is the result.

Learning points

- Risk scoring of pregnant women is best carried out using standard scales.
- Low-risk mothers can be cared for in the community.
- Many higher risk mothers can be cared for in the community if dedicated midwives are available.
- A significant number of admission days can be saved for hypertensive women using midwifery support at home.

References

1   Hern W (1975) The illness parameters of pregnancy. *Social Science and Medicine.* **9**: 365–72.

2   HMSO (1994) *Report on Confidential Enquiries into Maternal Deaths in the United Kingdom, 1988–1990.* HMSO, London.

3   Dawson A, Middlemiss C, Coles E *et al.* (1989) A randomised study of a domiciliary antenatal care scheme: the effect on hospital admissions. *British Journal of Obstetrics and Gynaecology.* **96**: 1319–22.

4   Middlemiss C, Dawson A, Gough N *et al.* (1989) A randomised study of a domiciliary antenatal care scheme: maternal psychological effects. *Midwifery.* **5**: 69–74.

5   Central Health Services Council Standing Maternity and Midwifery Advisory Committee (1970) *Domiciliary Midwifery and Maternity Bed Needs.* DHSS, London.

6   HMSO (1980) *Second Report from the Social Services Committee. Session 1979–80. Perinatal and Neonatal Mortality.* HMSO, London.

7   Maternity Services Advisory Committee (1982) *Maternity Care in Action. Part One – Antenatal Care.* HMSO, London.

8   Candelier C (1993) *Antenatal Care – Deprived Communities: The Effect of Enhanced Domiciliary Care.* MD thesis, University of Sheffield.

9   Hobel C J, Hyvarinen M A, Okada D M *et al.* (1973) Prenatal and intrapartum high-risk screening. *American Journal of Obstetrics and Gynecology.* **117**: 1–9.

10 Report of the RCOG Working Party on Antenatal and Intrapartum Care (1982) Royal College of Obstetricians and Gynaecologists: September; Appendix 2.

12

Mothers as partners in antenatal care

Kevan Thorley and Trish Rouse

Introduction

Writing in 1989, Chalmers stated that antenatal care in Britain follows a pattern which has evolved with little scientific basis. He went on to suggest that it is uncertain which procedures performed routinely are effective in promoting the health of pregnant women or their babies. In many areas of care, the available data derived experimentally are inadequate to support strong inferences about their effects and in others there are no data available[1].

The reduction in perinatal mortality in the twentieth century is frequently said to be due to 'Good Antenatal Care'. However, other factors have improved at the same time, and it is 'unscientific' to assume that antenatal care has been responsible for this improvement[2]. Perinatal morbidity is now relatively low, and any further improvements will be marginal. However, in those areas of the country with social deprivation and where educational and nutritional standards are poor, high perinatal mortality persists.

Education to improve nutritional standards and to reduce maternal smoking and alcohol consumption might produce better results in terms of lowering perinatal mortality than would the clinical measurement on which antenatal care is based. Women are often told to attend antenatal clinics every month or every fortnight irrespective of their needs. Hospital clinics can be inaccessible to the populations in greatest need, times are inconvenient and there are frequently long waits.

This chapter describes a more rational system of care which involves mothers in discussions about its provision. The process of development of this system is described elsewhere[3].

Too often, the main objective of antenatal care is to screen for abnormalities, when no pathology may be present. Little account is taken of the physical, emotional or social needs of pregnant women.

Whilst there may be good reasons for checking blood pressure, testing urine and palpating the abdomen, there is no evidence about how frequently these should be done[4]. Such measurements tend to become the major focus of care at the expense of the woman's feelings and concerns and her other physical and psychological needs.

In an attempt to address these problems it was decided to change the pattern of antenatal care in our practice of 3500 patients, who live in an area to the south west of the Potteries. The practice population is mixed, consisting mainly of blue collar workers, a small council estate close to the surgery, a 'professional' belt in a suburban area, and a site for travellers.

There are about 50 births each year: most are booked for the GP Unit at North Staffordshire Maternity Hospital; a small number are referred for consultant care; and an increasing number of mothers request home birth. The practice has its own ultrasound scanner, and both the doctor and midwife have been trained in its use.

New approaches

The aims of the new method of care are as follows:

- to provide antenatal care which is sensitive to the needs of pregnant women

- to maintain a high standard of clinical care, while reducing clinical measurements

- to provide a comfortable setting for a group of mothers where education takes place through discussion

- to introduce flexibility of timing and availability of care

- to make a wide range of therapies available

- to audit these changes to ensure safety for mother and baby.

The clinical procedure

The focus and starting point of the clinic is a meeting for the women, the midwife and the doctor, sometimes with a guest speaker or facilitator. Some aspects of pregnancy are discussed. Women are encouraged to question the professionals and to share their own experiences and feelings. This usually takes about half an hour but may last up to an hour. Afterwards there is time for informal discussion over a cup of tea. The midwife and the doctor are then available for individual consultation and to perform routine check-ups. Five attendances are standard – at booking, 22, 30, 36 weeks and term, a pattern proposed by Hall[5]. Mothers may consult or have a check-up if they feel the need for it at any other time during their pregnancy. They may attend the clinic as often as they like. The midwife or doctor may also suggest extra attendances if they consider this necessary for clinical reasons.

On confirmation of pregnancy, women are given a leaflet which explains the way the clinic works, and gives some information about pregnancy and birth and services available. We aim that the clinical component of care should be minimal but of high quality, encouraging women to take responsibility for themselves and for their births, and to give them the necessary information to make informed choices. They are also encouraged to take control of their births – the position they will adopt, the methods of pain relief they will use and how the births will be managed. This encouragement is given during the meetings by discussions among the mothers themselves and with staff and guests.

The development of a cohesive support group among the women is of the greatest importance and is of benefit before and after the birth when new mothers can feel very isolated. Mothers who have delivered recently are encouraged to bring their babies to the antenatal clinic.

Data gathering

Data were collected from all mothers who attended the clinic from four years before to four years after the introduction of the new approaches, and the following outcome measures were investigated:

- *safety*: birth weight, and number of low birth weight babies (below 1500 gm)

- *intervention*: caesarean section rate, forceps and ventouse rate

- *transfers*: to consultant care from GP Unit or home

- *maternal morbidity*: episiotomy and perinatal tear rates

- *breastfeeding*: the number of mothers breast feeding at discharge, at six weeks, three months and six months post partum

- *mothers' satisfaction*: measured by a questionnaire using visual analogue scales

- *attendance*: the number of attendances for each mother and partner.

Results

Baby outcome

There was no clinically or statistically significant change in birth weight or admissions to the Special Care Baby Unit.

Intervention

Table 12.1 shows that in the first two years after the change to the new clinic the caesarean section rate fell from 7% to 4% of deliveries (the difference of 3% had a 95% confidence interval of –3% to 10%). During the same four-year period, DHA rates for caesarean sections increased from 11% of deliveries in both 1988 and 1989, and to 13% in 1990 and 1991. The DHA's episiotomy rate increased from 26% in

Table 12.1 Comparison of old and new style antenatal clinics at the Higherland Surgery in terms of instrumental deliveries and perineal damage 1988–91

Variable	Old clinic (1988–89) (n = 87) No. (%)	New clinic (1990–91) (n = 108) No. (%)
Total births	88 (100)	108 (100)
Normal deliveries	70 (80)	94 (87)
Forceps	8 (9)	6 (6)
Ventouse	2 (2)	1 (1)
Breech	2 (2)	3 (3)
Caesarean section	6 (7)	4 (4)
Episiotomy	29 (33)	24 (22)
Tear	29 (33)	26 (24)
Intact perineum	30 (34)	58 (54)

1989 to 29% in 1991, whilst for the Higherland Surgery it reduced from 33% to 22% from 1988 to 1991. No figures were available for 1988.

Forceps and ventouse percentages both dropped and intact perineums rose by 20% to over a half.

Bookings and transfers

Similar numbers of bookings and transfers to consultant care were found during the two periods of study (Table 12.2).

Breast feeding

The number of women breast feeding was significantly higher at all periods after the change to the new clinic compared to the old, as shown in Table 12.3.

Patient satisfaction

Enjoyment of the new clinic showed an increase in mean Visual Analogue Score of 10.5%.

Attendance at the clinic

We excluded mothers who attended both forms of antenatal clinic from analysis of attendance.

There was a small fall in the average number of clinic attendances per patient from 9.2 (SD 3.9) to 7.9 (SD 2.8) after the introduction of the new clinic, but there were fewer mothers who made less than our minimum standard of five attendances.

Table 12.2 Comparison of old and new style antenatal clinics at the Higherland Surgery in terms of place of booking and transfer to consultant care 1988–91

Bookings	Old clinic (1988–89) (n = 87)			New clinic (1990–91) (n = 108)		
	No.	(%) births	% of bookings	No.	(%) births	% of bookings
GP Unit:						
Bookings	60	69	100	68	63	100
Deliveries	39	45	65	52*	48	76
Intra-partum transfers	10	11	17	13	12	19
Ante-partum transfers	11	13	18	4	4	6
Total transfers	21	24	35	17	16	25
Consultant unit:						
Bookings	20	23		20	19	
Deliveries	41	47		40	37	
Home births:						
Bookings	7	8		20	19	
Deliveries	7	8	100	16	15	80
Intra-partum transfers	0	0	8	4	4*	20
GP Unit and home transfers	21	24	31	21	20	24

*Includes one intra-partum transfer from home to GP Unit.

Table 12.3 Comparison of old and new style antenatal clinics in terms of numbers of mothers breast feeding

Breast feeding	Old Clinic (n = 87) No. (%)	New Clinic (n = 108) No. (%)	P value
In first week	46 (53)	76 (70)	<0.01*
At 6 weeks	33 (38)	57 (53)	<0.01
At 12 weeks	23 (26)	51 (57)	<0.01
At 6 months	17 (20)	20 (37)	<0.01

χ^2 test with 1 degree of freedom.

Nine mothers made less than five visits to the old clinic, compared with seven to the new clinic. Three came twice to the old clinic and one only once. No mother attended the new clinic less than three times. Under both clinic arrangements, attempts were made to follow up infrequent attenders by home visits from the midwife.

Costs

Costs involved in maternity care seem difficult to estimate since the Trusts giving provision of care calculated costs only in terms of block contracts. The estimates we were able to find showed that a delivery of any kind on the Consultant Unit costs £699, compared with £425 on the GP Unit. This presumably reflects the greater costs involved in caesarean section and other forms of intervention. Increasing GP bookings therefore saves £274 per mother for those mothers who deliver in the GP Unit. Each antenatal visit costs approximately £30. A reduction of five visits per mother will on average therefore save £150 per mother. Our aim was not to reduce the cost of care but to increase women's autonomy and choice by giving them information. Our results show substantial reductions in maternal morbidity and intervention rates and therefore should be associated with reduced costs both to the individual women and to the NHS. The additional resources in terms of professional time in the antenatal clinic amount in our case to an extra half hour per week of midwife and medical time. The gains in terms of health and monetary savings we have demonstrated have, we feel, offset this small additional resource input by a large sum.

Discussion

The involvement of mothers was the most important element in planning and developing change in our antenatal care. As the needs of mothers change, we are prepared to make further changes, taking medical evidence into account. We feel we must concentrate on clinical methods which are useful for individual mothers.

The group is a very important part of antenatal care. It develops informally in antenatal clinics in different settings where people are thrown together while waiting, but we have given this process recognition and structure which enables mothers to use our group more effectively. Occasionally it fails to function, as all groups will, but the mothers know it offers a source of support and information. They appreciate the facility the group gives them to ask questions which they may find difficult to voice individually.

It would be possible to run such a group, with modifications, in a hospital antenatal clinic, and we suggest that if a consultant obstetrician became involved in the group, this may provide one answer to women's frequent charge that they never saw the consultant responsible for their care.

Giving mothers the responsibility of choosing when to attend the clinic may seem risky but we find this method improves attendance by previous defaulters. Mothers appreciate the greater flexibility.

There has been an increase in home births since the introduction of the new clinic. Greater opportunity for discussion among mothers and midwifery and medical staff in the new style clinic may be an important factor in this increase. Mothers who had experienced home birth encouraged those considering it.

The Government's proposals in *The Health of the Nation*[6], set targets of 75% of infants to be breast fed at birth, and 50% at six weeks. If the improvement achieved so far continues this target should be met. We believe that partnership with mothers is the key to achieving these targets nationally.

Marsh[7] suggested that longer consultation time, a leisurely atmosphere and more opportunity to talk during antenatal visits would improve antenatal care, and that such a model although resulting in fewer visits to the clinic was preferable to the old 'conveyor belt' style. We have extended this model to include the group process and thereby provide even more opportunity for exchange of information between mothers themselves and the professionals. Fewer mothers defaulted from the smaller number of clinic attendances, presumably because they preferred the new clinic to the old. The aim has been to give them a greater understanding of their antenatal care and their need to attend.

The practice incurs costs in time and expenses paid to visiting therapists – though most are able to offer their time free of charge. There has been some capital investment in equipment – the transcutaneous electrical nerve stimulation (TENS) machines, ultrasound and the birthing pool. The additional time needed to run the clinic is about half an hour to an hour weekly, but we believe that this is more than offset by a reduction in consultation time because of the educational value of the clinic.

Our clinic certainly gives greater satisfaction to doctor, midwife and mother. We feel that this model of care is capable of use with adaptation in any centre offering antenatal care, whether hospital or community based.

The Expert Committee on Maternity Care[8] recommended that 'the woman having a baby should be seen as the focus of care; and that the professionals providing that care should identify their needs and develop arrangements to meet them which are based on full and equal co-operation between all those charged with her care'. This is the philosophy we have aimed to follow and we welcome the report and its recommendations.

Learning points

- Consumers should be involved in planning new services.

- Mothers-to-be, given the necessary information, will make informed choices.

- Groups are an important component of antenatal care.

References

1   Chalmers I, Enkin M and Keirse J N C (1989) *Effective Care in Pregnancy and Childbirth*. Preface, Vol. 1. Oxford University Press, Oxford.

2   Tew M (1990) *Safer Childbirth, A Critical History of Maternity Care*. Chapman and Hall, London, pp. 8–12.

3   Thorley K J and Rouse P R (1993) *British Journal of Midwifery*. **1(5)**: 216–19.

4   Lindmark G and Chattinguis S (1991) The scientific basis of antenatal care. *Acta Obstetrica et Gynaecologica Scandinavica*. **70**: 105–9.

5   Hall M R, Chang P K and MacGillivray I (1980) Is routine antenatal care worthwhile? *Lancet.* **i**: 78–80.

6   Department of Health (1991) *The Health of the Nation, A Consultative Document for Health in England.* HMSO, London.

7   Marsh G N (1985) New programme of antenatal care in general practice. *British Medical Journal.* **291**: 646–8.

8   Department of Health (1993) *Changing Childbirth (The Report of the Expert Committee on Maternity Care).* HMSO, London.

13

Preventing low birth weight

Gaynor Bussell

Introduction

The issue addressed in this chapter is the incidence of low birth weight (LBW) – below 2500 g – and the consequences for health service and other public sector expenditure at a later date. The problem, tackled from a dietitian's view point, is divided into two sections.

- Preventing LBW during the preconception period, i.e. a time of three to six months before conception and, although not technically correct, including the first few weeks after conception when the mother may not realize she is pregnant.

- Preventing LBW during the antenatal period; i.e. the time from when the mother realizes she is pregnant up to the birth of her baby.

Preventing LBW in the preconception period

Considerable evidence has accumulated suggesting the diet a mother eats before she is pregnant is more important to her baby's health than her diet while she is pregnant. For example:

- *The so-called Dutch Hunger Winter of 1944–5*[1]: mothers who were malnourished before and early on in their pregnancies had a significantly higher rate of perinatal mortality and congenital malformations compared with those who conceived before the famine. Birth weight was also reduced. Malnutrition experienced after conception resulted only in a lowered birth weight.

- *The diet of some women in the East End of London and the subsequent birth outcome*[2]: here, maternal diet correlated strongly with birth weight for babies up to 3270 g. This was most significant for diet during the first trimester of pregnancy, where it can be assumed the mothers' intake resembled most closely that before conception.

- *The American Special Supplement Program for women, infants and children*[3]: it was shown that an improved diet following one pregnancy and before the next increased mean birthweight and length and reduced the risk of LBW in the second pregnancy.

Why is preconception nutrition important?

Poor nutrition in *late* pregnancy affects fetal growth; but *after* birth babies can usually catch up, central nervous system (CNS) and brain development are not affected, and head circumference will be average. Poor nutrition in the preconception period, and in the early weeks of pregnancy, affects development of the embryo and its ability to survive. The CNS is particularly affected and both body and head circumference will be small. Catch-up growth cannot occur as the total number of cells is reduced[4].

There are several reasons for vulnerability at the very early stage of pregnancy:

- there is rapid cell organization, differentiation and organogenesis taking place – poor nutrition will slow this down and/or disorganize it[5]

- factors affecting the rate of cell replications have most of their effect during the first six weeks of pregnancy[5]; and therefore even a small decrease in number of cell divisions in the early part of pregnancy can mean the difference between having a normal birth weight baby (NBW) or a LBW one (Figure 13.1)

- a poor maternal diet will produce a lower level of essential hormones as well as nutrients, and a lack of nutrients causes a falling off in the number of cells (Figure 13.2)[5].

For all these processes to run smoothly in the embryo it must also have the right environment. At this stage there is no placenta to concentrate nutrients or produce the correct level of hormones and prostaglandins[5]. Indeed, an optimum nutritional environment can even offset the damage that some adverse agents such as drugs, alcohol, tobacco and heavy metals might do.

What are the results of poor preconception nutrition?

These can be summarized as:

- LBW (below 2500 g)
- congenital malformations, particularly of the central nervous system[6]
- reduced IQ[7]

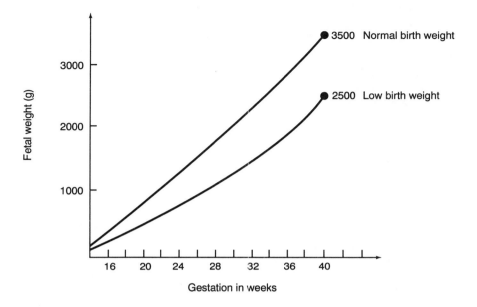

Figure 13.1   Preconception. Two fetal growth curves differing by one half a cell number doubling during the first trimester

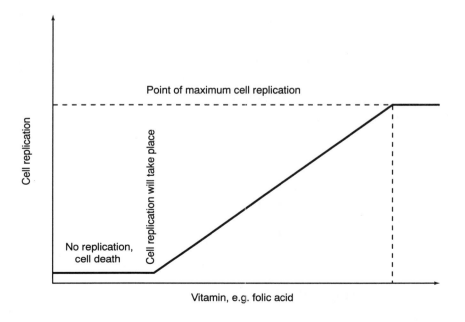

Figure 13.2   Relation between maternal vitamin intake and fetal cell replication

- reduced immunocompetence

- behavioural problems[6]

- faulty 'programming' leading to diseases such as diabetes and high blood pressure in later life[8]

- allergies.

These create a major cost to the health and education systems – for example, expensive medication or special schools are needed – and the emotional drain on the family is considerable.

Two pieces of data suggest where resources should be targeted[9]:

- perinatal death rates:
  - LBW babies: 92.6/1000
  - NBW babies: 2.8/1000

- national average for LBW:
  - 7% (has not significantly changed over last 30 years)
  - two-thirds of LBW babies are born to working-class mothers.

What actions are needed?

Research
Research is required to try to discern reasons for poor diet in the preconception stage and establish a firm link between LBW, non-genetic congenital abnormalities and poor preconception diet. Some key knowledge and behavioural indicators include the following:

- 16–34 year olds know least about healthy eating and find it hard to follow healthy eating advice[10]

- women with limited income would welcome cookery demonstrations using cheap but nutritious ingredients[11]

- 93% of 7–11 year olds know how to play computer games, but 54% do not know how to boil an egg[12].

The author is currently carrying out a study on the attitudes, beliefs and nutritional intake of mothers who have had a Small for Gestational Age (SGA) baby. The study will compare their results to those mothers who have had a NBW baby. It will hopefully enable the planning of a strategy to help mothers at risk of producing LBW babies.

At University College London Hospital (UCLH) *preconception advice* is offered by the dietitian as part of a Well Woman and Family Planning service. Local GPs and Health Centres have also been leafleted about the service and uptake is slowly on the increase. This voluntary uptake tends to be mainly from well motivated women who, although feeling they have learnt and benefited from the advice, are not so needy. To take it further, GPs and hospital consultants could adopt a *screening scheme* where at risk mothers could be referred to the dietitian or a practice nurse for preconception advice. A simple questionnaire with a scoring system that could take a few minutes to complete could include the following questions:

- previous LBW baby?

- low maternal weight, below a body mass index (BMI) of 19?

- history of miscarriage or other fertility problems?

- smoking, alcohol or drug misuse?

- poor social circumstances?

The author is devising a system of 'catching' those mothers who have given birth to a LBW baby in hospital and giving them healthy eating advice to reduce their risk of subsequent LBW baby. If a mother has had a LBW baby there is a 1 in 3 chance of having another LBW baby at the next pregnancy[13].

'Educating the mother-to-be'

Educating the mother before she is pregnant is vital, and important basic facts need to be conveyed:

- what is a healthy diet – special emphasis on iron and calcium

- how to cook healthy meals even on a budget

- importance of breakfast and how eating breakfast cereal can help[14]

- dangers of strict dieting

- food hygiene and the dangers of salmonella, listeria and toxoplasmosis in pregnancy

- the danger of liver and hypervitaminosis A during pregnancy

- the importance of folic acid both before and during pregnancy[15]

- how close birth spacing can cause LBW.

Schools should be providing a consistent message across what is taught in the National Curriculum and what is taught by example in the provision of school meals and the tuck-shop service.

Often when new mothers come to Parentcraft classes they leave in a dazed and worried state muttering, 'If only I had known that earlier'; for example, about not eating liver or taking folic acid supplements. If it is part of their basic education then they will enter pregnancy knowing what is best to eat or to avoid to improve the chances of a healthy pregnancy.

Promoting the nutritional value of breakfast cereals could save millions of pounds; and it has been shown that women who eat breakfast cereals have a larger intake of micro-nutrients, including folic acid[14], and are less likely to have LBW babies[13].

Slimming diets

Women on slimming diets, who may go on to conceive, should be warned about dieting too strictly and of aiming for an unreasonable low weight. 'Weight for height tables' used by some slimming groups still aim their target weights too low. If the woman then becomes pregnant, she may go on to have a LBW baby. Dietitians do not like the terms '*going on*' and '*coming off*' a diet. They prefer to talk of following a healthy eating diet . . . for life!

Women with a BMI of less than 19 at the start of pregnancy have three times greater risk of having a LBW infant than those women with a BMI that is between 20 and 25[16]. To minimize the chances of producing a LBW baby and maximize fertility a BMI of 24 is the ideal[16].

Fertility treatment

Anyone undergoing fertility treatment should receive mandatory preconception advice. Indeed many underweight infertile women might improve their chance of conceiving by increasing their weight. A very underweight woman will not ovulate at all. However, with increasing body weight or with drugs that produce ovulation a woman is able to become pregnant despite her body still not being ready to deliver a healthy baby of normal weight at full term. This period of time is called *penumbra*.

At UCLH, more and more women are beginning to be referred for dietetic therapy along with or instead of the regular treatment for fertility.

Educating health workers

Educating other health workers on the importance of preconception nutrition is something that is done regularly at UCLH. The message can then be spread to a wider audience. Not all doctors, for example, are aware of the importance of avoiding anaemia in young women (the incidence is on the rise): a low iron status in the preconception period has been shown to give rise to babies that are small compared with the placenta size[8]. Some researchers suggest this could have long-term detrimental health implications, such as high blood pressure.

Poverty

In *The Health of the Nation*[19], there was little attention given to poverty, but two-thirds of LBW babies are to mothers who are poor. As part of its work, the Montreal Diet Dispensary in Canada has, since 1948, prepared regularly and revised minimum family budget standards that are sufficient to maintain health. These are presented to the Government who act on them and raise income maintenance programmes if necessary.

Preventing LBW during the antenatal period

Attention to diet during pregnancy can help increase birth weight and prevent the birth of weak babies who may have reduced immunity. Several areas of action are important.

Weight gain

More attention needs to be paid to the weight gain of the mother, particularly if she is underweight at the beginning of her pregnancy. For an average weight mother the gain should be 13–20 kg (23–35 lb). The further implication of this figure is that even an overweight mother (BMI 26–29) should gain 8.5–14 kg (15–25 lb), while an underweight mother (BMI < 19.8), or a teenager who is still growing, needs to gain 16–23 kg (28–40 lb).

Teenage pregnancies

As well as correcting appalling diets, teenage pregnant girls warrant special attention as they are also still growing, to include:

- calcium 1500 mg
- vitamin D 10 μg
- iron 14.8 mg.

Nutrition education

Women are usually very receptive to nutrition education while they are pregnant, giving the opportunity to promote healthy eating. Nutrients such as iron which can be low (due to the declining intake of red meat) and calcium (due to the fattening and allergy causing image of dairy products) need special attention. The importance of these minerals should be stressed with examples of foods in which they can be found, including non-meat sources of iron and non-dairy sources of calcium.

Screening

Screening during pregnancy may allow targeted advice by observing indicators such as:

- previous LBW baby
- low weight prior to pregnancy
- smoking, alcohol or drug misuse
- close birth spacing
- use of contraceptive pill just prior to conceiving
- age below 19, or over 35.

UCLH runs midwife education sessions with one of its aims being to screen pregnant women and refer them to their dietitian.

Timing

The dietitian would like the opportunity to see pregnant mothers as early as possible. This would save a lot of mothers' anxieties and comments about 'Wishing they knew that sooner'. Advice could be given on: folic acid, nausea, alcohol intake, food hygiene, and liver and vitamin A.

Conclusion: What actions are required by governments?

Perinatal mortality has decreased in the last 30 years, unlike the incidence of LBW, but this is mainly due to improved perinatal care such as expensive Special Care Baby Unit equipment. Surely it seems logical to look at the root cause of these LBW babies who require this expensive support.

The Government must now realize that channelling resources into improving the health of mothers in their preconception period is a way of saving much expenditure later on. It needs to acknowledge the general importance of women's health in the preconception period. There are considerable resource releasing possibilities.

Learning points

- Prevention of LBW must occur before conception.

- LBW must also be countered during the pregnancy.

- Dietitians should be involved at an early stage.

References

1   Stein Z *et al.* (1975) *Famine and Human Development: The Dutch Hunger Winter of 1944/45.* New York, Oxford University Press.

2   Doyle W, Crawford M A, Wynn A H A *et al.* (1990) The association between maternal diet and birth dimensions. *Journal of Nutrition and Medicine.* **1**: 9–17.

3   Caan B, Horgan D M, Margen S *et al.* (1978) Benefits associated with WIC supplemental feeding during the inter pregnancy interval. *American Journal of Clinical Nutrition.* **45**: 29–41.

4   Personal communications with neonatologist, UCL Hospital, London.

5   Wynn M and Wynn A (1983) *The Prevention of Handicap of Early Pregnancy Origin: Some Evidence of Good Health Before Conception.* Foundation for Education and Research in Childbearing, London.

6   The Scottish LBW Group (1992) The Scottish LBW Study: survival, growth, neuromotor and sensory impairment. *Archives of Disease of Children.* **67**: 675–81.

7   The Scottish LBW Group (1992) The Scottish LBW Study: language attainment, cognitive status and behavioural problems. *Archives of Disease of Children.* **67**: 682–6.

8   Barker D (1993) Maternal nutrition and coronary vascular disease. *Nutrition and Health.* **2**: 99–106.

9   Smith A and Jacobson B (eds.) (1989) *The Nation's Health: A Strategy for the 1990s.* King Edward's Hospital Fund for London, London.

10   Taylor Nelson (1993) *One Year on From the Health of the Nation. A Survey Conducted for Boots the Chemist.* Taylor Nelson, London.

11   Price S and Sephton J (1991) *Just Desserts: Influencing Food Choices: Food Behaviour and Strategies for Change.* Horton, Bradford.

12   National Food Alliance (1993) Mori poll Commissioned for the Get Cooking Project. National Food Alliance, London.

13   Doyle W, Wynn A H A, Wynn S W *et al.* (1991) The diets of 28 mothers of LBW babies. *Midwife Health Visitor and Community Nurse.* **27/2**: 44–6.

14   Crawley H F (1993) The role of breakfast cereals in the diets of 16–17 year old teenagers in Britain. *Journal of Human Nutrition and Dietetics.* **6**: 205–15.

15   Wald N, Sneddon J, Densem J *et al.* (1991) Prevention of neural tube defects: results of the Medical Research Council Vitamin Study. *Lancet.* **338**: 131–7.

16   Van der Spuy A M, Steer P J, McCusker M *et al.* (1988) Outcome of pregnancy in underweight women after spontaneous and induced ovulation. *British Medical Journal.* **296**: 962–5.

17   Wynn A and Wynn M (1990) The need for nutrition assessment in the treatment of the infertile patient. *Journal of Nutrition and Medicine.* **1**: 315–24.

18   Naye R L (1979) Weight gain and the outcome of pregnancy. *American Journal of Obstetrics and Gynecology.* **135(1)**: 3.

19   Department of Health (1992) The Health of the Nation. HMSO, London.

14

Value for money in health promotion
Jeremy Corson

Introduction

Questions are asked frequently about how cost-effective health promotion is and whether it can release resources. This chapter, drawing mainly on the experience of the Heart Beat Wales project and the work of the Welsh Health Promotion Authority (Health Promotion Wales) over nearly ten years, shows that considerable effort has been devoted to addressing such questions, and that it provides already a solid basis for future action. There remains, though, plenty of scope to develop further this tremendously important area.

One must be careful not to over-simplify the issues. Those involved in public health are faced by all sorts of operational demands, and involvement with health promotion over a ten-year period reinforces the need for realism. It is an 'art' as well as a 'science', and indeed the definition of public health includes the words art and science. One must look at the possibilities as well as the problems.

Thinking about a strategy requires a view of the destination and of the route, and these were defined when Heart Beat Wales was started. But it is not enough looking just at efficient use of resources or at effectiveness. Along the way the programme itself must be evaluated and improvements and modifications made as appropriate. It is perfectly legitimate to refocus, so as to reach the target population, or to avoid unwanted side-effects. It is not just drugs which can cause these; even screening programmes can have side-effects, for example raised anxieties.

Heart Beat Wales

Figure 14.1 summarizes some of the inputs and outputs of the project. On the right-hand side are costs and benefits, but that is not all that needs to be looked at

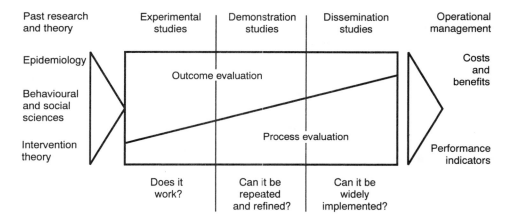

Figure 14.1   Developmental model for the evaluation of health education programmes

when evaluating a programme such as this; outcomes are in fact a particularly difficult area in health promotion because some of them may be quite long-term. A focus on process is quite legitimate, as long as it is done carefully. There is not just one question, 'Does it work?'. In this type of project others are valid too, such as:

- can it be repeated?
- can it be refined?
- can it be implemented widely?

The comments of Geoffrey Rose about the need to look at the population perspective in addition to the individual one is very important[1], because if we have an effective intervention, unless it can reach the entire population, it is not going to be as effective as it could be.

A lot of thought went into how Heart Beat Wales should be organized. Wales is such a varied country, geographically and historically, that it would be absolutely impossible to find within it both a control area and an intervention area. This can be done with closed systems and indeed some of the evaluations of Heart Beat Wales have been done on that sort of basis. In general, the evaluation has to take into account the simultaneous implementation of interventions by a number of agencies and to try to get some idea of how that relates to the outcomes in different parts of the country and in different groups.

This underlines the difficulty in measuring outcome. To supplement existing monitoring systems through which changes in mortality and to a lesser extent in morbidity can be tracked, specially designed survey mechanisms have been established since 1985, looking at risk factors, behaviours and personal characteristics.

The Heart Beat Wales programme as launched in April 1985 was originally set up as a five-year demonstration project, with evaluation built in, based around a wide consensus, represented by reports by the Royal College of Physicians and the Welsh Medical Committee. Several factors were identified for study. These were:

- smoking

- food and nutrition

- alcohol consumption

- physical activity

- social support

- health knowledge and attitudes

- cardio-pulmonary resuscitation

- screening and health service contact.

The programme was clearly very limited in its initial approach, taking in just a few risk factors, which was felt to be the most practical way of tackling what was one of the major public health problems.

Figure 14.2 shows the original plan. There was and indeed there still is a reference area somewhere in the UK. Surveys were undertaken in 1985, 1988, 1990 and 1993 involving around 18 000 completed questionnaires. The questionnaires were very detailed and were from all over Wales. This allowed information to be fed back on a district basis, which was helpful not just in terms of outcome, but also in maintaining recognition at a local level that the programme was relevant.

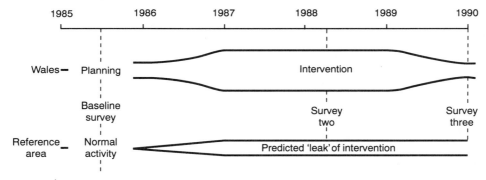

Figure 14.2   Welsh Heart Programme. Planned programme development, 1985–90

Building alliances

The funding was £250 000 a year for five years. This is perhaps not a great deal compared with the budget of a district health promotion unit. But it was enhanced by collaborating closely with other bodies.

- Working with Tescos on food labelling effectively contributed another £200 000. This was because the agendas overlapped, with them looking for a market edge, and other supermarket chains quickly followed suit.

- Wales has about three million people and 12 million sheep, and the agricultural interest is clearly an important one. The Meat and Livestock Commission and project staff worked very closely on identifying incentives for both farmers and butchers to produce leaner animals.

- The media were very interested and effectively Health Promotion Wales secures about £400 000 worth of free media coverage a year.

- Other partners have included the School Curriculum Council, the Sports Council for Wales, voluntary agencies, Red Cross, St John and the Women's Institutes.

- Environmental Health departments were also important, since their officers inspect routinely the kitchens of restaurants and other facilities. The opportunity was taken to suggest that when they did this they could also look the menu and see that a certain area in the restaurant was non-smoking.

Parallel developments occurred elsewhere. Very shortly afterwards, following a WHO International Conference the Ottawa Charter was published. Its principles were to:

- build healthy public policy

- enable, mediate, advocate

- create supportive environments

- strengthen community action

- develop personal skills

- re-orientate health services.

These emphasized the importance for health promotion of healthy public policy, community involvement, personal skills, and what is now increasingly seen, the re-orientation of health services. Within two years of the programme's start, colleagues in Glasgow and in Northern Ireland had established excellent projects and the Look After Your Heart initiative was launched in England.

Widening the focus: Health Promotion Wales

In 1987 at the same time as the Health Education Authority was created in England the Health Promotion Authority for Wales was set up. This took over the Heart Beat Wales programme and other functions previously handled by the Health Education Council, which had had responsibility for both England and Wales.

Following this, a quite wide ranging consultation exercise was undertaken, involving both professionals and the public. The professionals generally had a feel within their own particular fields of what they thought the priorities were, and over time the process of developing consensus has been studied in some detail. The views of people working in the field are often close to the priorities which might be identified with more detailed studies. The public were also consulted, both individually using mail-outs and through various organizations, to see what they thought the priorities were.

Because the additional resources made available to the new authority were small, compared with the much wider remit, expansion was managed carefully.

- Alcohol was early taken on board as an issue, with a greater effort to collect data in this area.

- There was a focus on healthy sexuality, since the AIDS epidemic was becoming quite strongly established.

- Cancer was included insofar as some of the risk factors for heart disease were in common with those for cancers – particularly diet, smoking and alcohol.

- The consultation highlighted the need for an emphasis on young people.

- It was intended that later, as resources became available, accidents, mental health and the needs of older people would be addressed more specifically.

Despite the changes, the original surveys and a lot of the interventions were still running and by 1990 some shifts were evident:

- smoking rates had come down quite dramatically

- intake of meat and saturated fat and total fat had decreased, and that of fruit, vegetables, fish, fibre had increased

- in common with many other places, the problem of overweight, if anything, had slightly worsened

- there was a marginal improvement in uptake of physical activity, but this was not really significant.

The outstanding challenges became evident.

Evidence of effectiveness: the case of smoking

What evidence was there that using focused health promotion interventions had had a significant effect? As stated earlier, the economic evaluation of health promotion is not easy, since there may be many influences on outcome, which in turn may be long term. But one area where a lot of interest has focused is smoking, and here several studies from Wales and elsewhere are now available.

- The Smoking Epidemic series, including *Counting the Cost*[2] and *A Prescription for Change*[3] provides a simple but striking summary of the cost to the NHS of diseases which are attributable to smoking. These do grab the public imagination, and provide a very good focus for discussion.

- Several studies have attempted to address broader economic issues. Catford *et al.*[4] reviewed 11 studies which showed benefit : cost ratios of smoking interventions which averaged about 2 : 1.

- *The Economic Consequences of Smoking in Northern Ireland*[5] discusses a range of issues including the effects on individuals, the workplace, health and social services, government, and the tobacco industry itself.

- More recently Nutbeam *et al.*[6] have undertaken an economic analysis of Heart Beat Wales' non-smoking programme. Data show that in Wales, as elsewhere, young people have been smoking more. There is, nevertheless, quite an encouraging reduction overall among those aged 18–64. The costs identified in the study included the programme itself and those elsewhere across society, such as sickness and absence, and the question of full employment, always a difficult one, was also confronted. The approach at least gives some sort of indication of the magnitude of some of the potential benefits, broken down by some of the individual conditions.

- Because it is very difficult to say that the project itself was responsible for all of the benefits, a range of different 'attribution rates' have been looked at, from 100% down to 10%, the 10% here meaning that one assumes that the project was only responsible for 10% of the reduction. Even at a 10% level, and including other adjustments such as discounting for future benefits, taking the economy more broadly, there will be a benefit. Table 14.1 indicates some of the costs and benefits, the latter amounting to as much as £7 million for the NHS and nearly £40 million for the general economy.

- Studies of individual interventions have also been undertaken. Nutbeam *et al.* in an evaluation of two school smoking education programmes[7] concluded that reduction of teenage smoking would need more comprehensive interventions than school health education alone. An evaluation of the Health Promotion Wales Quit and Win contest[8] showed a 30% quit rate at one year, with an estimated cost of £42 per year of life saved, which is cheaper than other interventions.

Each of these studies must be interpreted appropriately, but further work in this field will increasingly inform decisions on appropriate investment of resources.

Table 14.1   Economic appraisal

Costs	Benefits
1 Health Promotion Authority	1 Savings to the NHS from reduced morbidity, displaced mortality
2 DHA Local Programmes	
3 Commerce and industry/employers	2 Reduction in lost output from reduced morbidity, displaced mortality

Interestingly some other recent studies have shown no significant difference between individual projects and the control. That suggests that the way that it has been done in general practice over recent years perhaps has not been effective; it does not mean that health promotion in general practice cannot be effective.

Improvements in quality of life may, of course, only be increasing the burden on the health services at a later stage. But does that matter? It is also important to recognize that health promotion may not always release resources, but should also be seen as an investment in health, and considered in the context of alternative interventions. The strategic approach to health service planning in Wales, *Strategic Intent and Direction*, supports the principle of balancing investment, in contrast to the past pattern, when traditionally most of the money went into treatment and investigation. This approach feeds into Local Strategies for Health in Wales.

Health Promotion Wales has continued to develop, and has recently been subject to an efficiency scrutiny. It is now very much structured to try to respond to those who use its services. It is a tight operation, spending a little over £3 million per year against total NHS Wales expenditure exceeding £2000 million. Strengthening the focus at local level, following the scrutiny, commissioners were required by the Welsh Office to move towards spending 0.75% of their budget on health promotion.

What are the achievements?

There has been a significant lifestyle change, at what is a comparatively small cost. The 1993 survey results have now been published[9], and they show a continuation of the trend from 1985 to 1990. The fact that we now know that the diet of young people and smoking frequency among young women are getting worse is not a condemnation of the programme. It can be argued that rather the improved data allow refinement of target groups and more focused efforts for improvement. The surveys are now established: they have run in 1985, 1988, 1990 and 1993, and there is a Youth Survey which is part of a European Study, allowing international comparisons.

A focus on measurable health outcomes is now part of the NHS strategy in Wales. Of course, reorientation of the health service has so far occurred only at the margins and one would not expect it to move too quickly, but nevertheless there is pressure for further movement, and within Wales changes over a broader area over the next 20 years are being studied.

There have been significant achievements in working through the other sectors – education, industry and so on. It is important to maintain this broad focus, to counter the danger of thinking only in terms of inputs and outputs related to the health services sector. This is important too in thinking about releasing resources. A narrow concentration on costs and benefits just within the NHS will perhaps rule out some options. There is a need both to work through other agencies and to include their inputs and outputs in the evaluation. The Welsh Health Promotion Authority has an innovative research and development strategy and research and development division, and this activity must be co-ordinated with the NHS research and development strategy to avoid duplication, because evaluation itself is quite a resource intensive activity.

Learning points

- There are pressures on all parts of the NHS and it is important that long-term, apparently less urgent issues are not squeezed out, such as health promotion and evaluation in all its forms.

- Building alliances increases the resources available.

- Evaluations in the health promotion field are not lacking, but evaluation is not enough.

- The next stage is for commissioners to ensure that the findings are actually put into practice.

References

1 Rose G (1987) Environmental factors and disease. *British Medical Journal.* **294**: 963–5.

2 Health Education Authority (1991) *The Smoking Epidemic: Counting the Cost in Wales.* Health Education Authority, London.

3 Health Education Authority (1993) *A Prescription for Change.* Health Education Authority, London.

4 Catford J C, Nutbeam D and Woolaway M C (1984) Effectiveness and cost benefits of smoking education. *Community Medicine.* **6**: 264–72.

5 Ulster Cancer Foundation (1986) *The Economic Consequences of Smoking in Northern Ireland.* Ulster Cancer Foundation, Belfast.

6 Nutbeam D, Prowle M and Phillips C (1991) *The Heartbeat Wales No-smoking Intervention: An Empirical Study of the Economic Viability of a Health Promotion Programme. Heartbeat Wales Technical Report No. 22.* Health Promotion Authority for Wales, Cardiff.

7 Nutbeam D, Macaskill P, Smith C *et al.* (1993) Evaluation of two school smoking education programmes under normal classroom conditions. *British Medical Journal.* **306**: 102–7.

8 Health Promotion Wales (1994) *Evaluation of the Quit and Win Contest.* Health Promotion Wales, Cardiff (in press).

9 Moore L, Roberts C, Playle R *et al.* (1994) *Related behaviours in Wales 1985–93: Findings from the Health in Wales Survey.* Health Promotion Wales Technical Report No 8. Health Promotion Wales, Cardiff.

15

Health promoting hospitals in Europe

Dominic Harrison

Introduction

The Department of Health's mission statement identifies its function as protecting and promoting the health of the population. Its secondary task is to secure systems of health care for those who need it. Both elements are required to be delivered with maximum consumer involvement.

It is therefore important that hospitals review their organizational ability to involve consumers in the delivery of the health service's objective – good health for all the population. The consequent refocusing of activity within hospitals will require reviews of technical efficiency (doing things right) and allocative efficiency (doing the right things) if health gain in terms of demonstrable outcomes and tangible benefits is to be demonstrated. Hospitals who can develop consumer-orientated prevention activities as a part of their service delivery will attract income from commissioning authorities. It is these concepts that are at the centre of the health promoting hospitals initiative.

This chapter addresses some of the problems with current health investment strategies and reviews how the European Health Promoting Hospital network is working to develop practical solutions to the problem of releasing resources to achieve health gain.

Health investment strategies

The main purpose of using 5.9% of the UK Gross National Product for health is to keep people happy, healthy, safe and independent at home with their families and communities. Some argue that it should be used primarily to provide high quality illness treatment services for people who are sick. The necessity for such provision is largely a mark of the service's failure to meet its primary objectives.

A review of mortality trends for England and Wales from 1841 to 1985 shows that the investment strategy used for achieving this aim has not delivered the desired outcomes[1].

Figure 15.1 shows that the introduction of the hospital-focused NHS in 1948 (dotted line) made very little contribution to preventable mortality – it may even have slowed down the rate of health improvement that was already being achieved.

The improvement had been brought about by changes to the social, economic and environmental circumstances of peoples' lives, particularly in the areas of nutrition, housing, disposable income, a clean and accessible water supply, and the increased availability of family planning. It is still the case that such changes would bring about the biggest advances in public health, but most of the NHS budget is not directed to investment in this area.

The most expensive and least humane and effective way of dealing with the nation's health is to wait for people to become ill and then give them a hospital bed. Such a strategy misses the essential point that the stage at which intervention

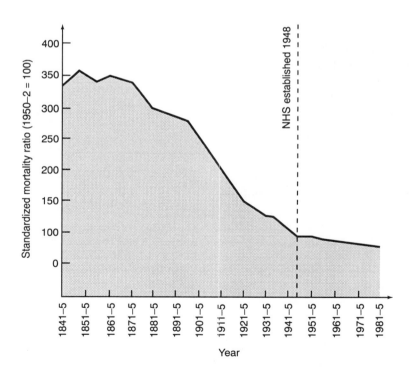

Figure 15.1 Mortality trends, 1841 to 1985 in England and Wales, all persons. The Standardized Mortality Ratio (SMR) is an index that allows for differences in age structure. Values above 100 indicate higher mortality than in 1950–2 and values below 100 indicate lower mortality. (Source: Department of Health (1991) *The Health of The Nation: A Consultative Document for Health in England and Wales*. HMSO, London)

would bring about the greatest outcome for a specific investment of health care resources – health gain – is within primary prevention when people are still well, in their homes, families, communities and workplaces.

The current distribution of health care investment is, as a result, ineffective, unscientific, inefficient and inequitable; but quick, radical reform is fraught with political and organizational difficulty.

The European Health Promoting Hospitals Project and Network

The main challenge for health policy reformers and the WHO is to develop political and organizational strategies that will assist managers and politicians to effect the transition to health gain focused services with the minimum of agony and maximum public understanding and support.

This is particularly true for hospitals, for although they command great public support and loyalty, only about 30% of their services have been evaluated as beneficial to their recipients by the standards of a double blind clinical trial.

Whatever their contribution to health, disinvestment from hospital services may be considered politically expensive. The next best thing may be to subvert the traditional concept of the hospital from within. This is perhaps the essence of the health promoting hospital strategy, although as a whole it is rooted in a much broader reform process.

During the 1980s the WHO Regional Office for Europe began developing practical strategies to try to refocus health services and reorientate health care investment towards the emerging socio-ecological understanding of health promotion. This followed the WHO strategy of Health for All by the Year 2000 (1977) which offered a focus for progressive change in concepts of health that resulted in 38 targets being set in 1984.

The Ottowa Charter for Health Promotion (1986) recognized:

> that policy decisions in areas other than health make a key contribution to health; that supportive physical and social environments are important in establishing the conditions for health and the parameters for health behaviours; that the community can and must play a crucial role in undertaking action for health; that a broad range of personal skills for health needs to be developed; and that existing health services need to be reorientated.

WHO reasoned that, if the most promising improvements in health can be created by changing the social, economic and environmental contexts of peoples lives, then it is efforts directed at changing these settings that may be most effective in achieving health improvement.

Thus the Healthy Cities movement was born in 1986, an approach later extended to workplaces, homes, schools and in fact any setting which provided an opportunity for planned and systematic interventions to promote health. In 1989 the concept of Health Promoting Hospitals was developed jointly by the WHO Regional Office for Europe and the Ludwig Boltzmann Institut Für Medizin und

Gesundheitssoziologie in Vienna in partnership with a local 1000-bed general hospital, the Rudolfstiftung. The health promoting hospital initiative formalized its aims, concepts and criteria at a conference in Budapest in 1991 where the Ottowa Charter advocated action within the context of a hospital setting.

Since 1991 an international network of 20 pilot health promoting hospitals has functioned as part of the multi-city action plan of the health cities project. Their role is further to develop the concepts and processes involved in becoming a health promoting hospital and identify externally validated health gain outcomes. Interest in the network has been shown by over 21 countries from the European Region, plus Australia, Canada, New Zealand and Japan.

To be a pilot hospital the following conditions have to be met:

- managerial commitment to the Ottowa Charter for Health Promotion and the Budapest Declaration on Health Promoting Hospitals

- establishment of a management group with a designated co-ordinator and an external validating institution

- adoption of at least five hospital-based health promotion sub-projects. Ideally these are health gain targeted action/research interventions, that use existing internal resources.

The concept of a health promoting hospital is still evolving. In addition to increasing consumer involvement and undertaking preventive activities within existing resources, a health promoting hospital uses mediation, advocacy and alliance building with the community it serves to deliver health gain outcomes.

Becoming a health promoting hospital

The steps to develop a UK Health Promoting Hospitals project are as follows:

Step 1 – secure management agreement

It is important to gain hospital management agreement to the Ottowa Charter and to the principles of the Budapest Declaration. These commit the management of the hospital to change the concept and role of the hospital within the community. The Budapest declaration in particular commits them to specific action, audits and validations.

Step 2 – expand stakeholders

This step involves hospital staff, unions, departmental managers and clinical directors in order to facilitate support and co-operation. The success of a Health Promoting Hospital Project may well depend on how well this process is managed. The development of a health promoting hospital cannot just be added on as another project to a few departments – it should be a core process throughout the organization.

Step 3 – develop healthy alliances

The key alliance should be with an academic or other research institution whose role would be to assist with the planning, documentation and evaluation of the overall project as well as future sub-projects. The most important long-term role of this partnership is for the institution to offer independent monitoring of the project's health gain outcomes. Other partners in the project will depend on how the future sub-projects develop.

The academic or research institution will need to be near the hospital and may well require financial support for the work it will undertake, although there are ways in which collaborative research can be undertaken without financial commitment from the hospital e.g. some institutions are willing to supervise undergraduate or postgraduate research free of charge. Also, NHS staff could register for supervised academic research degrees which both reduces costs and gives staff a payback on their investment in the project.

Step 4 – appoint or nominate a project coordinator

The project coordinator should be in a senior position with a high level of administrative skills. The individual should have a working knowledge of research processes, organizational development and, most importantly, the principles and practice of health promotion.

Step 5 – establish a project committee

A Health Promoting Hospital committee to manage the project should ideally be chaired by the chief executive. Members should include the project coordinator, staff of the academic institution undertaking the research or evaluation and key sub-project managers.

Other significant members could include the chair of the medical executive committee, trade unionists, or leading members of the local medical executive committee. The management group should meet monthly to review and support the project's development.

Step 6 – plan organizational structures and processes

The structure should be explicit and mission, roles and responsibilities should be identified. Consideration should be given to the management processes of organizational development and change within the hospital as a whole, and to the development of at least five separate sub-projects which should be developed jointly between NHS staff and the academic or research institutions.

The sub-projects might ideally be aimed at issues related to the Health of the Nation targets and should be developed as intervention studies with clearly defined protocols agreed in advance with the academic or research institution. This is particularly important because only careful planning at this stage will ensure validated outcomes from the sub-project interventions, so allowing efficiency and effectiveness. All sub-projects should be planned within the existing resources of the hospital and should be focused on the causes rather than the consequences of hospital admission.

The projects can be a completely new initiative e.g. developing an environmental audit process for the hospital, or an extension of existing work that meets the criteria of the Budapest Declaration e.g. developing and extending a coronary rehabilitation programme to cover primary prevention of CHD with families of patients.

Step 7 – Implement, popularize, evaluate and network

The initial five projects should run for up to five years and managers, staff and project participants should be encouraged to publicize the positive benefits and evaluated outcomes of the projects.

The process of building healthy alliances and networks should evolve along with the experience and skills of all staff participating, and close links should be developed with schools, workplaces, primary health care teams, community groups and other local institutions who can promote health.

Step 8 – Promote integration and ensure quality assessment

After the initial stages of project development have been established within the organization, long-term consideration should be given to how the hospital can develop processes to require all departments or clinical directorates to redirect their resources in the ways shown by the initial sub-project 'product champions'.

One strategy for achieving this is to establish a stakeholders' conference with the general public and hospital users to allow them to set the agenda for changes they would wish to see. This would then be integrated into the planning and contracting process. Another model is to integrate the Health Promoting Hospital approach into the total quality management strategy of the hospital. Work on both these integration strategies is now underway amongst the European network hospitals.

Experiences and outcomes within model hospitals

Each of the 21 hospitals in the European Network of Health Promoting Hospitals reports on progress at least annually to a standing committee. These reports cover both the development of the overall projects and the success of the specific sub-projects.

Responsibility for overall documentation and evaluation of the network's work is undertaken by the Ludwig Boltzmann Institute in Vienna. Hospitals in the network vary in size and type and operate within quite different financial, and political and administrative frameworks. This has resulted in a wide range of sub-projects being developed. Some examples are:

- The smoke free hospital project – Padua, Italy

- Improving dietary habits among hospital staff – Warsaw, Poland

- Health promotion in hospitals through job and organizational development – University of Bielefeld, Germany

- Hygiene in hospitals: cost-effective measures against hospital acquired infection – Basle, Switzerland

- Training of diabetic and the outpatient department as interface between in- and out-patient care – Vienna, Austria.

Evaluation strategies vary and most projects are far from complete. Participating hospitals are achieving success in innovation and service development towards health gain, but the identification of extra resources for the external validation process seems to present a significant problem for most hospitals.

Preston Acute Hospitals NHS Trust – England's pilot hospital in the European network – has undertaken a considerable amount of work on the concept since being accepted into the network in February 1993. In association with the Health Education Authority it ran the first English Health Promoting Hospitals Conference in April 1993 and published proceedings. In September 1993 it undertook a major public and staff consultation exercise on health promoting hospitals, the results of which are now being used as the agenda for change within the Preston project. In November 1993 it participated in a major NHS managers' consultation exercise established by the then NHS Management Executive aimed at market testing the concepts for the development of future national guidance. It has since worked with the National Health Service Executive and others to develop guidelines for all English hospitals which was due for publication and release from the Department of Health in the summer of 1994.

In addition to these national developments, Preston has developed its own five sub-projects in association with the Lancashire Centre For Medical Studies, jointly established between the University of Central Lancashire and Preston Acute Hospitals NHS Trust. The sub-projects are summarized below.

Project 1: accident prevention

This uses data and staff resources from the accident and emergency department. The aim is to reduce accidents and accident and emergency admission by a mixture of organizational, educational and outreach strategies.

Staff from the Accident and Emergency department had already established an 'extended triage' system for admission where potential attendees could telephone for immediate advice on first aid or self-care. Consideration is being given to the teaching of self-care skills for regular attendees who could potentially deal with minor ailments if they felt more skilled, knowledgeable and confident.

Outreach work is being undertaken to prevent the causes of admission. This work is being undertaken in alliance with both NHS community staff such as school nurses, and commercial organizations. A notable success so far has been the identification of burns and scalds to children under two living in nearby Blackpool DSS bed and breakfast accommodation. Action was taken by a nurse on the burns ward involving collaboration with the Hotel and Caterers Association to remove kettles with flexes from rooms and published guidance throughout the resort has already brought about health improvements, with burns and scalds admissions reduced significantly.

Project 2: the storage, collection, transportation and disposal of domestic and clinical waste

This aims to improve the environmental effect of the hospital on the community. It involves all aspects of health promotion in the collection and disposal of waste. A baseline study has determined the existing pre-intervention practices and data from this are being used to produce practical, measurable improvements. Considerable investments in capital equipment has been allocated to this project and it is hoped that the improvements demonstrated will act as a model for other local industries and hospitals.

Project 3: the management of post-coronary patients

This project aims to extend and evaluate the existing health alliance between the hospital's coronary care unit, the University of Central Lancashire and the voluntary sector charity Heartbeat. It has involved coronary care staff and the University of Central Lancashire in a programme of teaching sessions for patients and carers, and Heartbeat staff in a programme of primary prevention within schools.

Ex-patients work closely with the programmes that have been developed, and the alliance is developing the means of monitoring the outcomes.

Project 4: the health promoting hospital in the community: developing health networks and alliances

This is process-based and seeks to identify and evaluate the benefits and outcomes of health alliances developed as a result of the health promoting hospitals project.

Project 5: health at work in the NHS

This project aims to improve staff health by a wide range of evaluated interventions which vary from policy initiatives to one-to-one health education. Evaluation and monitoring has been built into the programme. The Occupational Health Department has purchased a lifestyle screening package and is currently completing a baseline study of a 10% sample of the hospital's staff. This screening includes medical data such as blood pressure as well as health behaviour measures and can act as a counselling tool for one to one health education.

The data collected in a second follow-up study will be used to review the effect of workplace-based interventions on a range of population indicators of health status.

Conclusion

There is no doubt that after the full five years of the European health promoting hospitals network's life it will be able to demonstrate a reorientation of hospital activity towards health gain activities. It remains to be seen whether it will be able to demonstrate validated health gain outcomes as a result.

However, the logic and inevitability of the change is not just for purchasers of health care services, but also will reshape the attitudes of providers. The medical director of a German privately funded hospital described this need for change at the 1994 European Health Promoting Hospital Network Conference in Hamburg. A review to identify the key criteria for a market leading organization in the year 2000 conducted in the hospital came up with three needs.

- To be closer to their local community, involving consumers in service delivery, improving quality and adding value to their service portfolio by delivering earlier more cost-effective interventions. Such interventions would likely be with well people identified by increasingly effective screening.

- To 'break through the walls' of the hospital and extend into peoples homes, thanks to developments in medical technology. This would reduce bed numbers and require reskilling and reorientation of the staff and buildings.

- To be a learning organization dedicated to public health improvement and health maintenance if it was to attract future commissions for the provision of health services.

This managerial and commercial diagnosis led the hospital management to conclude they should become a health promoting hospital. Whether looked at from the purchaser or the provider side of health care provision, there are sound strategic, ethical and commercial reasons for developing health promoting hospitals.

Learning points

- Tremendous opportunities for health gain exist through health provision.

- Shifting the focus within current budgets may be easier than trying to move budgets.

- A carefully managed process is likely to be necessary to maximize the process.

Reference

1   Department of Health (1991) *The Health of the Nation: A Consultative Document for Health in England.* HMSO, London.

16

Shifting the focus in dental care

Wayne Richards

Introduction

This chapter examines the health promotion role of the general dental practitioner. The earlier suggestion[1] that there is room for improvement in how health promotion is delivered through general medical practice is true also for general dental practice. It is recognized within primary health care that availability and accessibility of services are potential barriers to the receipt of care[2], but there is another important factor, often overlooked, and that is acceptability – the acceptability of the type of care delivered by clinicians. It is very difficult for individuals to look at themselves and ask 'how acceptable is my performance as a clinician from the patient's viewpoint? What effect am I having on my client group?' This chapter is a description of a patient-centred delivery system, developed by a dental practitioner team based in Swansea, in South Wales.

Creating an image

In dentistry, at the moment considerable energy is being concentrated on the image of general dental practice[3]. What patients see from the outside creates, in part, that image. For the Swansea team the image is middle of the road, not up-market, not down-market. The image the team wants to project is one of self-help and health, not an image of 'drill and fill' and repair. They have a logo, which is of mother and father with a child, and the mother and father have taken control of that child's dental health, through self-help. That logo is used through the whole building (Figure 16.1).

The building provides the structural environment, but it is the people working within the building who deliver the care and form the health-driven environment of care and support. The team consists of two dentists and eight support staff. Seven

Figure 16.1   Logo of the Swansea dental team

dental surgery assistants (DSAs) are trained to National Examining Board for Dental Surgery Assistants (NEBDSA) level and all are also trained or training to be dental health educators. So they are not just DSAs, but dental health nurses, taking opportunities with patients to deliver health education messages whenever possible during a patient visit. The eighth person is specifically in charge of looking after a computer system which keeps the patient base active; his remit is just to keep patients attending.

Aims and objectives

The practice has rules and the team know the team rules because they are written down. There is a quality assurance systems manual and a quality assurance procedures manual. The systems manual provides the structure for managing change. The quality assurance procedures manual is updated according to the desires of the team. This is an invaluable tool which is audited to the BS5750 standard. Within the systems manual, there are a mission statement, aims and objectives. The aims are:

- to register 8000 patients by the end of 1995

- to keep patients with enough teeth to eat, smile and be happy for life[4].

Throughout the patient's dental career, the goal is to minimize discomfort, disability and discontent[2]. This applies to *all* the practice population, including those with dentures. A dental practitioner's role is to monitor for soft tissue health *and* to screen for oral disease, such as oral cancer. Many full denture wearers are unaware of this. They are a target group for care and that is why the team homes in on mouth, teeth and gums (MTG), not teeth alone. With full denture patients the health card will be scored for M only. Some patients who would benefit from dentures are quite happy without them. Providing they experience no discomfort, disability or discontent and are screened for oral disease, it is inappropriate to insist they have dentures.

In support of achieving the aims of the practice the team have three objectives:

- to encourage a segment of the community to register and attend the practice as prescribed

- to train the clinicians and support staff to acquire appropriate levels of skill in assessment, treatment planning and treatment delivery

- to promote healthy habits through informed choice so that patients take responsibility for their own dental health[5].

The challenge to the team is to convert the aims and objectives into reality. From the onset it should be emphasized that the practice's philosophy is based very much on the social model of health.

A partnership with patients

So how do the patients view what the team is trying to do? What does it communicate to them? They are told what they can expect of the practice through a patient's charter, which every member of the team agrees to and signs. Two elements of the charter are of importance here. One deals with the very practical issue of appointment keeping and time keeping. Patients are expected to be with the team for about an hour, this is the time needed for all the assessments to be done, and information exchanged. The other more important element is that the practice is committed not only to attending to patients' voiced dental problems, but also to making them aware of diagnosed problems of which they may be unaware and which may not be a problem for them.

When the patient first attends, the staff register him or her using a 'credit card type' registration card (Figure 16.2) which the patient signs, thereby forming a psychological contract. They are told about the practice through an information leaflet which tells them how the team would like to care for them on an ongoing basis. This promotes the concept of the patient's long-term dental career as opposed to involvement in just a one-off problem-solving session.

The first appointment will be an anxious experience for many patients. Therefore, it is appropriate to explain in advance that this appointment will include an information-gathering process regarding the state of, not just their teeth, but their mouth and gums too. Following the information-gathering stage there will be a diagnosis followed by treatment options from which they choose.

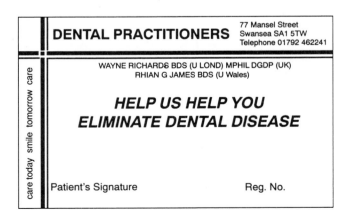

Figure 16.2   Patient registration card

A very simple colour code system is used to describe health and disease: white and green are healthy colours, yellow and red are diseased colours. This is not a scientific measure, it is a user-friendly communication tool, similar to a visual aid a teacher might use with a class of students. It could be used in conjunction with objective clinical assessments and statistical tests to establish clinicians' sensitivity and specificity to tooth decay or periodontal disease. Essentially it is used like this:

- white – never had a filling and healthy now
- green – fillings present but healthy now
- yellow – disease present
- red – much disease present.

Each clinician using this index will own his or her clinical opinion.

The practice declares, as a team, both verbally and non-verbally, that it would like its patients to be healthy i.e. in the white or green category. The final choice, however, must lie with the patients themselves. Whether health or disease is chosen, it is accepted by the team. For example, if the attendance programme is suggested for a patient and the patient does not comply, there is no reprimand when a problem instigates the next visit; instead the dentist thanks the patient for coming back, sorts out the problem and offers an alternative approach to long-term care in the future. This increases the chance of converting an irregular attender into a regular attender[6]. Even irregular attenders cross the registration 'hurdle' in such circumstances, and that places the onus of responsibility of care on the dentist. This must be the first step towards health if the dentist follows through with care based on sound behavioural science principles.

After diagnosis and colour coding, a health card (Figure 16.3) is provided for the patient. This addresses two issues:

- the reason for attendance, the health code making the patient aware that oral health is being checked
- the specification of future attendance requirements[7].

YOU'RE HEALTHIER ITS BETTER TO BE REGULAR BECAUSE ITS CHEAPER AND YOU'RE HEALTHIER ITS BETTER TO BE REGULAR

WAYNE RICHARDS **RHIAN G JAMES**

Tel:462241 Out of Hours Emergency Service 650583

Name . . . . Date . . . .

Year	Date	HEALTH CATEGORY				
		WHITE	GREEN	YELLOW	RED	OVERALL

© 1993

Figure 16.3 Patient health card

Mouth, teeth and gums are scored, the overall score is based on the greatest extent of disease. This again consolidates the fact that *both* dentist *and* patient share responsibility in the patient's dental career.

Making it work

Several theoretical principles underpin the approach adopted. First, there is a recognized need to manage the process of *communication*. There must be a message, it must be consistent, it must be fun, the lay-out must be clear. The literature must be appropriate, the range must be appropriate, it must be interesting, it must be readable and it must involve the patient[8].

Based on the scientific basis of dental health education[9], the message is four-fold:

- leave long gaps with an empty mouth – about 2–3 hours

- keep plaque less than 24 hours old

- use a fluoride toothpaste

- attend the dentist for appropriate advice.

Figure 16.4 shows the reverse of the dental health card which tells them that message. Other practical methods include providing a children's room as an appropriate environment for a 0–10 target group and using the surgery ceiling for communicating to a captive audience. These are just a few practical examples of how the team puts theory into practice.

All too often people make an assumption that communicating a message is enough to instigate a behavioural change. It is not, so different methods are needed for *influencing behaviour*. To do this, one must apply a 'can do' philosophy and understand self-efficacy, set goals, provide reward reinforcement, use time frames,

> Thank you for coming to see us. We would like you to have healthy teeth and gums by practising healthy habits.
> **(1) Regular effective brushing with a fluoride toothpaste.**
> **(2) Long gaps (about 2½ hours) between food and drink.**

Figure 16.4   Reverse side of dental health card

understand the concept of locus of control, again use involvement and give people permission to behave as they wish[2, 10–12].

An example of the application of the above for children is to reward attendance by giving them prizes, regardless of their health status. The value of the prize can be linked to health status – yellow or red and you get a toothbrush, white or green and you get a bar of chocolate. This is an important element of using permission, thus transferring responsibility to the parent. Providing direction is given to the parent as to when the chocolate should be eaten, an interactive involved learning process is experienced.

Another key element is *risk assessment*. There is much in the literature at the moment suggesting that low-risk patients should attend the dentist less frequently than high-risk patients. The need for routine six-monthly dental check-ups has been questioned by some academics[13,14]. How can risk be established? Clearly, when a dentist monitors a patient's dental career the dentist is able to build up a history of the disease experienced by the patient over a period of time. Consistent health scores (green or white) over a two-year period indicate low risk and annual recall examinations are deemed appropriate. Low risk patients are invited to attend at any time if they think care is needed. New patients are considered high risk until a history of disease experience is obtained. High risk patients may be asked to attend as appropriate for the individual. Obviously a dentist can care for a greater number of low risk patients.

Evaluation is also vital. The health index can be used as a monitoring tool to establish a practice health profile. The practice monitors baseline registration health code and current health code. Figure 16.5 shows the practice health profile at February 1994. All those in black have stayed the same, the ones in italic type have benefited and the ones in bold type have not benefited from the care delivered.

	Start totals	Red	Yellow	Green	White
Red	1300	*827*	**290**	**182**	1
Yellow	3215	67	*2282*	**843**	22
Green	1238	10	250	*960*	17
White	1056	5	67	60	*924*
Totals		909	2889	2045	964

Figure 16.5   Practice health profile, February 1994

Registrations are monitored to establish practice growth, be it positive or negative. The Dental Practice Board provide annual treatment profiles which enable comparisons between self, area and national average. The author's patient registrations at 31 March 1993 were 3484, with an average cost per claim of £27 compared with the lower quartile for the local FHSA of £28.30 and national average of £34. The rate per hundred adult item of service claims shows that diagnosis and prevention only (check-ups) was 51% compared with the upper quartile for the local FHSA of 47% and national average of 42%. These are performance indicators that can be used to audit practice outcomes against the national and local average.

Conclusion

We know that disease levels are higher in lower socio-economic groups, and that often these are the groups who do not register for care. At present the prevailing view is that resources *appear* to be sufficient to care for roughly 50% of the population, with the average practitioner caring for the needs of roughly 2000 patients. However, based on the author's experience and the opinions of such workers as Aubrey Sheiham[15], one can argue that if a philosophy based on the social model of health instead of the medical model is adopted a given resource could provide care for a much larger group. Indeed, it has been suggested that practitioners, in the not too distant future, with a team of auxiliaries could look after 20 000 plus. Others in health promotion would certainly agree with the need for dentists to change their approach (e.g. Gift, Blinkhorn)[16,17]. The problem is one of reorientation of the practitioners as opposed to the patient.

Evaluation data suggests that the sort of health promotion approach to the delivery of dental care outlined above is producing different outcomes. Whether these are *clinically* significant has yet to be evaluated. This approach has been developed from theoretical concepts; whether the mission aims will be achieved will only be revealed with time. But, if clinically significant outcomes are present then this could have significant implications for dental manpower. The author would welcome research to clarify this.

Learning points

- Dentistry does not have to be a 'drill and fill' service.

- The patient as a partner can put significant resources into a programme of care.

- A shift in emphasis to health promotion is possible in this area.

- Bringing together a variety of skills allows each team-member to concentrate on best use of individual expertise.

References

1   Corson J (1994) Value for money in health promotion. In: *Releasing Resources to Achieve Health Gain*. Welsh Health Planning Forum and the King's Fund, London.

2   Jacob M C and Plamping D (1989) *The Practice of Primary Dental Care*. Wright, Oxford.

3   British Dental Association (1990) *Masterclass, The Practice Development Programme*. BDA, London.

4   World Health Organization (1982) Goal for oral health in the year 2000. *British Dental Journal.* **152**: 21–2.

5   Ashley F P (1989) Role of dental health education in preventive dentistry. In: Murray J J (ed.) *The Prevention of Dental Disease*, 2nd edn. Oxford Medical Publications, Oxford.

6   Geboy M J (1989) *Communication and Behaviour Management in Dentistry*. B C Decker, New York.

7   Richards W (1993) Look at it from where I'm sitting – I'm a patient. *The Probe.* **35**: 5.

8   Blinkhorn A S, Fox B and Holloway P J (1980) *Notes on Dental Health Education*, 2nd edn. Scottish Health Education Group/HEC, London.

9   Levine R S (1989) *The Scientific Basis of Dental Health Education*. HEC, London.

10 Bandura A and Adams N E (1977) Analysis of self efficacy theory of behaviour change. *Cognitive Therapy and Research.* **1**: 287–310.

11 Lazarus R S (1966) *Psychological Stress and the Coping Process*. McGraw-Hill Books, London.

12 Rotter J B, Chance J E and Phares E J (1972) *Applications of the Social Learning Theory of Personality*. Holt Rinehard and Winston, New York.

13 Sheiham A (1977) Is there a scientific basis for six monthly examinations. *Lancet.* **ii**. 2, 442–4.

14 Elderton R (1985) Six monthly examinations for dental caries. *British Dental Journal.* **158**: 387–9.

15 Sheiham A (1992) The role of the dental team in promoting dental health and general health through oral health. *International Dental Journal.* **42**: 223–8.

16 Gift H C (1988) Awareness and assessment of periodontal problems among dentists and the public. *International Dental Journal.* **38**: 147–53.

17 Blinkhorn A S (1993) Factors affecting the compliance of patients with preventive dental regimens. *International Dental Journal.* **43**: 294–8.

17

Podiatric surgery: early interventions in foot health care

Nick Gilbert and Tom Galloway

Introduction

This chapter attempts to describe both resource release by simple internal adjustments to a chiropody service and the costing required to prove the case and the need for a new surgical specialty, podiatric surgery. The resource release is a short-, medium- and long-term project in regard to this approach.

The history of chiropody in the health service

The benefit of being able to offer suitable patients surgical correction for their painful foot problems is self-evident but its cost-effectiveness has not been adequately explored to date. Since the inclusion of chiropody within the NHS as part of the 1974 Reform Act, registered chiropodists have been providing regular palliative treatment to thousands of National Health Service patients. Some of these patients could have benefited from corrective foot surgery, a number of whom might subsequently have needed less or no chiropody care at all. Difficult referral routes, long orthopaedic waiting lists and failure on the part of the orthopaedic surgeons to satisfy demand effectively prevented chiropodists from referring their patients for orthopaedic surgery. This lack of an accessible curative surgical option continues to place enormous strain on NHS chiropody services. Many chiropody services are inadequate, but this inadequacy is not recent and many organizational strategies have been tried to improve matters. The Department recognized in 1974 that lack of chiropodists restricted access to the service for the existing priority groups. In 1977 it issued advice to health districts in dealing with the intractable long chiropody waiting lists. In 1980 district chiropodists felt that access could only be achieved by doubling the number of chiropodists in the service[1]. This was reiterated in 1983[2] and in 1986[3] using the association of chief chiropody officer's figures. These publications and the Wessex Report[4] suggested the wider use of foot-care assistants and other strategies to make chiropody services more efficient, but the main conclusion was that an immediate massive increase in the number of chiropodists was needed. Since those surveys were conducted there has been an increase in the number of NHS chiropodists and major changes in the NHS structure. There has also been a general steady increase in foot-care assistant numbers, but the problem of long chiropody waiting lists and low discharge rates remain commonplace. The strain on services is likely to increase with the planned reduction of growth of resources in many districts, and many districts are currently unable to fund vacant chiropody posts.

The development of podiatric surgery

The most recent and by far the most radical strategy employed to improve the care of foot problems has been the introduction of podiatric surgery. This approaches the problem of allocating limited resources to a wider group of patients by providing curative treatments where possible, thus freeing resources for other patients. The emphasis is on increasing the opportunity for discharge identified by chiropodists but unmet by orthopaedics.

The foot health service in Hereford provides a comprehensive service to meet the foot health needs of the area. It comprises a community chiropody service providing special chronic and high-intensity chiropody care, routine chiropody care, and foot care only clinics. To meet the genuine unmet need for their patients, several health authorities have now set up podiatric surgery units based on the Hereford model and tailored to their situation, and many districts and trust managers are considering podiatric surgery as a future development.

Integrated foot health service in Herefordshire

All chiropody is undertaken in twin consulting rooms allowing the chiropodist and the foot care assistant to work appropriately and efficiently. Chiropodists refer patients as necessary to the Orthotic clinics and the hospital-based diabetic and rheumatology chiropody clinic or to the hospital-based department of podiatric surgery. Thus the old-style chiropody service has been changed completely into an integrated foot health service, coining the term 'tiered levels of care in foot health'[5]. However, to achieve tiered levels of care in 1986 a fundamental change in philosophy was required of the existing chiropody staff. The assessment of all patients attending chiropody and of those on the waiting list, determined that at least 50% did not require the service of a state-registered chiropodist. Of the remaining 50%, a conservative estimate of at least 15–18% would have benefited from foot surgery leading to discharge from the service, or occasional treatment from the chiropodist or foot care assistant. These changes in Herefordshire reduced the number of state registered chiropodists from 11.1 whole-time equivalents to 3 full-time equivalents state registered chiropodists, thus releasing resources to

employ 5 whole-time equivalent foot-care assistants and two whole-time equivalent specialists in podiatric surgery. The aim of tiered levels of care is to use the
available staff for their skills in surgery, chiropodial and foot care, so as to optimize
the patient care and the efficiency of its provision. Care level is based on a treatment
plan made following assessment of the patient by the chiropodist. Each patient has
access to treatment determined by the clinical need. The innovations of this
Hereford model service are:

- the high level of integration of the tiers

- the provision of podiatric surgery

- the emphasis on educating and training foot health staff and other health care
  professionals in the appropriate referral patterns.

Since the introduction of tiered levels of care in foot health in 1986 chiropody
treatment frequency has been decided solely by the patient's need determined by
the chiropodist. Waiting lists have been eliminated by increased resources due to
the greater increase in efficiency and the availability of podiatric surgery which
allow the discharge of many patients and the reduction of the levels of foot care
needed by the remaining patients.

Podiatric surgery in practice

Podiatric surgery can be described as surgery performed on extremities distal to
the ankle and foot, by specialists in podiatric surgery usually carried out under
local anaesthesia on a day case basis[6]. This definition has been adopted by the
Working Party of the Royal College of Surgeons looking into podiatric surgery and
the range of practice accurately described the work of the Podiatric Surgery
Department in Hereford. It has become the major provider of foot surgery in the
district. The service has proved to be extremely popular with patients, foot-care
staff and in particular, the GPs. Podiatric surgery was conceived and developed in
the USA, which always seems to be about 20 years ahead of the UK.

Objections to the service

The internal costs of providing a podiatric surgical service is a common reason for
preventing managers supporting the introduction of the specialty. Secondary
objections are:

- philosophical objection to the new specialty[7,8]

- the practice of surgery by non-medically qualified practitioners

- a lack of trained podiatrical surgical specialists locally

- lack of theatre and/or other physical resources

- lack of other physical resources.

The problems of establishing podiatric surgery as a new specialty are not unique and it is perhaps unsurprising that the services already in existence react defensively. Porter in his book *Competitive Advantage* in 1985 defines a model for the intense competition in industry in which five forces are constantly present. This model is quite applicable to health care professionals and managers in understanding the problems of introducing a new service (Figure 17.1).

However, industry is geared towards profitability and the model for health-care management is geared towards viability. The professional antagonism of the established providers to the new entrant, that is podiatric surgery, can be seen in the light of this model as an inevitable result of these competitive forces. But with business managers taking a more influential role in NHS and trusts now and in the future, the economic strength of any development may well be better considered. The cost objection is the most readily addressed by analysis and yet no scientific work has been published in this area. Economic evaluation is now an accepted tool for the appraisal of health care programmes[9]. The scientific study outlined in this chapter examines the long-term cost saving or benefit outcome of podiatric surgical intervention and its effect on general health care provision and will hopefully encourage informed consideration of this important subject. To date, orthopaedic surgery has been unable to meet the need for foot surgery over the last 15 years or so. It has also been accepted that the results of podiatric surgery are as good as or better than that of orthopaedics. Despite this acknowledged history of orthopaedic uninterest in feet, an alternative to the development of

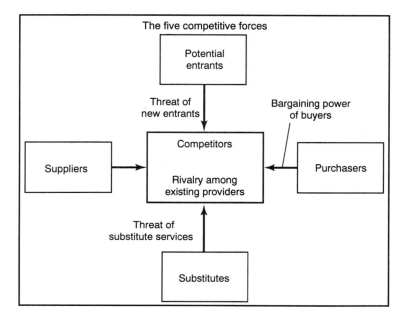

Figure 17.1   The forces causing intense competition (Source: Porter M (1985) *A competitive advantage.* MacMillan Publishers, London)

podiatric surgery remains in departments of orthopaedics or accident and emergency departments, who could also undertake foot surgery.

Cost-effectiveness comparison

Therefore, in analysing resource release, cost comparison are with orthopaedic surgery and accident and emergency departments is essential. In order, therefore, to study the possibility of genuine resource release, a study was carried out on podiatric surgery in Hereford in the form of a cost-effectiveness analysis. This is the most common form of economic evaluation because of its simplicity. This type of analysis deals with relative efficiency and having assumed that the goal was worth achieving, it shows the best means to achieve it. Cost-effective analysis also involves comparison of at least two other options with the same goal. The Department of Podiatric Surgery in Hereford as part of its pioneering role, has amassed many case histories where both surgical and non-surgical management and resources have been used. These records have been used to test the hypothesis that in appropriate cases surgical management of foot problems can be the cost-effective solution as well as the ideal clinical solution for the patients' individual needs. As the primary purpose of this study was to compare the cost-effectiveness of chiropody against podiatric surgery, computer-based podiatric surgery data were collated with the chiropody clinical records of the same patients. The subject population was of course therefore pre-ordained. The subjects were all NHS patients who had been treated within the community or hospital chiropody service in Herefordshire. The inclusion criteria were that all subjects must have:

- been referred for podiatric surgery by a state registered chiropodist

- had at least two years of chiropody history at an NHS clinic in Herefordshire before referral for podiatric surgery

- had at least two years post-surgery period follow-up confirmed by the community chiropody service

- been referred for the management of one or more of the five most important chronic chiropodial problems, which are painful involuted nails, painful thickened or gryphotic nails, mycotic nails, painful digital corns, and painful intractable corns under the lesser metatarsal heads.

As this is a cost-effectiveness study for resource release, it has been assumed that a cost-benefit analysis will show that the goal of providing some sort of health care service was worth allocating at least the present resources. The cost-effectiveness study as previously mentioned, compares the two or more contrasting forms of management[1]. In this case, chiropody only or podiatric surgery with chiropody as necessary. The cost-effectiveness of these two alternative strategies is measured using the measure of benefit, the economic outcome of the patient's subsequent need for chiropody care following podiatric surgery. This was measured by costing each sample patient's chiropody treatment pattern before and after podiatric surgery. The surgery could be said to be cost-effective therefore if the cost of that surgery and subsequent post-surgery chiropody cost resulted in a cost that was less than continuing to provide the pre-surgery chiropody care. The study, therefore, excluded costs of community services, ambulance services, voluntary services and soon.

Costings

The included costs were staff costs based on current rates of pay at July 1992 calculated to include on-costs as used in the health service. Staffing levels of the various forms of chiropody and surgical treatment, both podiatric and otherwise were based on known standard practice. This particular study assumes that it is in the best possible interests of the patient for all surgery where possible to be carried out by the most skilled practitioner available, which is in line with recent Department of Health advice. Therefore, the salary costs were as for consultant orthopaedic surgeons, casualty consultants, specialists in podiatric surgery, and senior chiropodist. It is accepted that nail surgery in casualty departments and foot surgery in orthopaedic departments is often performed by the most junior clinical staff. Nail surgery is performed by chiropodists in community clinics and chiropody may be performed by chiropodists lower than senior one level. The costs used in this study, however, were chosen to reflect the best model of podiatric practice and therefore the true cost of providing podiatric surgery and its alternatives by the acknowledged specialists in those areas. The orthopaedic and casualty surgery costs have had to be calculated from known costs, i.e. consultant and other salaries of typical orthopaedic casualty theatre teams and extrapolations based on typical working practice. These factors included theatre and out-patient department facilities, in-patient beds and nursing staff for an average patient's stay. Unknown variables that have not been included include special consultant pay enhancements that remain secret, occasional variations in working practice and the use of community care staff for post-operative dressings and stitch removal.

In an attempt to eliminate the effect of inflation and to reflect the real resource use cost, both surgical and non-surgical, the known costs are used for the base year of 1992. An attempt to reflect the effect of inflation on the various aspects of the different treatment regimes would have been difficult to achieve in view of the many variables. The common costing mechanism, discounting, has been avoided as this aspect of the calculation would only be of particular use in high inflationary periods and again is subject to the difficulty of deciding what future level of inflation to account for. It was felt that in keeping to costs for a base year there was no need for these enhancements.

Using spread-sheet formulae, the record of each subject's pre-surgery chiropody treatment need over the 2 years was costed, averaged over 1 year and projected forward to the average life expectancy of a patient of that age and sex. This was based on the most up-to-date life tables available from the West Midlands Regional Health Authority[10]. This allowed the total cost of such patient care, projected for the life of the patient, to be obtained. This is option one. The post-surgery chiropody need was costed by averaging the 2 year post-surgery chiropody and projecting this forward to the patient's average life-span. The cost of the surgical care and the post-surgery chiropody need was thus calculated. This is option two. Any saving therefore resulting from subtracting option two from one was deemed to be the measure of cost-effectiveness.

The pre-surgery chiropodial patterns and the post-surgery chiropody and foot care patterns were compared using the Chi square test to investigate whether there was a statistical difference between the pre- and post-surgery patient pattern. This method of analysis was chosen because it is well suited to investigate the significance of any difference between the two groups of non-continuous data.

Results

Out of a total of 5656 referrals to the department of podiatric surgery, 204 cases met the criteria for inclusion in the study (Figure 17.2). The largest proportion were digital surgery followed by first metatarsal and lesser metatarsal surgery, total nail ablations (Figure 17.3) and partial nail ablations. The largest client group is elderly females between the ages of 65 and 84 by a ratio of 4 : 1.

In the comparison of chiropody for life (option one) surgery and chiropody for life (option two), expected savings can be plotted against the remaining life-span of the patient (Figure 17.4). An important factor is early intervention. Obviously the earlier the better, and the more resource savings occur. A total saving for the sample group of £34 722 was made which is an average saving of £170 per patient (Table 17.1). The Chi square test confirmed the reduction in the post-surgery need

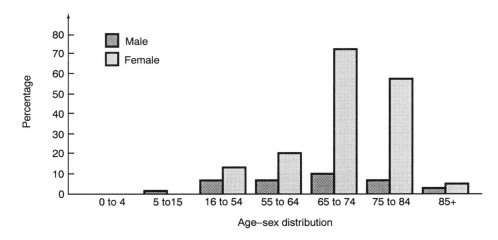

Figure 17.2 Podiatric surgery sample (n = 204): age–sex distribution. Ages grouped in Department of Health Data-set form. ▨= Male; ☐= Female

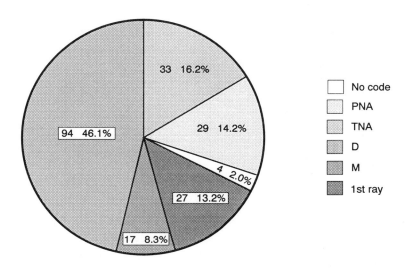

Figure 17.3   Procedures in sample group (*n* = 204). No code denotes procedures not fully matching the five groups. PNA = partial nail ablation; TNA = total nail ablation; D = digital surgery; M = lesser metatarsal surgery

Table 17.1   Costs for sample surgery activity level

Surgery type	No.	Podiatric	Casualty	Orthopaedic
Nail surgery	62	£5 322.08	£8 390.46	£15 175.12
Digital or metatarsal surgery	111	£24 626.46	N/A	£78 535.83
First ray surgery	27	£7 371.00	N/A	£26 527.50
Totals	200	£37 319.54	N/A	£120 238.45

N/A = not applicable

for chiropody. The cost comparisons for the surgical provision based on the study sample shows 318% greater costs for orthopaedic surgery over podiatric surgery. Casualty is not included in all cases because they only do some of the nail surgeries.

Summary

The provision of podiatric surgery for patients with foot problems and who are suitable for such surgery is a cost-effective alternative to the provision of life-time

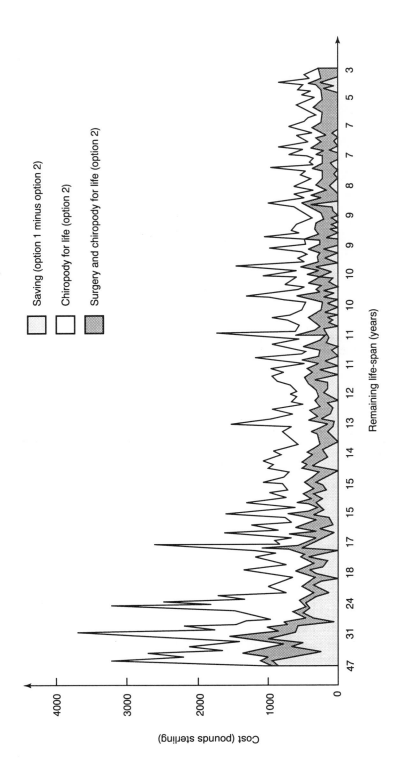

Figure 17.4 Costs of treatment options plotted against remaining life-span ($n = 204$)

palliation in the form of life-time palliative community chiropody care for the same patient. There are evident resource releasing implications. The subsidiary investigation showed podiatric surgery was a cost-effective alternative to a more traditional vision of surgical management to foot problems through orthopaedic departments. The cost comparison methods described in this chapter can be easily used and utilized by other health service districts and trusts to assist in the identification in cost benefits of introducing a podiatric surgical service in this country.

Learning points

- An integrated foot health service can demonstrate a release of resources through appropriate management of foot problems by
  - chiropodists
  - podiatric surgery
  - foot-care assistants

- Podiatric surgery can be introduced to tackle a need unmet by orthopaedic specialties.

References

1 Association of Chief Chiropody Officers (1988) National manpower survey of the registered chiropody profession, Aylesbury.

2 Kemp J and Winkler J T (1983) *Problems Afoot. Need and Efficiency in Footcare.* HMSO, London.

3 Cartwright A and Henderson G (1986) *More Trouble with Feet.* HMSO, London.

4 Wessex Regional Health Authority (1988) Wessex Feet. *The Chiropodist.* **43**: 152–68.

5 Galloway T and Gilbert N G O (1985) *Tiered Levels of Footcare.* Herefordshire Health Authority, Hereford.

6 Chiropodists Board (1987) *Statement of Conduct Footnote on Ambulatory Surgery,* Council for the Professions Supplementary to Medicine, Park House, Kennington Park, London.

7 British Orthopaedic Association (1981) *Statement on Podiatry* (1981) British Orthopaedic Association, London.

8 British Orthopaedic Association (1991) *Annual General Meeting Minute G27/91(f).* British Orthopaedic Association, London.

9   Donaldson C (1990) The state of the art of costing health care for economic evaluation. *Community Health Study.* **14(4)**: 341–56.

10   West Midlands Regional Health Authority (1991) *Statistical Information to GP Budget Holders.* WMRHA, Birmingham.

Note: This chapter draws on a degree thesis: Galloway T (1992) The cost effectiveness of podiatric surgery. University of Brighton.

18

Psychological aspects of early treatment interventions

Sue Gardner

Introduction

Early intervention can be defined as some form of helpful input provided shortly after a need has arisen. Its aims are to reduce distress, shorten the episode of care, minimize the intervention required and to reduce costs. Beyond this there are the issues of minimizing dependency and enhancing coping. There is evidence to show that early intervention is useful and effective but there are some problems which prevent implementing the lessons from successful schemes.

There is also debate about the difference between prevention and early intervention. For the purposes of this brief overview any helpful input influencing the beginning of an episode of need will be regarded as an early intervention. A full account of this debate and the lessons to be learned are given in the works of Newton[1,2]. However, there is clearly an overlap as early intervention is intended to prevent additional needs developing. In addition, preventive strategies may increase the demand for early intervention by raising public awareness of a problem or need and of the services that can be provided.

Issues in early intervention

Some evidence has emerged about service directions which will increase the usefulness of early interventions.

- Strategies must be designed to increase public awareness generally about psychological distress.

- Programmes to reduce vulnerability of high risk groups should be targeted.

- The needs for primary prevention (to avoid the occurrence of illness or disability), secondary prevention (for early diagnosis and treatment to shorten episodes of illness), and tertiary prevention (to limit the effects of disability and handicap) must be ascertained.

- Information and support should be provided which increases the individual's capacity to cope rather than creating dependence.

- The use of existing natural community and voluntary support networks must be maximized.

- The timeliness of interventions is important to improve coordination and increase the efficiency and effectiveness of professional support.

It is the timing of an input that identifies the 'early' from the 'late', 'too late' or 'too early' intervention. Even if a problem can be seen to be developing, help may be difficult to offer or accept until a point is reached where the need is or has to be acknowledged. This point often occurs as a crisis. A crisis has several central features:

- there is usually a triggering event or an accumulation of long term stress

- the individual experiences distress

- there is loss, danger or humiliation

- there is a sense of uncontrollability

- the events are experienced as unexpected

- there is disruption of routine

- there is uncertainty about the future[3].

Whilst a crisis is a horrible event to experience it does offer opportunities for learning, personal growth and life changes to occur. A crisis can represent a time when people want or need to change and an intervention at this point can be very effective.

When faced with crises, human beings, in common with other animals, show the 'fight', 'flight' and 'freeze' reactions. Whilst these may be useful initially in preventing emotional overloading they may not be useful strategies to adopt over the longer term. Support and help to enable people to cope with crises include:

- tolerating the feelings

- thinking about the issues

- facing the facts

- obtaining information and practical help

- taking care of oneself and managing stress

- regaining confidence

- finding control

- resolving difficulties.

Crises can therefore be a recognizable point for the use and provision of a helpful input; and focused early intervention must centre on recognized 'trigger' events or on those whose vulnerability may be high.

Areas for intervention

Early intervention is difficult to evaluate but there are five groups for which it has been shown to be effective. They are:

- the under fives and their families
- vulnerable adolescents
- people with psychological problems presented in primary care settings
- people with long-term mental health needs at the point of relapse
- elderly people who need help to avoid mental health problems.

Some examples of each group are given below.

Under fives and their families

The NEWPIN project is an early intervention scheme offering a befriending service for isolated mothers with young children. It aims to enhance self-esteem, break destructive patterns in relationships and prevent child abuse and neglect. The befrienders are trained volunteers who work with women in their homes. There is also a drop-in centre where group sessions are held. The women are referred mainly because they are judged to be depressed.

Many mothers became befrienders after receiving help from the scheme. Whilst it has been difficult to complete a cost–benefit analysis hidden resources which are attractive offset some of its costs. Similar schemes are operating in other areas.

Evaluation shows that the main benefits to accrue in terms of the women's relationship with partners and children – 62 % improved or had been resolved. Levels of depression recovered at about the same rate as other local work by psychiatric and primary care services. No child was returned to care after the mother had been involved in NEWPIN and 70 % of mothers reported improvement in child management.

Vulnerable adolescents

Adolescents leaving care to enter the world as young adults are known to be at risk. A scheme in Bradford offers support and practical advice to enable them to cope. A similar scheme to help teenage mothers at St Michael's in London has also been evaluated and shown to be effective.

Psychological problems in primary care

In primary care settings people present with psychological problems requiring information, counselling, support and crisis intervention. Ninety per cent of mental health needs are dealt with in primary care settings and the recently increased emphasis on community care has raised awareness among secondary and tertiary services of the importance of GP practices in mental health issues. Examples of improved information services include libraries of self-help material and greater access to voluntary groups via GPs.

Counsellors are a more recent addition to primary care, and there are mixed reactions to this development. Advocates point to the advantages of counselling here and in other settings such as breast screening and diabetic clinics as well as with bereavement (CRUSE) and couples' relationships (RELATE). They argue that GPs do not have sufficient time or training to counsel effectively. Patients' expectations are rising and the psychological aspects of many conditions require a counselling intervention component.

Concerns have been expressed about the use of primary care resources for the 'worried well' depleting resources for those with long-term mental health needs. Also, the wide variations in training and experience of counsellors reduces confidence in their contribution. There are studies underway to evaluate their effectiveness in primary care settings. However, there is already evidence to suggest that counselling in primary care results in quicker recovery with fewer consultations and less medication.

The voluntary and self-help agencies are expanding in many areas to provide invaluable first-hand practical and psychological support, especially for carers. Most conditions, from Alzheimer's disease to acquired immune deficiency syndrome (AIDS), now have support groups and they are often seen as more useful in improving quality of life than the statutory agencies. Early reaction to problems is a common theme.

Also in primary care come crisis intervention teams, which link tertiary experience with primary care settings to offer a rapid response and short-term intervention. Their actions are aimed at helping families to support the identified client using existing social networks. One study in Tower Hamlets has shown that for the cost of two hospital beds over 12 months, a crisis intervention team supported 117 families over the same period. The crises referred to the team included the threat of violence, psychosis, suicide and family breakdown.

Relapse prevention

The fourth area in which early intervention has been shown to be effective is with relapse prevention for people with long-term mental health needs. These services exist in several places such as Croydon, Salford, Birmingham and Buckinghamshire. The main thrust here is to help people monitor their own mood and behaviour so that maintenance levels of medication and support can be increased if changes occur which are predictive of another acute episode. The service also aims to improve family problem solving and to enhance coping by the client and family.

Avoidance of mental health problems for the elderly

It is now known that supporting independence and offering choices can contribute to maintaining health and motivation in older adults. Even in residential care settings this approach can prevent or delay mental health problems arising: early intervention can reduce premature dependence.

How, then, can all services have an early intervention component? Most human service systems are based on reactive behaviours whereas early intervention requires a more proactive approach. To be more proactive and have an early intervention element, services have to be able to manage demands better and cope with a range of pressures. They have to feel that ultimately they can stem demand through empowering their clients to help themselves. Even services set up specifically to provide early intervention should have to cope successfully with these issues.

If there is commitment to the provision of early intervention then managers and clinicians, purchasers and providers have to address the problems outlined here. The benefits for the clients and for ourselves would be worth the effort.

Learning points

- 'Early interventions' are overlapping concepts and are often confused.
- Early intervention is effective with certain groups: the under fives and their families, vulnerable adolescents, in psychological problems in primary care, in acute relapse for those with chronic mental health problems, and in elderly people to avoid mental health problems.

Better use can be made of early interventions by removing obstacles such as:

- Poor links between research and practice.
- Lack of meaningful feedback to practitioners to help them monitor their own practice.
- Poor management – too much control or not enough direction.
- Rigid professional boundaries preventing a flexible coordinated approach.
- Resistance to new ideas.
- Failure to accept and work with the available resources.
- Lack of planning at all levels.
- Unrealistic timescales for planning and managing change.
- Being daunted by the complexity of the situation.

References

1   Newton J (1988) *Preventing Mental Illness.* Routledge, London.

2   Newton J (1992) *Preventing Mental Illness in Practice.* Routledge, London.

3   Parry G (1990) *Coping with Crises.* British Psychological Society, London.

19

Tertiary preventive programmes

Peter Donnelly

Introduction

Preventive programmes are usually described as primary, secondary or tertiary[1]. The definitions of prevention are:

- *Primary* – Aimed at reducing incidence of disease and other departures from good health

- *Secondary* – Aimed at reducing disease prevalence by shortening duration

- *Tertiary* – Aimed at reducing complications.

Thus tertiary prevention merges with rehabilitation. Indeed many from both the general public and from the medical profession will fail to perceive such measures as truly preventive. Yet in this area of tertiary prevention, the reduction in the complications caused by illness, there is much scope for releasing resources. If we consider two examples the strength of this argument may become more apparent. The first is the introduction of a cardiac rehabilitation programme and the second the aggressive management of early osteoporosis.

In considering the safe introduction of any interventions, the following questions must be answered:

- Does it work?

- Is it cost-effective compared with alternatives (including doing nothing)?

- Is it ethically acceptable?

Some would quibble with the ordering of these questions, arguing for the paramountcy of ethical approval. However, no ineffective treatment can ever be ethical and when operating within a limited budget neither can an intervention which is not cost-effective. The ordering of the questions is therefore logical in that whilst efficacy and cost-effectiveness are not sufficient for ethical approval they are at least necessary prerequisites.

Cardiac rehabilitation after a heart attack

Does this work? The evidence is neatly summarized in two reviews[2,3]. Both demonstrate that overall mortality is reduced by 20–25%, that cardiovascular mortality is significantly lowered but that there is no change in the number of non-fatal heart attacks. So whilst it would be desirable to reduce the number of non-fatal events the principal aim of tertiary rehabilitation, namely to prevent complications (in this case sudden cardiac death) is met.

Is the programme cost-effective? Ades[4] showed in 1992 that cardiac rehabilitation produces a 40% reduction in re-hospitalization costs, and Oldridge in 1993[5] demonstrated that the cost per 'quality adjusted life year gained' was a relatively modest $9200.

Is the programme ethical? Well, given that it works and its benefits are commensurate with its cost we may proceed to consider issues such as whether it is appropriate to patients' perceived need and whether it is free from adverse effects. There is no evidence that such a programme increases patient or relatives' anxiety. On the contrary a properly conducted programme has both psychological and social as well as physical aspects, and enhances patient autonomy by decreasing medical dependence. Also the philosophical objections to primary and secondary screening programmes so eloquently argued by the late Petr Scrabenek[6] do not apply to this tertiary preventive situation where the patient is manifestly acutely ill to start with.

All of the above would lead one to believe that cardiac rehabilitation programmes should thus be commonplace if not universal. Such is not the case, despite a recent expansion (Figure 19.1). A report for the British Cardiac Society in 1991[7] stated that 'large areas of the country have no provision at all' and one-third of districts had 'no interest' in developing any. Why should this be? Rehabilitation has never attracted the kudos that comes with acute clinical work. It has the apparent disadvantage of being 'low-tech', community orientated and patient centred. Clinicians willing to become involved have to be prepared to relinquish their leadership role in favour of an unfamiliar enabling one. Responsibility for running cardiac rehabilitation is often not sought! Of course, the very features which apparently make the provision of a cardiac rehabilitation service unpopular in terms of medical careers arguably make it particularly appropriate in terms of patient needs – the demedicalization, enhancement of autonomy and building of confidence that a good programme provides may make the physician feel unneeded but it also makes the patient feel well!

How does such a tertiary preventive strategy compare with a programme of primary or secondary prevention for coronary heart disease? Certainly preventing the uptake of smoking, helping those who do smoke to stop and encouraging

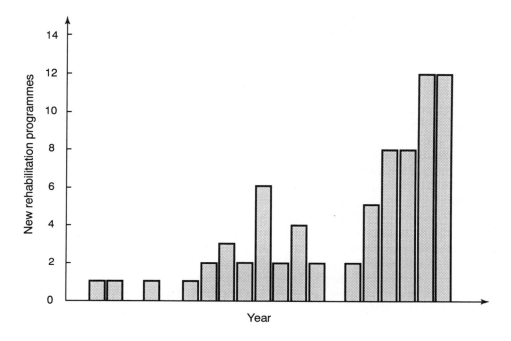

Figure 19.1   New cardiac rehabilitation programmes per year, 1969–89. (Source: Reference 7)

weight loss through exercise and a balanced diet all have a role but in many instances the evidence for the effectiveness of the intervention in achieving the desired result is lacking. For example, weight reduction diets are notoriously ineffective over the longer term and a large proportion of the population apparently enjoy their sedentary life-style.

As if this were not difficult enough, there is also the problem that a number of interventions may have significant unwanted effects. Consider the example of the use of cholesterol-lowering drugs for those with mild or moderate increase in serum cholesterol. A decrease in cardiovascular mortality certainly is seen to follow their use but this is compensated for by a rise in deaths from other causes probably resulting in no overall reduction in mortality[8]. Opinions differ over the interpretation and implications of such data but a general consensus against treatment (albeit for differing reasons) seems to be emerging[9]. How ethical is it to advocate such preventive measures when, compared with cardiac rehabilitation, their efficacy, safety and cost-effectiveness is so much in doubt? No one is seriously suggesting that GPs and others should stop trying to get patients to quit smoking but perhaps they should also spend time acting as patient advocates in insisting on the local provision of a well-organized, comprehensive cardiac rehabilitation programme.

Osteoporosis treatment following first fracture

The loss of bone density with age is a universal and physiological rather than pathological process. However, a point may be reached when this bone density loss is so marked that fractures – typically of the wrist, spinal vertebrae and hip – may result from very minimal trauma. The resultant health problems are extensive. In the first year following a fractured hip excess mortality exceeds 20% and the mortality in the year following a second hip fracture approaches 80%. Pain and other difficulties following hip fracture are also a great problem. Many never return to their former life-styles or accommodation. Mobility and confidence can be greatly impaired and the cost to both the individual family and the state are considerable. Yet much of this expense and misery is potentially avoidable.

Typically, those with osteoporosis follow a fracture career which starts with a Colles' fracture of the lower arm in their sixties, progresses through vertebral fractures in their seventies and culminates with a hip fracture in their eighties. Tertiary prevention would involve picking up individuals at the time of their first fracture and aggressively treating their underlying osteoporotic condition. Does it meet the criteria? Several treatments have been shown to be effective in reducing loss of bone mass including hormone replacement therapy (HRT) and calcium supplementation[10]. More importantly there appears to be good evidence that at least one treatment, HRT, reduces fracture rates[11,12]. These treatments are not on the whole expensive, have few adverse effects and appear to be well tolerated.

How would such a programme compare with alternative existing primary or secondary prevention? Primary measures such as ensuring that peak bone mass is maximized through exercise and avoiding smoking when young[13] undoubtedly have a role, although interestingly their implementation may depend more upon the actions of educational rather than health authorities. Secondary prevention through screening is much advocated but unproven. The current position is that even the most sophisticated testing available through bone densitometry has insufficient predictive value[14] in terms of picking out those likely to fracture to make population screening viable let alone cost-effective. Testing of highly selected populations, for example those who have already fractured or those with secondary osteoporosis, is justified as a means of monitoring the effect of treatment.

Another alternative strategy that has been advocated is the universal giving of hormone replacement therapy (HRT) to all post-menopausal women. Proponents argue that not only does HRT delay loss of bone mass but it has other beneficial side-effects – for example in reducing cardiac risk. In practice, however, such a strategy may meet with widespread resistance. A health policy which suggests that half of the population over the age of around 45 should be on permanent and (not universally beneficial) medication will quite rightly raise ethical issues. For example, how do we regard non-compliers: as misguided deviants who deserve their fractures in later life, or as individuals who are sensibly sceptical of a one-pill-cures-all approach to the health problems of middle-aged and elderly women?

No such ethical issues impinge upon tertiary prevention – a manifestly ill patient is offered therapy which not only will help prevent recurrence but may also speed her recovery. Should she decline therapy then she is no worse off than she would be under current practice.

Conclusion

So both cardiac rehabilitation and the aggressive treatment of osteoporosis provide us with examples of tertiary preventive measures which appear to confer benefits commensurate with their cost and are ethically defensible in that they are triggered by a patient's presentation with illness, speed recovery, reduce chances of recurrence and perhaps most important of all help maintain and enhance patient autonomy and confidence. There is little doubt that they have the ability to release resources. Purchasing authorities must therefore take the courageous decision of resisting further new acute developments in favour of funding tertiary preventive measures such as these. In truth, they probably should have done so some time ago but as in the clinical situations we have considered, it is never too late for an early intervention!

Learning points

- Any interventions, before their introduction, should satisfy the following criteria:
    - Does it work?
    - Is it cost-effective?
    - Is it ethically acceptable?

- Tertiary prevention programmes, aimed at reducing complications, can meet these criteria, for example for cardiac rehabilitation and osteoporosis.

- Such approaches should be evaluated and practised alongside other more established services in the first instance.

References

1   Last J M (1988) *A Dictionary of Epidemiology*. International Epidemiological Association and Oxford University Press, Oxford.

2   Oldridge N B, Guyatt G H, Fisher M D *et al*. (1988) Cardiac rehabilitation after myocardial infarction: Combined experience of randomised clinical trials. *Journal of the American Medical Association*. **260**: 945–50.

3   O'Connor G T *et al*. (1989) An overview of randomised trials of rehabilitation with exercise after myocardial infarction. *Circulation*. **80**: 234–44.

4   Ades P A, Huang D and Weaver S O (1992) Cardiac rehabilitation participation predicts lower rehospitalization costs. *American Heart Journal.* **123**: 916–21.

5   Oldridge N *et al.* (1993) Economic evaluation of cardiac rehabilitation soon after acute myocardial infarction. *American Journal Cardiology.* **72**: 154–61.

6   Skrabenek P and McCormick J (1989) *Follies and Fallacies in Medicine.* Tarragon Press, Glasgow.

7   Horgan J *et al.* (1991) *Working Party Report on Cardiac Rehabilitation.* British Cardiac Society, London.

8   Davey Smith G and Egger M (1994) Commentary on cholesterol papers: statistical problems. *British Medical Journal.* **308**: 1025–7.

9   Law M R and Wald N J (1994) Commentary on cholesterol papers: disagreements are not substantial. *British Medical Journal.* **308**: 1027–9.

10   Baran D and Sorensen A (1990) Dietary modification with dairy products for preventing vertebral bone loss in premenopausal women: a three year prospective study. *Journal of Clinical Endocrinology and Metabolism.* **70**: 264–70.

11   Kiel D P *et al.* (1987) Hip fracture and the use of oestrogens in post menopausal women: the Framlingham Study. *New England Journal of Medicine.* **317**: 1169–74.

12   Nassen T *et al.* (1990) Hormone replacement therapy and the risk for first hip fracture: a prospective population based cohort study. *American Internal Medicine.* **13**: 95–103.

13   Valimaki M J *et al.* (1994) Exercise, smoking and calcium intake during adolescence and early adulthood as determinants of peak bone mass. *British Medical Journal.* **309**: 230–5.

14   Melton J, Eddy D M and Johnston C (1990) Screening for osteoporosis. *Annals of Internal Medicine.* **112**: 516–28.

Part Three
Doing Things Differently

20

Overview
Morton Warner

Introduction

The task of this chapter is to look at why and how we might do things differently – how health service delivery will possibly change. It starts by looking at the major pressures for change.

Major pressures for change

Figure 20.1 suggests that these fall into several categories[1,2], as described overleaf.

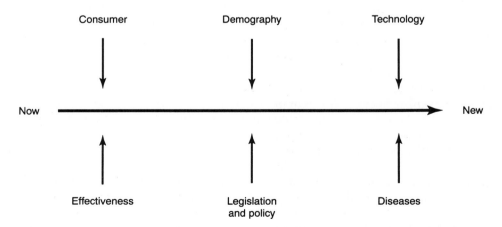

Figure 20.1 The pressures for change. (Reprinted with permission of the Welsh Health Planning Forum)

Consumerism

The position of the consumer has changed quite dramatically over the last ten or 15 years, and even more in the last two or three. By contrast, in 1974 when the Community Health Councils were introduced they were not as influential as they might have been. Now we have the Patients' Charter and an expressed intention by government that there shall be information flowing to consumers which allows them to make better choices about what they want.

Demographic changes

Again these will cause the NHS to do things differently. The over 85s will not peak in number until around 2015, but they are going to be significant in their require-ments between now and then. Through health promotion activities there may be some compression of morbidity, but people will still get ill, although maybe in a shorter period of time at the end of their lives. The NHS will still have to look after them.

Legislative changes and policy

Social services are increasingly involved in what was previously health service activity, and this will probably continue. Economic constraints on public sector spending will probably cause a shift in financial responsibility to individuals and the family. But beyond that, little is clear.

Disease patterns

At a World Health Assembly some 15 years ago somebody was rushing around at a time of considerable excitement about the birth of Health for All 2000, saying 'It won't be Health for All 2000 it will be AIDS for all by the year 2000'. There was little realization from participants that the HIV problem was going to be on our doorstep, with a consequent resurgence in tuberculosis – particularly of an antibiotic-resistant type. But 15 years ago only early indications were beginning to emerge of reductions in coronary heart disease in North America and Australia, which have now been followed in most countries in Western Europe.

The other item is the issue of occupation-less health – the health problems associated with long-term unemployment. Richard Smith provided a very good series of articles on this in the *British Medical Journal*[3], bringing together the literature in this field. It is quite clear that people will have more physical and mental illness problems if they are long-term unemployed. We have seen an unceasing increase in the UK, and across Europe, in the numbers of long-term unemployed. A Danish futurist at a recent World Health Organization meeting predicted only dire things in Europe in terms of civil unrest and local war that would be exacerbated by long-term unemployment, which is an unhealthy situa-tion to be in.

Efficiency and effectiveness

This is doing the right things right. In the 1980s emphasis was on greater efficiency in public services – value for money (VFM). Archie Cochrane in 1971 described a health service that emphasized efficiency. He said:

> 'I once asked a worker at a crematorium, who had a curiously contented look on his face, what he found so satisfying about his work. He replied that what fascinated him was the way in which so much went in and so little came out. I thought of advising him to get a job in the National Health Service.'[4]

However, few health care interventions – no more than 20%, according to Brook and Lohr[5] – have been evaluated as useful against the gold standard of randomized trial control. At the other end of the scale, a perhaps similar proportion are of no value. In between lie the majority of interventions in which varying degrees of confidence can be placed (Figure 20.2). Where further evaluation is required, the quest to target the application of resources more accurately will, during the 1990s, become a subject of central concern to the Central Committee on Research and Development as they determine their investment priorities.

The influence of technology

Here we are talking about future technology and care ranges from home and clinic to inpatient acute services. The examples suggest a potential for a shift of activities closer to home. Figure 20.3 shows some of the major technological substitutions envisaged. At the *inpatient or outpatient* end of the spectrum several key trends emerge:

* advances in the use of endoscopy, in combination with lasers, will increase the proportion of surgical work undertaken by minimal access therapy (MAT), perhaps to about 80% in the early years of the twenty-first century

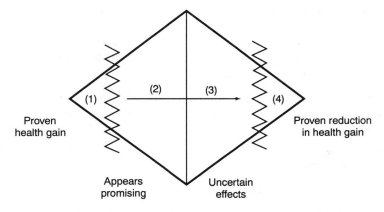

Figure 20.2 The health gain rhomboid. (Reprinted with permission of the Welsh Health Planning Forum)

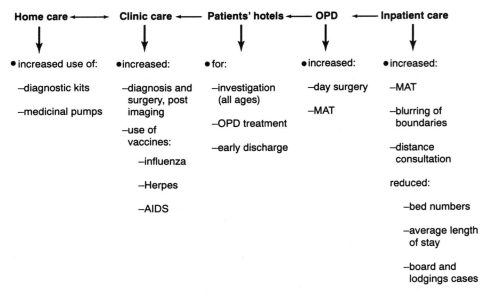

Figure 20.3   Future technology and substitution. (Reprinted with permission of the Welsh Health Planning Forum)

- the average length of stay for procedures will reduce

- the proportion of surgical work carried out on a day-care basis will rise to about 60% by the year 2000

- the boundaries between medicine, surgery and radiology will become increasingly blurred

- patients' hotels will emerge as half-way houses between acute district general hospitals and primary care. They will accept individuals from early discharge from acute hospitals who still need a supervised environment, and take in patients referred by GPs for complex investigative work.

At the *community care* end of the spectrum, substitution for acute hospital care will occur by actively keeping people out of hospital, or away from general practice surgeries. Growth can be anticipated in:

- primary health care for diagnostic and surgical activity, especially when imaged material can be transmitted digitally between general practice and the acute hospital

- the development of vaccines for such conditions as AIDS and herpes, and better influenza vaccines

- the use of diagnostic kits using monoclonal antibodies

- the availability of high quality medical pumps for treatment of chronic conditions and relief of pain, and controllable through telemetry.

Extending the theme of substitution, we can look at locational and staffing substitutions. There is an important message we have to get over in response to the challenge, 'that's all very well, but the public will perceive it as closing down hospitals'. I think a massive educational community-based campaign will have to be undertaken by the health service if it is going to follow through on these ideas, the sort put out in NAHAT's paper, *Reinventing Healthcare*[6]. We are talking about really quite dramatic shifts that are not easily understood by people who understand the 'bricks and mortar' of hospitals, and do you blame them? That is where they have, for many years, received care when they have been in life-threatening situations.

Most importantly, achievement of health gain will not be possible if new technologies are viewed merely as additional costs to an already over-burdened health service. They must be chosen on the basis that they can assist in the necessary shift of resources across levels of care and can lead to a re-thinking about the organization of care itself, and to the release of resources from acute district general hospitals in particular.

Organizational issues

The central change will be the disappearance of the district general hospital as we know it. With the emergence of new technologies it is likely that both the size and the role of district general hospitals will change.

Opinions vary on the subject of size, suggesting bed reductions will be possible of between 30% and 50%, with a total size of no more than 250 beds. The only inpatients using the highly specialized units that the district general hospital will become will be those who are very sick, and those with day-care surgery needs which demand a specialist response. Other cases will be looked after in small local or neighbourhood hospitals serviced by consultants and GPs, and providing for inpatient and day-care surgery patients. Maternity care will be provided at both sites, but only high-risk cases will go to the specialized obstetric unit.

As now, most treatment and care will be provided through general practice and in the home. Strategically, an ideological shift will become evident whereby primary care is supported by the hospital system rather than the reverse; and health promoting activities will have greater currency.

So what sort of release of resources might be expected from the shifts that are emerging? It may be no more than 10–25% of revenues. But this would be a considerable sum to invest in the primary care system to achieve health gain.

Training and redeployment issues

Figure 20.4 suggests a major need to redeploy and re-train staff. The issues arising from this are the subject of major inquiries by government, the Royal Colleges and professional associations. The Chief Nursing Officers (CNOs) have been particularly active and leading the way with their *Heathrow Debate* document[7]. Will Project 2000 nurses be fit for tomorrow's tasks? The CNOs conclude that they will, but post-registration training will require further scrutiny.

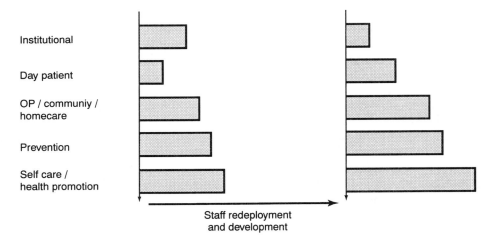

Figure 20.4   Shifts in care, 1989–2000+

Moves towards general care

Twenty years from now most of our current assumptions and practices will have been undermined by the waves of change that will certainly hit us. We cannot predict the future but can envisage how it might be.

A vision for the future must be clear enough to win acceptance and serious attention, but not so precise that people will quarrel over details. The framework shown in Figure 20.5 avoids discussion of precise institutions, and concentrates on the elements that will offer a rational overall service 20 years hence. It is assumed that organization will be tailored to match purpose.

The circle represents the area within which the NHS will do most, though it will not act alone within the circle and it will also reach out beyond. On the boundary are clustered *general care teams*: within it are *specialized* care services:

- more will be done in the general community to maintain health. More people will be more conscious of their own health, and more willing to take control

- home care supported by peripatetic staff, telemonitoring and portable equipment will be commonplace. There will be more choice about birth location

- when people look to expert help, the greater part of their health care needs in the broadest sense will be met through general care services

- where a level of expertise beyond that available at the general care level is required, then the individual will use specialized care services.

General care teams will meet most basic health and social care needs including active efforts to promote and maintain fitness, health education and advice, initial diagnosis and assessment of problems, most forms of treatment, antenatal and postnatal care, and social support for the elderly, infirm or disabled. Current distinctions between health services and social services will have blurred.

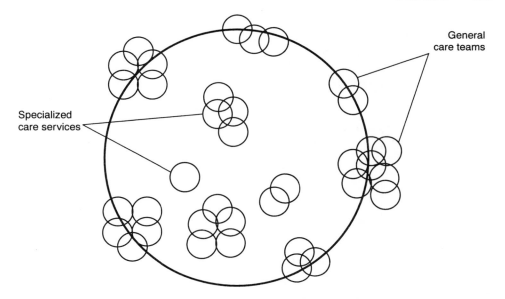

Figure 20.5   The pattern of the future care framework. (Reprinted with the permission of the Welsh Health Planning Forum)

An essential element in the concept is the idea of a *cluster* of services. Services in the community will be richer and more diverse, including what is now available, new services, and some currently available but not in the mainstream. All of these will be integrated much more closely than now, to eliminate incompatibilities in policy, culture and funding. How skills and services are grouped into clusters will differ from place to place, taking into account locally developed expertise and geographical social, economic and other factors.

For cases which the general care services are unable to deal with adequately there will be *specialized care* services. The difference between general and specialized care will not be precise nor will it be defined as tends to be the case now in terms of job titles and location. The key determinants will be efficacy (for certain conditions a skill possessed by only a small number of providers can provide optimum outcome), and efficiency (some resources will have to be concentrated on economic grounds). In total, though, the emphasis will be on achievement of health gain using the least possible resources. Much of the release of resources for this must come from the existing secondary sector, especially in a tightening economy.

Moving on

In the next 10–15 years many assumptions held in the early 1980s about the provision of diagnostic, treatment and rehabilitation services will need to change. Figure 20.6 illustrates one way in which current approaches to health care may change radically.

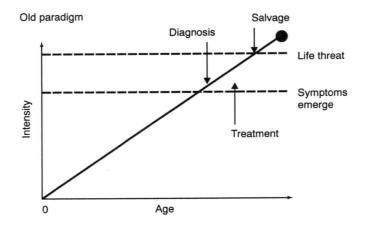

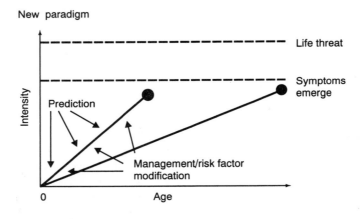

Figure 20.6   Old and new paradigms of chronic disease management (Source: Goldsmith J (1992) The Reshaping of Healthcare Part 1. *Healthcare Forum Journal*; May/June: **21**)

Here, the old paradigm represents intervention for chronic disease management only once symptoms have emerged. In the future, a 'predict and manage' approach which is triggered by a genetic screen and followed by further testing and regulation prior to the symptom stage, will be the dominant paradigm.

The perennial question remains: how will resources be released from existing services to undertake work in this new and important field?

Learning points

- Many pressures for change are beyond the control of the NHS – consumerism, demography and disease processes, for example.

- Technological innovation will be a major force to be reckoned with in the final part of this century.

- 'Substitutions' of location, manpower and technology will mean many services closer to peoples' homes.

- Watch for the new paradigm of 'predict and manage' in diagnostics and therapeutics.

References

1 Welsh Health Planning Forum (1994) *Health and Social Care 2010: A Report on Phase 1*. Cardiff: WHPF.

2 National Association of Health Authorities and Trusts (1994) *Closer to Home – Healthcare in the 21st Century*. Research Paper No. 13. NAHAT, London.

3 Smith R Occupational health (series). *British Medical Journal.* (1985) **291**: 1409–12; **291**: 1563–6; (1986) **292**: 137–8.

4 Cochrane A L (1972) *Effectiveness and Efficiency: Random Reflections on Health Services*. Nuffield Provincial Hospitals Trust, London.

5 Brook R H and Lohr K N (1985) Efficacy, effectiveness, variations and quality. Boundary-crossing research. *Medical Care Journal.* **23, 5**: 710–22.

6 National Association of Health Authorities and Trusts (1993) *Reinventing Healthcare*. NAHAT, London.

7 Department of Health (1994) *Heathrow Debate. The Challenges for Nursing and Midwifery in the 21st Century*. Department of Health, London.

21

Supporting self-care: the buck stops here

Bill Holmes

Introduction

Gather together any group of GPs, and conversation turns to their work, and the problems they face. High on this list is a lack of time to satisfy the needs of patients, administrators and the increasing volume of paperwork. Though it is almost to let the side down, I do not share this problem, or at least do not let it get me down. This is not because of particular skills, talents or industry, but rather because my goals in each working day are clear and my work is organized to meet them. Developing efficient working practices is a skill which empowers GPs, enabling them to work efficiently and economically, and to derive professional satisfaction from their efforts. Developing that skill is rarely encouraged.

Much of the work in general practice deals with self-limiting illness. There is a great deal of such 'dis-ease', and my firm belief is that we must develop the skills to encourage patients to manage these episodes themselves. Partly this is to make the lives of GPs easier, but more importantly because it discourages patients' dependency upon the medical profession in general, and drugs (especially anti-biotics) in particular. Such dependency is good for neither party. My thesis – itself an apparent paradox – is that the more available we are to patients the easier it is to encourage self-reliance. It is not easily or quickly achieved, but requires the consistent application of a clear plan of management. The better organized we are, the clearer our aims, the closer we get to this goal.

General practice activities cost considerable sums of money, and referrals to hospital, a prime example, have 'knock-on' costs. Savings can be made, although this is not an aim to which many GPs feel committed. This chapter describes some thoughts about the provision of general medical care, with examples of working practices which I have found helpful, and which, almost incidentally, save money in my practice.

The title is 'the buck stops here' because it is a sentiment which most GPs will recognize. Whatever happens in committees, may be decided by eminent working parties or be written in government planning papers, patients will continue to present themselves to their family doctors with illness and discomfort, and GPs will sort them out. Whatever the general issues, GPs deal with the particular and the individual. Historically, it is not a discipline where forward planning and managerial skills have had a high profile. Primarily, GPs are 'copers'; it is the strength of general practice.

The traditional strengths of general practice

Though not without its problems, the provision of medical care in Britain is a considerable success. The average citizen may be unfamiliar with the motto that medical care is universally available and free at the time of need, but he or she knows that they can expect competent medical attention when needed and not have to pay for it.

There are several factors which contribute to this success, and the skill of Britain's doctors is only a part. Of greater importance is a national temperament which has traditionally derided introspection in matters of health, and is suspicious of lawyers. There is also an affection for general medical practice. Although unlikely to spend time thinking about the qualities of primary care, and still less praising them, most patients value the relationship with their GP. Though often imperfect, it is personal, continuing and usually family based. A good relationship between GP and patient overcomes many shortcomings.

When GPs take pride in their work, when patients have confidence in their GPs acting both as personal physicians and as advocates for their interests – in short when primary care flourishes – many perceived and actual shortcomings in the NHS are tolerated and difficulties surmounted. This is a bonus of GPs' professional pride; general practice should remain the bedrock upon which the NHS is built. This is not to undervalue the skills and achievements of physicians and surgeons, but rather to suggest that when primary care is at its most efficient, benefits are felt in secondary care through reduced pressure on facilities and by lessening the annoyance which accompanies unnecessary or inappropriate referrals. Financial savings should also accompany these improvements.

The last few years have been a time of great change in general practice. This is a time when GPs have been expected to provide medical 'services' – such as 'health promotion' – previously outside their remit. These activities have costs, some potentially very expensive. Anything which reduces GP availability (for example by increased management responsibilities) or reduces the quality of their consult-ations (for example by disenchantment) dilutes continuity of care. Do patients value activities such as 'health promotion'? Perhaps some do, but they might not if they felt the cost of their provision included less access to surgery appointments or the production of disheartened doctors.

Previously, GPs might have felt that they knew what their work entailed. In a time of change, where the pace is being set by others, GPs would be wise to define their goals, and develop a strategy to achieve them without losing traditional skills or burning themselves out.

Can I believe what he says?

It is always wise to question the applicability of an individual doctor's practice to the discipline as a whole. Traditionally, GPs have shown a shrewd suspicion of research which claims improved performance such as an impressive uptake of screening invitations. The perception, often unvoiced among the rank and file of primary care, is that such achievements may relate more to characteristics of the population under study, or to the resources they enjoy, than to the process of care described.

I have a small, inner-city practice with markers of deprivation at or above the local average (Table 21.1). There is no special nursing or clerical support. The explanation for any achievements or failings must be sought elsewhere.

What savings does he make?

It has proved notoriously difficult to measure costs in general practice. GPs who find themselves castigated for high spending costs may justly point to the qualities of the population they serve, or may argue that their high prescribing is offset by lower rates of investigations or hospital referrals. Any GP could make a case that the overall cost of GP activity, corrected for the characteristics of the community being cared for, is really the only figure which would provide a true comparison.

However, such data are not yet readily available, and until then, other measures are needed. Two such markers are prescribing costs and out-of-hours work. Table 21.2 displays these and other markers of my practice activity. Currently, prescribing figures are 33% below the FHSA's average. This translates into a cash saving of £83 624 annually for a two-partner practice.

Night visits are similarly at best only an indirect marker of out-of-hours work. Some feel that it is unfair that those who have been successful in reducing the demand for night visits by increasing daytime availability should find that element of their income reduced.

Table 21.1   Practice profiles at July 1993, single-handed practice

	Data for this practice	Average for Notts FHSA	Range for Notts FHSA	Compared practice with Notts FHSA
Size	2350	1950		
Jarman	17.62	7.62	−22 to +44	+10
Townsend	4.04	2.46	−4 to +9	+2
Unemployment	12.98%	10.55%	0.3 to 22	+2.43%
Ethnicity	8.76%	3.93%	0 to 17.7	+4.83%
Patient turnover	11.69%	8.84%	0.3 to 16	+2.85%
No car in family	33.92%	27.28%	0.5 to 53	+6.64%

Table 21.2   Activity for this practice compared with Notts FHSA average

Item	Comparison (%)	Note	Source
Prescribing	–33	£83 624*	PACT 07/94
Night visits	–70.4		FHSA 6/93
Maternity	+14		FHSA 6/93
Vaccination and immunity	+48.5	99% primary vaccination	FHSA 6/93
Cytology	+86	90% done in practice	Practice audit

*Annualized saving, two partners.

Techniques for an efficient practice

Choice is the basis of success

Encouraging self-care ia a long process. Patients have to believe that recommendations reflect their interests, that their GP is 'on their side'. This requires a relationship of mutual respect, a process which begins when patients enquire about registering. When setting out their stall, the most variable quality which doctors offer is themselves. It is naïve to think that any one physician's consulting style will suit every patient, and surely GPs display a degree of arrogance in thinking they are capable of doing so. Every patient wishing to join my list is offered an opportunity to meet the GP. They can visit the practice, meet the team of staff who work there, and have some experience of the style of medical care offered.

In this way *patients* make the decision whether or not to join the practice. This is not always easy, for most patients moving home do not bother to register with a new doctor until they fall ill. This is a poor time to choose a new GP, for the exercise of choice is heavily influenced by the need to have prompt attention. Separation of the two tasks is possible by making it clear that I will be happy to sort out any immediate problem on the basis of temporary registration, and leaving them to decide at their leisure if they wish to have this particular GP as their family doctor.

The aim is to emphasize that the GP values the relationship with patients. The GP will provide medical services of a certain range and style and patients will contribute to the success of the practice by valuing those services and using them wisely.

Few patients decide not to join: indeed, most are frankly amazed that a GP takes the trouble to meet them first. It is very rare for me to decline to take on a patient, and never on the basis of matters of health. The usual reason is gender; patients wanting a female doctor are unwise to join the list of a single-handed male.

Certainly, this all takes time. However, the relationship between GP and patient may last for many years, and is likely to have to survive episodes of stress and pain. It should be entered into thoughtfully. Such introductions represent time well spent. I am surprised that not every GP accords a high priority to the act of patients joining their list.

Availability demonstrates commitment

Encouraging self-care requires me to be readily available and to offer continuity. These principles are translated into two working practices:

- every patient is seen on the same day they request an appointment

- when a patient needs to talk to me at night or at weekend, they can usually do so.

Both are difficult commitments. My motives are entirely selfish; to make this work easier and personally more rewarding. In theory, it is easy for patients to undermine them. Being human, a GP whose surgeries run on for hours, or who is regularly woken at night would be forgiven, at least by his or her colleagues, for throwing in the towel. However, when one treats patients reasonably, they respond in kind; and paradoxically, the more available I make myself, the less I am troubled out of hours. This is hardly a novel observation, and many retired GPs report that their professional lives began in that way. It *can* still be that way, though not without effort and thought.

Most patients, even in the deprived inner cities, have telephones. Patients know that when they phone out of hours they can speak to me. Most concerns can be addressed over the telephone without needing to call upon the arrangements made to cover my absence.

When given rapid access to convenient appointments, patients will use them wisely. Most are still reluctant to abuse out-of-hours services – but not if they experience difficulty being seen during the day. Patients need a choice.

When these two working practices were introduced it was hard for a while. But now the amount of work involved is small. They are the two primary goals. Only when they are achieved do I turn to 'health promotion activities', the 'business plan' and 'annual report'. Certainly these latter activities are required because remuneration is linked to them. But my patients value prompt attention more highly than efficiency in paperwork. The same is surely true of patients in other practices, and FHSAs would be wise to encourage it.

Unfortunately the average GP's experience and perception is that advice is given either by colleagues with a messianic zeal to work hard, or by those who do not share our day-to-day problems (for example from members of university departments of general practice or Government agencies). The record of change in primary care over the last twenty years is impressive, yet little of the impetus for those changes came from legislation. Doctors have considerable professional pride which, when used wisely, is a powerful tool for progress.

Making availability work for doctor and patient

In hospital, one begins one's working day by seeing the sickest patients, and gradually works through to those who are recovering. It seems eminently sensible to start, for example, in the intensive care unit, to move to coronary care, then to the wards and gradually to review the patients ready for discharge.

General practice traditionally works in an opposite manner. Most GPs begin at, say, 9.00 am in the morning, and see first those patients who booked their appointments some time previously; patients, for example, who require repeat prescriptions for the contraceptive pill, who need to have their blood pressure checked, their treatment and investigations reviewed and sickness certificates renewed. In many practices the demand for appointments exceeds their supply, and at the end of the morning the GP is often late and stressed. Traditionally, GPs then start seeing – as 'extras' – those patients who are acutely ill. Typically, these will be patients who have felt unwell overnight and who have had to argue with a receptionist for an appointment to be seen that morning. Such consultations are frequently a far from quality experience for patients or doctors.

So consultations are different in my practice. I start at 8.45 each morning with no routine appointments booked until 9.15 am. Any patient in the practice can walk into surgery at 8.45 and be seen without question and without an appointment. Patients don't have to argue with or seek permission from a receptionist, they just come in, sit down and are seen in turn. Most mornings there are no patients to be seen during this time, and so it is an opportunity to have a cup of coffee and go through the mail.

This single act, putting aside an unstructured half an hour each day, has had a powerful pay-off. It has decimated the amount of out-of-hours work. Requests for attention at night, are few and far between. This is as it should be, for significant medical emergencies are rare events.

It is not how long it is, but how you use it that matters

Many doctors get terribly wound up about the length of the appointments they offer patients. This phenomenon arose during the 1950s and 1960s when research about the 'consultation' began to appear. Rightly, this work demonstrated the central role which the process of consultation has in primary care. Brief consultations came to be frowned upon; for it was implied that 'quality' was to be achieved through longer appointments. Training schemes for general practice encouraged young doctors to aim for longer appointments, and consulting 'by appointment only', a marked change from the previous decades, became *de rigueur*.

Although longer consultations undoubtedly have some advantages, they are often achieved by making patients wait longer to see their doctor, both in the waiting room and by making appointments more difficult to obtain. Patients value neither, and although many patients when they are well say that they want longer consultations, when they are ill they want prompt attention.

Furthermore, one has to make allowance for a proportion of patients who cannot cope with an appointment, and who turn up at surgery unannounced. Like most GPs in the inner cities, my practice has a fairly large number of unemployed and alcoholic men who will never cope with the social niceties of telephoning in advance or calling in to the surgery to make an appointment.

There may be GPs around who are sufficiently under-worked to be able to provide both long and easily available consultations. Most cannot. Individual doctors need to make a choice. The length of my consultations has to vary to accommodate the number of patients who want to be seen that day. My goal is to see every patient on *that* day; all other targets, including the length of an individual appointment, are a secondary consideration.

Therefore with only half a dozen patients, it's nice and relaxed. But there are some days when 20 people are seen in the morning. Patients are never turned away, and of course no more time is available. So I have to work quicker. A 'booking procedure' with receptionists has been established so that appointments are booked in at ten-minute intervals, but when needed, spaces in between are used to accommodate demand. Consequently, appointment length falls steadily from 10 to 7.5 to 5 minutes as needed.

These are two simple ideas. They are neither revolutionary nor original, but they have revolutionized my practice. Has it translated into savings? The prescribing costs and night visit claims suggest it does.

What about unreasonable patients?

Changing one's consulting habits is hard. GPs feel that, like the boy with his finger in the dyke, they are holding back a potential flood of demand. And they are right: unreasonable patients have the capacity to destroy any system in primary care. They represent a problem which needs to be addressed, but which is frequently swept under the carpet.

If one were to inspect the medical cards issued by the 'panel' or the community insurance system established at the turn of the century, one would find certain rules about calling the doctor: 'if you want a visit, you must phone before 10 am. You must not call the doctor after seven o'clock at night for problems which can wait until the next morning. You should not call the doctor for trivial matters'.

Those rules sought to curtail unreasonable behaviour because such behaviour raised the costs of the service. Those costs were borne, not by idle doctors or office-bound administrators, but by the patients in the scheme.

That message has been forgotten. Nowadays in discussing 'unreasonable' patients we tend only to consider the way that unreasonable behaviour impinges on the doctor. Unreasonable behaviour by a small proportion of patients produces in doctors behaviour which affects adversely the availability and quality of care offered to everybody else on their list. It is in the interest of *patients* and not just doctors that unreasonable behaviour should be curtailed.

Whose task is it to address that problem? Well it certainly should not be left to doctors, who will understandably tend to defend themselves. It is relatively easy, for example, to draw a line at 7 o'clock, refuse to see extra patients and to switch over to a deputizing service. It is to the considerable credit of general practice that so many doctors do not behave in this way.

To use an expression familiar to most GPs, 'something must be done'. No one, however, wishes to grasp the nettle. If the balance were redressed, a considerable amount of goodwill could be translated into constructive behaviour.

If the future of health care continues to involve individual GPs providing personal services out of hours, change must happen. The idea that doctors are terrified to say 'No' to patients who demand a night visit for trivial matters must be overturned. GPs are afraid to address individual problems because they fear that, however unjustified, a subsequent complaint to the FHSA will trigger a complaints procedure which generates discomfort out of all proportion to the effort required to meet the original request. When faced with the opportunity to do so, many GPs have withdrawn from providing care out of hours, and many more would like to do so. The discomfiture of GPs is not a good reason for change; the weakening of primary care is.

Summary

Patients old enough to remember GPs' surgeries of 20 years ago would hardly recognize their modern counterparts, which now enjoy all time high levels of staff and resources. It is strange, then, to find primary care disillusioned, and an unpopular career choice for young doctors.

Increasing personal and professional satisfaction in general practice will bring rewards for GPs and patients. Encouraging self-care of minor illness plays a small but important role in that process. It cannot be achieved without organization and commitment. Agencies charged with administering and supervising primary care would be wise to facilitate those processess.

Learning points

- Encouraging GPs to work at what they do well, to be available and to provide continuity of care is good for the profession and for patients.

- It may also reduce costs.

- Allowing the skills and traditions of general practice to be lost either through neglect or by being channelled into fashionable activities is likely to prove a very expensive alternative.

22

The community pharmacist

Michael Chapman

Introduction

This chapter examines the contribution that can be made by community pharmacists in health care and in self-care.

The current image of community pharmacy

There is a view that community pharmacists are underused. This may in part be due to problems created by the profession itself. There are, however, several things which community pharmacy can offer in the area of self-care. As with other health care professions, community pharmacy is required to respond to a rapidly changing world, indeed, a rapidly changing health service. Doctors have faced that in the past and have done so successfully over the years but pharmacists may not have done that to as great an extent. And therein lies one of the problems. Leaving the safety of financial security of an established pattern of service and passing through the transitional state towards something that is new is not easy and some pharmacists are reluctant to move from their current position. Human beings are resistant to change, and, that is the case in community pharmacy.

Community pharmacy is also suffering an identity crisis. The difficulty is that pharmacists wear two hats or two coats, firstly as shop-keepers but also as professionals providing a service, dispensing prescriptions, giving advice to patients and supporting the GP's role. The difficulty lies in the public perception of the pharmacist as a shopkeeper rather than a professional. So pharmacy's image needs improving. Its worth and potential are not exploited sufficiently, or even recognized to any extent by fellow health professionals. But pharmacists are equipped by their training to make a greater contribution to the area of health promotion and indeed the whole area of health care. They are well placed to tackle opportunities for ill health management and prevention and the promotion of positive health more proactively than in the past.

Historically, pharmacies are recognized as being rather quaint with many coloured bottles lining the shelves, carboys in strategic places and a pharmacist in a white coat who would spend most of the time in the rear dispensary, compounding and formulating foul tasting and smelling potions. Care obviously had to be taken to advise a doctor on a physical or chemical incompatibility, in case two or more prescribed medicines interacted. But there was less in the area of in vivo drug interaction. As the pharmaceutical industry developed, a wide range of ready-to-use products came onto the market and many of these utilized improved delivery systems and dosage forms. Therefore there was less compounding and preparation and more counting, pouring and weighing. That is not exactly an inspiring job. It does not need a pharmacy degree to count tablets into a bottle although of course there are important skills involved in the dispensing process. But that role is now being passed on to pharmacy technicians to release the pharmacist to take part in wider initiatives.

The wider role of the community pharmacy

The role that is emerging is one that includes advice on medicines. Potent medicines require precise instructions and guidance on administration. There is a great need for compliance where a patient follows the doctor's and pharmacist's directions. New drugs are also very expensive and patients should be encouraged to comply with dosage instructions. Compliance is a very important factor in the achievement of better health care.

A community pharmacist's role in primary care is one of instructing and informing patients as to how they can take medicines in the most efficient and beneficial way, reinforcing the GP's instructions. The doctor may have explained what he wants the patient to take, he has written it down on a piece of paper, but the patient leaves the surgery and forgets what the doctor said; was it twice a day, three times a day or four times a day, was it before or after food? A pharmacist's job is to reinforce what the doctor has said in order that the patient may be acquainted with the best way of taking the prescribed medication. In many cases it is a question of expanding and explaining how the patient should take the medicine in terms of dose, frequency and length of course. It may be necessary to talk to patients, in certain instances, about side-effects. The doctor may well have done that but the patient may ask the pharmacist about those side-effects. In a cautious way the pharmacist would try to explain what may happen. There are also certain precautions that one needs to take in taking medicine. Patients need an explanation of how to take medicine in the best way. There are certain compliance issues as well – health gain through compliance enables pharmacists to assist people in self-care.

Assistance with patient compliance

Compliance aids are useful. For example, monitored dose units are being used effectively in some residential homes to assist in compliance. However, instead of making these universally available, a more appropriate approach is to persuade patients to be responsible for their own medicine, for taking the medicine in a self-care approach so that they understand what they are doing and why they are taking it at a particular time and in a particular way. Other compliance aids include a daily 'Medidose' container, Braille labels, labels with large type and patient information leaflets. However, leaflets containing too much information written in a technical way may prove to be a deterrent to compliance.

Another deterrent to compliance is the click-lock top, the security cap which prevents people gaining access to their medicine. Patients who have difficulty using safety closures will, on request, be supplied with a more easily removed cap.

Participation in the primary health care team

The role of the pharmacist is evolving in the primary health care team. Historically, pharmacists contact doctors by phone and tell them what has happened to their prescription, that they have made a mistake in dosage or in strength, etc. As part of the evolving role, assisting with patient problems encourages seamless care. For example, a patient may have a problem with the tablets they are taking and it may be useful to try an alternative dosage form. It may be that there is an alternative product that could be used. The pharmacist could advise on the generic equivalent. Indeed many pharmacists, particularly in Wessex and the South West, are seconded to a practice to give support to the GP in producing a formulary and to work along with the doctors in the area of rational prescribing. Pharmacists can also provide support in the area of drug interaction, not only those that arise through prescribing but particularly drug interactions between prescribed medicines and over-the-counter medicine. In support of that work there is also an opportunity to back up the work that is done in clinics on demonstrating inhaler techniques, use of peak flow meters and blood glucose monitors. The use of different dosage forms very often needs explanation – there is the story of the headmaster who went along to his GP with a frozen shoulder and he was prescribed some indomethacin suppositories. He went back to the GP and said his shoulder was no better. The GP was confused and mystified; something should have happened. He asked him a few questions and then said 'you are using one of these at night aren't you?' 'Yes', he says 'I put it under my arm every night and nothing seems to happen – it just makes a mess of my pyjamas.' So it is important that the patient should have an explanation on the use of their medication eg to remove the outer wrapping from suppositories and to use them correctly. Judy Clarke (see page 31) refers to the use of sustained-release medication as being a means of compliance, in that medication once or twice daily is often better than four or five times daily. However, it is important to be aware of the danger of overdosage particularly with confused patients. This interaction with the primary health care team and with other bodies is important. If there is a policy in an area then it needs to be disseminated through various bodies, one of them being community pharmacy. For example, the infestation treatment policy needs coordination and direction so that all health care workers are aware of the current treatment.

Support for patients

Currently several pharmacy services within the community are being developed in line with the *Health of the Nation*[1] and the regional strategy initiatives. Health promotion is taking place in the community, in schools, in general practice but it is also supported through Family Health Service Authorities (FHSAs) who have targeted the community pharmacy as being a strategic centre to convey health promotion messages. Community pharmacy is well placed to meet patient needs in this direction by virtue of its location in the community and exposure to the general public. It is estimated that some 6 million people a day visit a pharmacy.

This provides an opportunity to convey appropriate information and health care messages, but the opportunity needs to be used more proactively. The pharmacist is accessible without appointment, is captive in the pharmacy during the opening hours, is available by phone, and works in familiar, non-threatening centres. There is no charge for services or advice and recommendations may be advice or referral to the GP or it may be the sale of an over-the-counter medicine. Modern pharmacy has the potential to convey the message of health care to a large slice of the population. How successful this move will be depends on the influence of pharmacy's own professional bodies and the FHSA and it will require a spirited co-operation and willingness to adapt and change coming from pharmacy owners.

There is a pilot scheme in Somerset for health promotion through pharmacies and this is being done through verbal advice and leaflets in several areas, including smoking cessation. There is an opportunity to recommend patches or chewing gum and other means of giving up smoking. Patients are encouraged to return to the pharmacy so that the use of patches and gum can be reviewed and to sort out any difficulties that may arise. In another area of health promotion advice can be given to patients on the harmful effects of exposure to the sun. There are also opportunities in the area of infestation. Another pilot is being run in the area of blood pressure testing, peak flow monitoring and pregnancy testing, and the results of this pilot will be available in early 1995. These are all carried out using guidelines developed in conjunction with the Local Medical Committee (LMC), and indeed the initiative has been developed with the health promotion unit of the District Health Authority.

Another area in which specific pharmacies are involved is the syringe/needle exchange scheme. Government policy is to limit the spread of AIDS and it is doing this by encouraging addicts to use clean 'works', and exchanging 'works' that are used. It provides an opportunity to give advice and help to those addicts and to build a relationship with them which will support and encourage the use of needles and syringes in the correct way so that they will always use clean equipment and not share. It is an opportunity to build trust and confidence in those clients in an area of confidentiality. Many appreciate the opportunity of being involved in that way and helping themselves.

Another initiative has been the reclassification of several products which hitherto have been available only on prescription. They are now available for sale in a pharmacy, under licence and in certain circumstances and for specific implications. The pharmacist should determine the appropriateness of a request, give advice and, if necessary, refer the patient to the GP. Care is needed in giving advice to avoid missed referral indications. Several products have been made available in recent years including ibuprofen tablets and gel, ketoprofen gel, hydrocortisone cream and aciclovir cream which has recently been brought onto the market and is available for the treatment of cold-sores. Antifungals and H2 antagonists are other examples.

By encouraging people to purchase medicines GP consultation time is being saved, as well as the cost of the medicine itself. The pharmacist has a personal responsibility to ensure that such sales are appropriate, to prevent harm coming to the patient or missing cases for referral to the GP.

Patients' responsibility for their health

Patients need to take responsibility for their own health in addition to the role played by health care professionals and trained carers. Community pharmacists can assist in training carers, patients in residential homes, carers in the patient's own home and home helps. There is a training initiative taking place in some parts of the country to train those people and to help patients look after themselves. One example is in the social services level 3 assessment of the elderly. A pharmacist can be involved in this assessment and will be able to recommend compliance aids and special labels, monitored dose units etc. Several pharmacies in strategic areas are developing depots of aids for handicapped patients that will help normal living and support patients in those situations. In the area of discharge planning, there is a need to co-operate with hospital pharmacists so that patients will receive the correct information as they go into hospital, and pharmacists in the community will receive information from hospital to update records and to use patient medication records to the benefit of the patient and their overall care. In Liverpool pharmacists have been involved with psychiatric patients who have been discharged into the community. For example, it is important that these patients are able to take their medicines correctly and pharmacists provide support to those patients in clinics to help them understand why they are taking their medicine, to deal with side-effects and to encourage and give these patients support in medicine compliance.

Learning points

- Pharmacists must be confident that the change is appropriate and necessary.

- Pharmacists must receive training and support, from their professional bodies, FHSA, DHA and social services.

- The lay-out of community pharmacy premises must change, offering private consultation or advice areas. .

- Pharmacists should network, so a comprehensive range of services to patients can be provided.

Reference

1   Department of Health (1992) The Health of the Nation. HMSO, London.

23
Health promotion and self-care in later life
Janet Askham

Introduction

Health promotion in self-care among older people is a huge subject, which cannot be addressed adequately in a few words. Accordingly, this chapter will focus on the importance of health gain for elderly people:

- how health resources can be saved by both prevention of ill health and the promotion of positive health
- the role of health promotion and self-care activities.

These will be illustrated from recent or ongoing work.

The importance of health gain for elderly people

There are several reasons why self-care for older people is important. Self-care for older people is:

> 'Not merely a health device (like jogging for the sedentary affluent city dweller), but a reaffirmation of the dignity and autonomy of older persons . . . Too frequently older people are mentioned as individual and social problems (what shall we do about the elderly?) and the very act of urging that more, and more appropriate, services be provided may strengthen the popular image of a frail, helpless, confused group which needs to be looked after.'

This quotation is from a book entitled Self Care and Health in Old Age[1] and makes the important point that health gain and self-care are important in later life because they enhance the dignity of older people.

It is of course important too because older people as a group are the highest users of health services. How could this not be the case? Most people in our society now die in later life; therefore the illnesses which cause or hasten their deaths – and for which they need treatment and care – tend to occur in old age. It is also the case because 'the elderly' are such a large group, including people in an age group of 30 years and more. Although people are living longer, not all the years gained are disability free. There is controversy on the point, but the health study for the Carnegie Enquiry into the Third Age[2] concluded that:

> 'On balance the evidence suggests that most of the years of life gained are without major disability, but that there is also a small increase in the period of disability, especially for women.'

A recent analysis in *Population Trends*[3] assessed life expectancy with and without disability for men and women aged 65 at two points in time (1970 and 1980). It showed that while women had maintained their advantage over men in having a longer total life expectancy, they also maintained their disadvantage in that they could expect as many years with as without disability after the age of 65, whereas men could expect a higher proportion of disability-free years.

A high proportion of older people, particularly women, suffer from chronic illness and disability in their latter years. At the present time, as is well known, the number and proportion of *very* old people is increasing at a faster rate than that of the older population as a whole. Anything they can do to enhance their own health and to release resources is to be welcomed.

Health gain is important because health gain or maintenance in one area can promote gain in another. Perhaps this is particularly important in later life when multiple disabilities, illnesses and deficits can occur. For example, studies show that cognitive abilities do not decline until very late life provided physical health is good[4].

Finally, health gain is important for older people because of the roles they have to perform. It is a misconception that health gain is only important for people of working age. Older people need and want to be as fit as possible in order to fulfil their responsibilities. For example, they may help to care for someone else. A recent national survey[5] asked people whether they were helping to look after anyone who was sick, handicapped or elderly, and found that 13% of those who are 65 and over are carrying out such caring responsibilities (14% of men and 13% of women). Using the 1985 General Household Survey of Carers, a study of caring in the Third Age (for the Carnegie Enquiry) found that 19% of people in Britain aged 50–75 were carers, and 6% were looking after someone in the same household as themselves. Five per cent of this age group were providing 20 or more hours care per week[6].

Carers need to be fit, but it looks as though they are no fitter than non-carers – except at very late ages. Again, analysis of the 1985 General Household Survey shows that when people were asked whether they assessed their health as good, fairly good or not good, those thinking their health was good declined with age; and non-carers were generally more likely to say that their health was good except among those aged 75 and over (Table 23.1). Very old people may find it more

Table 23.1   Self-assessed health of carers and non-carers by age group (as %) – Britain 1985

Health during previous 12 months assessed as:	Carers			Non-carers		
	<50	50–74	75+	<50	50–74	75+
Good	66	51	47	75	50	34
Fairly good	24	33	37	19	31	39
Not good	10	16	16	6	18	27
Base for percentages	490	1124	110	9 594	4 972	1270

Source: Askham J, *et al.* (1992) Special Tabulations from General Household Survey 1985

difficult to be carers if they see themselves as in poor health. Caring for a sick or disabled relative has been shown to be very arduous, and therefore anything which can be done to improve such people's health will be welcomed.

It is also important to point out that in fact there is a good deal of such self-help and health-promoting behaviour already, and of faith in its efficacy. For example, a recent national survey for Age Concern England[7] found that though 'the family doctor is widely viewed as a common source of health advice, over 40% of those aged 55 or over said they would seek advice from a friend of their own age' *and* 'Over a quarter of those 65 or over are very confident that people can expect to be healthy in later life, as opposed to only 7% of 15–24 years old.'

Possible resource savings from the prevention of ill health and the promotion of positive health

The kind of health resources which can be saved through self-care and health promotion among elderly people are to some extent the same as for other age groups. But it is necessary to bear in mind the very high use made by older people of medication, and the huge financial cost of long-term institutional care. Although at any one time only a very small proportion of older people are living in institutions, a much higher proportion of people will experience such care at some time towards the end of their lives.

All the major causes of ill health and death among older people could be reduced by promotion of healthier lifestyles and changes in individual behaviour. These, of course, involve cutting down smoking or excessive use of alcohol, better eating habits and diet, more exercise, and preventive medicine, with special mention usually given to hormone replacement therapy (HRT) for women. Perhaps particularly worrying in the case of older people is lack of exercise. Dependence, the bane of late life, can often be avoided by continued maintenance of activity. Once given up, it may be gone for ever. Yet levels of exercise among older people are low. The 1992 National Fitness Survey showed that only 34 per cent of

55–64 year olds and 23 per cent of 65–74 year olds exercised sufficiently to maintain good functioning[8].

The value and role of self-care and health promotion activities

These activities include those where individuals work alone or in groups to improve their health and schemes involving older people helping each other or being assisted by younger people and/or professional people. Such activities can come about either through national or large-scale campaigns (for example national advertising) or through initiatives by individuals or small groups. All these are still scarce, and we certainly are not yet in a position to say which are more effective. A few examples can illustrate some of both the strengths and problem areas.

Schemes involving the individual and general messages

These comprise schemes where the individual acts alone in response to impersonal or general messages such as advertising, leaflets, health performances or shows. For example, Tester and Meredith[9] carried out a study in a socially deprived part of London to see whether:

- providing elderly people (aged 70 and over) with information on welfare and preventive services encourages them to use those services

- the provision of information was more effective when given personally on an individual basis;

- whether elderly people's well-being and quality of life can be improved as a result of acting on information received.

Using both action and control samples they found that:

> 'Information given in person was much more likely to be remembered than that delivered through the door. Impersonal information does, however, have an important role in reinforcing personally given information, in reminding elderly people or their relatives about the topics covered, or alerting them to things which were available, which they could then discuss with their personal contacts. The most useful sources of impersonal information for elderly people were television and local newspapers.'[9]

However, a recent national survey by Age Concern England[7] found that 'older people are much less likely than younger people to seek health advice from newspapers, TV or radio (18% of people aged 55 years and over as opposed to 32% of 35–44 year olds)'.

Another example of an innovative health promotion scheme is the Age Well Campaign set up in the early 1980s by Age Concern England and the then Health

Education Council. The aims of this national campaign were to promote good health in later life by a diversity of means:

- publicizing and advertising the importance of promoting the health of older people and the ways in which good health can be pursued (through Age Well shows and leaflets);
- providing small grants to help health-promoting schemes;
- building up and fostering networks of professionals and older people at local levels;
- working with a small number of innovative schemes whose achievements could be used as the material for a handbook to help others interested in starting similar innovations.

Looking just at the shows and advertising, it was clear that there were several lessons to be learnt for self-care and health promotion among older people. The methods used for assessing these were comparisons between two pairs of areas, and interviews with local workers involved with or potentially involved with health promotion. Findings showed that:

- campaigns run by national organizations can be seen as too distant and removed from the people they are trying to influence;
- low priority is generally given by agencies such as social services and health education units to health promotion in later life; they are either concentrating on younger people, or on service provision to older people;
- 'Good practice and innovation tends to depend upon isolated enthusiasts.'[10]

Problems of evaluation dog all innovatory schemes of this kind. If objectives are diffuse, as they often are, and if few of the diverse variables can be held constant, then it is often difficult to assess, let alone measure, outcomes.

Schemes using one-to-one or group interaction

This approach is generally acclaimed as more effective. Whether a professional or lay person is more effective as the facilitator depends on the nature of the behaviour being addressed, and perhaps also on the characteristics of the older people. Two examples where professional help seems to be beneficial can be given; one deals largely with self-care to prevent ill-health and the other to cope with it.

There are very few health promotion initiatives aimed at elderly black or Asian women. One of the few was carried out in West Lambeth, London, when a health visitor joined forces with an Asian Day Centre coordinator and set up a Look After Yourself course for elderly Asian women at the Day Centre. The health visitor herself provided translation/interpretation (a key factor); she adapted the course to suit the needs of her group. It covered, in particular, prevention of heart disease and diabetes, osteoporosis and osteomalacia, and aspects of women's health such as incontinence and arthritis. The authors of the article about the scheme[11] concluded that the particular characteristics of the health visitor were very important in the scheme's success, that 'the outgoing, flexible and responsive health promotion methods adopted appeared highly appropriate for this community'; and that the sessions were seen as safe and familiar being:

- for women only with a trusted leader
- in their own community centre
- specifically aimed at older women
- sympathetic and non-didactic in approach.

As far as self-care of those already with health problems is concerned an example from medication in sheltered housing may be taken to illustrate some general points to do with elderly people. As is well known, medication features highly in the lives of older people, especially in those of the very elderly. One study showed that 87% of people aged 75 and over were on a regularly prescribed medicine[12]. Other studies show that up 45% of older people on medication do not comply with the instructions. Many older people need help with their medication, help which often has to be given by lay carers or by, for example, sheltered housing wardens. In a recent small study we found that sheltered housing wardens did give considerable help, for which they had not been trained, and which they were not supposed to give according to their contracts and job descriptions[13]. With more information and advice on how and when to measure out and take their medication older people might need less help from professionals. Control over medication is a part of the sense of control over one's own life, and it is well known how important such perceptions are in the maintenance of independent living in late life.

As well as those with professional involvement there are also lay schemes. In particular there is the rising enthusiasm for peer counselling projects for older people. These have developed from the well-known Santa Monica Senior Health Screening Center's peer counselling project, set up originally in 1975. This scheme involved training older people themselves to counsel and advise other older people. Its success is usually couched in terms of:

- its great popularity among older people
- the ease with which they can be drawn in
- its ability to target specific groups of older people e.g. those from lower income groups or minority ethnic groups.

A new Ageing Well Initiative has recently been set up in England. It is managed by Age Concern England, and draws on previous peer counselling schemes, for example by training and using volunteer senior health mentors. The results of this will be awaited with interest.

Some conclusions

This is an area where we need far more evidence before any general conclusions can be drawn. However, some statements are relatively well supported. It is accepted, for instance, that older people can feasibly be targeted in self-care schemes. Research – from the USA though using some British material – suggests that 'it appears to be no less feasible to include adults up to age 74 in surveys, clinical research, and health promotion/disease prevention programmes than any other age group. Although recruitment periods may need to be extended, participation rates for this age group are either comparable or are only modestly lower than other age groups. Furthermore these older adults are good study participants. They comply with study protocols, and the quality of their responses to telephone and in-person surveys is comparable or only modestly lower than other age groups'[14]. It is only as people enter very late age that their participation rates decline.

We know very little, however, about what particular kinds of programme older adults are particularly likely to co-operate with, nor the kind which appeal to which types of older adult. There is some (not surprising) evidence, however, that those in higher social classes, and the more healthy, are more likely to co-operate.

It is also clear that professional support to self-care schemes is valuable. Professional endorsement can increase the scheme's acceptability and professionals are also often ideally placed to find and target older people.

There is a need for training, so that professionals involved with older people on all fronts are aware of the importance of health promotion and of how to encourage it. Plans or policies for health promotion among older people also need to bear in mind that they are not a homogeneous population, but that there are differences in age, sex, ethnic background and social class, and we need to respond to each appropriately. For example, it is calculated that differences in active life expectancy are greater by social class than by gender: 'Some research using international data suggests that men in the top fifth of the social scale have 6.3 years more life expectancy than those in the bottom, but 14.3 years more *active* life expectancy'[2]. There is therefore a more urgent need to concentrate health promotion activities on those in the lower than the higher social classes.

There is a vital need for evaluation and monitoring of schemes. There are far too many projects with no in-built evaluation. Without this the project's effectiveness cannot be assessed, the value of replicating it elsewhere remains unknown, and the state of our knowledge about the importance of health promotion and self-care to older people remains incomplete.

Learning points

- For many reasons health promotion for older people will probably include some expensive activities.

- There are examples of successful schemes, though broad general conclusions on the best approaches cannot yet be drawn.

- Training and professional support are valuable assets for such schemes and evaluation is essential.

- The greatest need is likely to be among lower socio-economic groups.

References

1 Illsely R (1986) Preface. In: Dean K, Hickey T and Holstein B (eds) *Self Care and Health in Old Age*. Croom Helm, London.

2 Grimley-Evans J, Goldacre M, Hodkinson M *et al.* (1992) *Health: Abilities and Well-Being in the Third Age*, Research Paper No. 9, Carnegie Enquiry into the Third Age. Carnegie UK Trust, Dunfermline.

3 Bebbington A (1991) The expectation of life without disability in England and Wales, 1976–88. *Population Trends*. **66**: 26–9.

4 Holland C and Rabbit P (1991) The course and causes of cognitive change with advancing age. *Reviews in Clinical Gerontology*. **1**: 79–94.

5 OPCS Monitor (1992) *General Household Survey of Carers in 1990. OPCS Monitor 17*. Office of Population Census and Surveys, London.

6 Askham J, Grundy E and Tinker A (1992) *Caring: The Importance of Third Age Carers, Research Paper No. 6, Carnegie Enquiry into the Third Age*. Carnegie UK Trust, Dunfermline.

7 Age Concern England (1993) *Ageing Well: Fact or Fiction (Press Release)*. Age Concern England, London.

8 National Fitness Survey (1992) *The Allied Dunbar National Fitness Survey*. The Sports Council and Health Education Authority, London.

9 Tester S and Meredith B (1987) *Ill-Informed? A Study of Information and Support for Elderly People in the Inner City*. Policy Studies Institute, London.

10 Nash C (1989) *The Age Well Campaign: A Research Report*. Report to the Health Education Authority. Age Concern Institute of Gerontology, King's College London, London.

11 Pharaoh C and Redmond E (1991) Care for ethnic elders. *The Health Service Journal*. **16 May**: 20–2.

12 Swift CG (1988) Prescribing in old age. *British Medical Journal*. **296**: 913–15.

13 Adams S, Askham J, Redfern S *et al.* (1993) *Medication in Sheltered Housing.* Anchor Housing Trust, Oxford.

14 Carter W, Elward K, Malmgren J *et al.* (1991) Participation of older adults in health programs and research: a critical review of the literature. *The Gerontologist.* **31(5)**: 584–92.

24

Benefits of additional staff in primary care

Denys Wells

Introduction

The key question in the debate on releasing resources into primary care is how to bring additional staff and services to patients in the general practice setting. There are certain issues to be considered by general practitioners and other primary care workers before these new services can start. The main ones are:

- how the service is currently managed
- the ethical issue of the reallocation of resources
- priority setting
- whether the proposed new services are necessary in the long term.

This chapter discusses these 4 issues in some detail and follows with examples of 'new services' provided in a fundholding practice since 1991.

Historical patient management

There were and are many reasons why general practitioners refer patients to hospitals and therefore consultant care. A simple division of the reasons behind these referrals could be clinical and administrative.

Fundholding has given general practitioners greater clinical freedom. For example in a case where the diagnosis is clear but a confirmatory test such as gastroscopy is required, in the past the GP effectively passed the patient over to the consultant, but now has more scope to specify and secure those services required for the patient and maintain direct control of the process.

Fundholding has also allowed general practitioners greater administrative control, for example through monitoring patient attendance at hospital clinics, unnecessary follow-up can be easily identified. Overall, greater administrative and clinical control brings many advantages to the patient – fewer trips to hospital, management by one or possibly only two doctors. For the general practitioner, however, it means new and increased responsibilities, and new staff may be required.

The ethics of resource allocation and priority setting

In setting up new services some possible ethical issues should be taken into account: justice, autonomy, beneference and malfeasance. For example, in the NHS as currently constituted, there is nowhere for the fundholding general practitioner to discuss the just use of the allocated budget when considering the comparative effectiveness of hip replacement or coronary artery work. Nationally these ethical debates tend to occur at universities or between the BMA and the Department of Health, but they need in addition to take place at local or regional level. There is also in setting up these services the question of the doctor/patient relationship and respect for the patient's autonomy. An effective treatment register could be produced, rather akin to the White and Black list of drugs, so that a fundholder will know that a certain type of treatment is effective, and whether or not the work can be undertaken in primary care.

Accountability for decision making, e.g. in diverting services into a new activity, is an area of interest investigated by the Audit Commission 18 months ago. The response was that GP fundholding was a very good return on investment. Professional accountability must also be considered in setting up a new service. The introduction of certain bulletins begin to address these issues e.g. Effective Health Care, MeReC, but are only a start. There is as yet no effective local 'ethical' forum for fundholders.

There are also the practical considerations to be addressed before a new service is provided, including questions such as: are the new staff a priority over other possible users of the resources? The legal responsibilities need to be considered too – if the work envisaged is carried out more quickly than anticipated what will that staff member subsequently do? Is the type of work going to infringe COSHH regulations or EC Directives?

In summary, when considering new staff and services the following should be considered.

- What are the services?

- What staff are needed to run that service?

- What equipment is required to produce the new service?

- Is the service already available? If it is available will the 'new' service produce a more cost-effective outcome?

- Is it necessary?

- How will it be funded?

- How long will the service continue for?

- Is there space?

- Will other people (patients not of the practice) in the locality be deprived of that service or can they be included?

Advantages and disadvantages of purchasing

Fundholding undoubtedly offers advantages and disadvantages when a new service is being introduced in primary care. The advantages are:

- the service may be cheaper, for example with chiropody

- specialists' time can be used more sensibly, for example to screen for important diseases such as glaucoma

- less travel for the patient – the West Midland experience of running two in-house out-reach clinics has shown ambulance usage has dropped dramatically; patients use their own transport or are brought to the surgery by friends or relatives

- the patient sees the same doctor or paramedic with an in-house service; at an outpatients clinic they will usually see a different person at each attendance

- the chance for general practitioners to talk to and learn from the person providing the new service leads to educational possibilities

- the practice is able to fulfil some aspects of the patient or practice charter more easily.

The financial arrangements can help. Fundholding budgets are allocated under four headings, but essentially there is one budget and uniquely within the health service, money can be varied between the different budgets. Setting up a new service under one budget might be achieved at the same cost, but will release funds in other budgetary areas. The first wave and second wave practices are probably going to be in a better position to enable resources to be released, but all practices and groups of practices are likely to find flexibility in the drugs budget. As an estimate, there are probably 30% savings on many drug budgets.

There are also disadvantages for patients and health care workers in starting new services in general practice. Probably the most important for patients is the potential loss of choice: if a practice employs a chiropodist the patient will be referred to a practice chiropody clinic. From the fundholders' point of view the patient will benefit because the service will probably be quicker and simpler and use common records: it will also be cheaper. But the patient loses the option of seeing the community chiropodist.

There are other potential disadvantages for the fundholder, mostly relating to problems of organization and management:

- the amount of time for the doctors to supervise the new service and the organization of the staff to run it

- issues surrounding the ownership of new equipment

- whether to upgrade or buy new equipment and the problems of quality control

- the cost of supplying staff to provide all the functions that would normally be done in outpatients – reception, general clinic secretarial duties

- how to deal with changing circumstances, as where the initial financial incentive of relocating a hospital service through cost and volume contracts may become financially less advantageous than at present

- ensuring that the financial means to provide a new service continues.

New patterns of services

In the first two examples that follow the additional staff were doctors. The first, eye services, required the purchasing of specialist equipment: and the second, orthopaedic services, highlighted particular issues in respect of organizing an outpatient-style clinic remote from other hospital based facilities such as the X-ray department.

Ophthalmic/orthoptic services

The single biggest cause of blindness is glaucoma. In the West Midlands screening for this condition is very patchy for people suffering from diabetes mellitus, and for their first degree relatives, those who are at greatest risk of developing the condition.

We therefore felt it would be sensible to start screening for glaucoma, initially amongst the high-risk group of patients. Such screening would require specialist equipment and the question arose as to whether, once the patient population at risk had been screened, the equipment would continue to be required. This question of whether the proposed service is required in the long term should, I believe, be considered before a new service is started.

The ophthalmic outpatients department was obviously overwhelmed by demand – as general practitioners we had little knowledge of why people continued to attend; information on altered treatment (particularly relating to glaucoma therapy) was scarce and people with often severe cataract disease were waiting for very long periods of time for initial review, and even longer for surgery. Fundholding allowed us to establish which patients were attending such clinics, though even this task required considerable time from our fundholding staff.

To have a consultant attend an in-house clinic for eye disease for our patients would not help the overall provision of ophthalmic services in our area. Discussion with senior staff at the Eye Hospital resulted in an Eye Associate Specialist being appointed to run clinics, initially every other week, but now weekly. It has given us 'administrative' control over the size of these clinics, which many patients had been reattending every six months for no good reason, e.g. to see how their cataracts were getting on.

This arrangement allows supervision of orthoptic staff who have to use the visual field equipment for glaucoma screening to proceed. The equipment is standardized and maintained by the Eye Hospital staff, a very different arrangement from that in high street retail ophthalmic optician outlets, where glaucoma screening equipment gives very variable results. The new service has resulted in identifying 30 new cases of glaucoma in the first 60 screened – two very severe but asymptomatic.

The attendance of the Associate Specialist has resulted in a greatly improved service for patients with eye disease. The waiting times for patients requiring initial review for other eye diseases, particularly cataracts, is now a few weeks, against a wait of 12–18 months before. Follow-up for glaucoma therapy has resulted in at least 150 fewer outpatient attendances from the practice and, an additional benefit for patients is that the time their appointment is booked is kept too. Those requiring laser therapy are seen and treated promptly; previously despite requiring urgent laser treatment they often waited 18 months. The number of ambulance journeys requested by the practice on behalf of patients has also fallen dramatically. The whole service costs approximately a third of the original one, including purchase of the equipment. This service is now run in several fundholding practices and our health authority will fund patients of other practices to attend these clinics. I do believe this particular service is a very good example of how reallocating the cost of an outpatients to be run in general practice shows the true benefit of fundholding.

Orthopaedics

The case of the second specialist, a consultant orthopaedic surgeon, was a little different. A recent retiree was chosen so the NHS was not deprived of consultant work. At the time, outpatients in orthopaedics waited up to 70 weeks for a first appointment. Only about 20% of orthopaedic referrals need to go on to surgery, so 80% probably need a clinical hands-on approach with some investigations. To enable the consultant to see the patient with the blood test and x-ray results that had been requested required a lot of organization of a type not previously encountered in general practice.

We have found that a full referral letter received by the consultant in week 1 has enabled us to arrange any further necessary tests by the appointment date in week 3.

A special contract was needed with the x-ray department to deliver x-rays and return them. The advantage is that the patients are in and out within about four weeks as opposed to 40–70 weeks. It has given fundholders a new level of responsibility. For example, a case initially suggesting Paget's disease was found by the consultant to be one of carcinoma and the patient was referred back to the general practitioner; previously the patient would have been sent to an outpatient department where the first consultant would have established the correct diagnosis and arranged an internal transfer to a further specialist. Now we have greater responsibility but the patient also benefits; the work up to the patient has a much greater opportunity for involvement in deciding whether to have specialist (possibly unpleasant) investigation and treatment of possible dubious benefit.

Orthotics

Many patients require some form of specialist appliance – lumbar support corset, special shoes, to name but two examples. Prior to fundholding, for a patient to be fitted and then refitted when the appliance wore out was a mast of extreme frustration – long delays, time consuming journeys and little choice in style of the appliance. The cost was often considerable. A polio victim required a new calliper and shoe; this was achieved in about 4 weeks at a cost of £293, the patient having been fitted at home with a choice of shoe colour. Prior to our employing an orthotist, the time taken would have been in the region of 11 months, the shoe would have been standard brown and several ambulance journeys to two different clinics would have been required. The cost would have been nearer £700 but nobody would have known or worried very much.

Further additional staff

The number and variety of additional staff and therefore new services that can be established in primary care is probably endless. Each practice or group of practices will need to consider the four issues I mentioned at the start of this chapter, but the new personnel most likely to be employed will be physiotherapists, psychologists, dieticians, chiropodists and counsellors. The latter are best supervised by the psychology service as this avoids difficult conflicts regarding confidentiality, psychologists. Some of these services many practices will have already, to others they will be new. All will require additional time from practice reception and secretarial staff.

One particularly useful new, or additional staff member is a completely new post – that of the practice pharmacy manager (PPM). This is a non-dispensing post best undertaken by a senior pharmacist (Grade D) with experience in community and hospital work and knowledge of adverse reaction reports and drug interaction problems. We initially employed a part-time pharmacist to help us produce a sensible, usable and cost-effective practice formulary. However, the task obviously required a full-time post to enable a proper control of the drug budget. The pharmacist's role is now to manage this budget – monitor PACT information, maintain the formulary and produce drug protocols and guidelines particularly in the area of expensive drugs. There is also a very important clinical role for the PPM in working directly with patients, supervising the repeat prescribing policy and ensuring sensible adverse event reporting. A third area of work is in fundholding and contracting with providers to ensure their use of drugs is consistent with that of the practice and vice versa. A further potential employee would be a practice pharmacy receptionist (PPR).

Traditionally, in every general practice any request for information relating to any pharmaceutical or medicinal product (particularly when the doctor(s) are away from the premises) has been dealt with initially by the reception staff. Extended training of some receptionists along lines similar to pharmacy technicians employed by community and hospital pharmacists would lead to a more controlled and so ultimately safer and more cost-effective area of work in general practice. The larger practices could undoubtedly have both a pharmacy practice manager and one or two practice pharmacy receptionists. To date we have, with the help of the practice pharmacy manager, moved from 7–8% below the local FHSA PACT data average to 20–25% below, or in national terms, about 12% below that for 1993.

The cost of this service is currently met from savings from the drug budget but the continued funding of such a position accounts for less than 5% of the total drug budget for the practice.

Equipment

An example in this area is a mini-lab. Mini-labs cost £12 000. They allow 12 or 16 blood tests to be carried out. Their advantages are tremendous. They have been performance tested, run and monitored by the main laboratory, under strict control of the hospital service, who come out and set the standards periodically. This ensures reliability and reproducibility. For example, in a patient with hypertension, kidney function can be monitored, leading to more appropriate prescribing. Another example is patients on non-steroidal anti-inflammatories for arthritis to check for anaemia; 90 seconds later the result shows the patient is anaemic, and non-steroidal treatment is stopped. Even without an audit, non-steroidal anti-inflammatory prescribing has probably decreased because of this machine. By having the immediacy of the test result, the patient is more inclined to allow changes in medication. Other examples include the purchase of air cushions and mattresses in constant short supply and in greater demand with the increasing emphasis on community care.

Conclusions

In primary care there must be a move away from services that are solely general practitioner led, to multi-professional partnerships. In the future, general practitioners will become purchasers of health care as well as providers. General practitioners are ideally placed to purchase effective health care in their locality. The additional staff we have employed or now work with have the first step to providing a 'one-stop' health care clinic, a place where health care in the widest sense can be delivered in the community.

A one-stop health care centre or primary health care unit, can combine the benefit of the smallness of general practice, a number of practices housed in one building each with their own front door, with access to a resource centre. The resource centre will actually fulfil many functions. It will bring in private health care, or private enterprise, because it will cover everything in the health care requirement of patients, from acupuncture to Zen Buddhism, including the undertaker. The hairdresser can be included because patients benefit from having their hair done. Other examples are the physiotherapist and the pharmacist. Our additional staff have started to create this resource centre.

The amalgam of two authorities – the FHSA and the DHA – will essentially become a commissioner. Health commissioning could involve the integration of all services including public health, education and social service, and so require a much greater integration of resources and management of people. It will probably include a supervisory role over the purchaser to ensure that there is purchasing of effective health care for the population base, and there will probably be yardsticks at a national level: for example, are hernias repaired in the right way and are they repaired at the right time? Is effective health care purchased? Health commissioning will be much more involved in the integration of all the services that go towards good health.

All of this will require health professionals to acquire new skills. All general practitioners will need to accept new roles often requiring greater clinical responsibility. The need to work with a greater range of health care professionals must be seen as enhancing the general practitioner's role, not as a direct threat. To ensure that it does so, those general practitioners setting out to employ or deploy new staff and services must first address the four issues stated at the start of this chapter. Is the proposed service better than that which is already there? What are the ethical issues of reallocating already limited resources? Is such action a priority? What are the long-term consequences of employing new or additional staff? If the answers to these questions are all positive, the service is likely to be a success – patients will benefit, the practice will enjoy a new and enhanced role, the doctors will appreciate it and the new staff member will find the role worthwhile.

Learning points

- Ethical thinking must be the foundation of resource allocation and priority setting.
- One-stop services benefit patients.

25

Nursing resources in primary care

Nesta Williams

Introduction

The NHS reforms have brought primary health care to the forefront of the provision of health services in the UK. The general practice setting is acknowledged as the first point of contact and the gatekeeper for an increasing range of health services. In support of this process, Staffordshire FHSA and First Community Health (FCH) are committed to the development of effective and efficient Primary Health Care Teams (PHCTs), valuing the individuals who work within the teams and providing a comprehensive range of client focused services.

Currently FCH is contracted by the South Staffordshire Health Authority to provide a range of services including community nursing and health visiting to a population of 350.000. In the area 123 GPs work in 50 practices of which seven are fundholding. FCH applies the principle of named nurse and health visitor for PHCTs, and staff can be attached to more than one practice. Provision of nursing resources has developed on an historical basis similar to the methods identified in the York report *Nursing by Numbers*[1], that is incrementally and often in response to demand rather than needs. The project described in this chapter was the first step in developing a more systematic approach linking the deployment of nursing resources to the assessment of health needs. The eight month project was funded by the FHSA and was led by a PHCT development manager. Four practices took part, two fundholding and two non-fundholding.

The project aims were to develop a framework or methodology which would facilitate the specification for community nursing and health visitor resources, to meet the health needs of practice populations in mid-Staffordshire, and to enhance health gain by improving the use of nursing resources through basing staff wherever practicable within PHCTs in a general practice setting. A number of specific objectives were identified:

- to develop a GP practice profile reflecting the holistic health needs of the practice population and the public health needs of the community serviced by the practice

- to develop a PHCT strategy for health gain, including common goals and objectives for all team members

- to adopt a PHCT approach to client-focused planning and commissioning for health care

- to maximize the use of nursing resources in the practice by encouraging a review of traditional roles and functions and facilitating changes in working practices

- to identify how to link nursing resources to individual GP practices or groups of practices

- to develop a timed, prioritized and costed implementation plan.

Drawing on that work, this chapter discusses the key areas of health needs assessment and better focusing of nursing resources.

Health Needs Assessment (HNA)

The priority of any PHCT must be to provide appropriate client-focused services for its practice population; and for this relevant, current information is essential. In carrying out an HNA for the practice population the PHCT needs to go beyond the medical or illness-oriented model to include aspects of physical, mental, emotional, social and societal health. Community nurses and health visitors already produce neighbourhood profiles, including information for example on education, housing, local facilities, voluntary and independent organizations, which has formed the basis for organizing their work. With the new emphasis on general practice it is appropriate to develop the neighbourhood focus into a practice-based assessment of need. Profiling and HNA are the first part of the cycle to achieve health gain, giving an indication of 'where we are now', including the existing resources available to meet the needs.

The project teams identified three stages of an HNA.

Stage 1

This involves gathering data identifying the needs. To be successful the process should meet certain key criteria:

- practice based

- holistic

- life-cycle based

- dynamic

- multi-disciplinary and multi-agency.

It should be based on the practice population, and all PHCT members should contribute and collaborate in the collection and collation of information. Statistical information such as morbidity and mortality should be enhanced by the neighbourhood information which community nurses collect. The agreed baseline information for a practice-based multi-disciplinary HNA is:

- Practice information:
  - age–sex breakdown
  - morbidity
  - mortality
  - disease register
  - cytology
  - breast screening
  - immunization
  - child health surveillance.

- Public health information:
  - demography
  - age–sex breakdown
  - mortality: perinatal,
      post neonatal and
      by disease (e.g. types of cancers, heart disease)
  - social class
  - deprivation
  - unemployment.

- Health visitor/community nurse profiles: information relevant to the practice population.

Health needs should be identified holistically, taking health as a continuum from good health and the absence of disease through to terminal care. All non-health factors which can affect health status should be identified e.g. socio-economic factors, environmental factors, unemployment, poverty and deprivation. A comprehensive age–sex breakdown of the practice population and identification of the factors that can affect health or ill health at each stage of the life-cycle are also essential.

Needs assessment is a dynamic process. There is no point when it is ever complete. It is a continuous cycle, a means to an end, rather than an end in itself. It is a cumulative process responding to changing demands, needing regular review and development if it is to contribute to health gain. It must draw in a wide range of services, if it is to be effective, involving all members of the PHCT and other agencies with which they liaise.

Stage 2

This involves identifying resources and services already available, primarily those of the PHCT, but also those relating to secondary care, local authority, social services and education and the voluntary and independent sector. Consideration should also be given at this stage to factors which inhibit or restrict both service availability and service uptake, such as the ethnic mix, transport issues, access problems and unmet needs.

Stage 3

This involves the team deciding on common goals and objectives designed to target the available resources effectively to achieve health gain.

After collating the information for the HNA, the teams developed action plans with targets designed to meet identified health needs and *Health of the Nation* targets. The previous approach had been to direct clients to available resources and services. Fragmentation of client care could result, particularly when the individuals providing the service worked to uncoordinated objectives. For the future, just as health needs have been identified by the team, the team will also agree a common strategy for the achievement of health gain. This will be based on a team action plan broken down into achievable targets which will be monitored, reviewed and evaluated on a cyclical basis by the PHCT (Table 25.1).

In part, these examples are an extension of the needs assessment – testing out whether an intervention will achieve health gain. However, they also represent a shift in service provision, as they are building a service around client needs rather than fitting clients into existing services. It has become apparent with all project sites that the HNA generates further work before decisions can be made on what action is needed to achieve health gain.

Table 25.1   Turning an analysis into an action plan: some examples

Area of concern	Action
The population 65+ and 85+ was identified as being above the local average.	A pilot study of both age ranges is being undertaken to develop a more detailed picture and to decide what resources are necessary to meet these clients' needs.
The quality of the management of leg ulcers needed improvement.	A member of the nursing team is to be trained in Doppler assessment and will develop a practice-based clinic to ensure that appropriate intervention is timely.
There was a high proportion of young people in age range 5–16 years with asthma, many of them not attending an asthma clinic at a surgery or hospital consultations.	A pilot study is being undertaken to review their status, and the need has been identified for a member of the nursing team to acquire the Diploma in Asthma Care to maximize effectiveness of asthma management in the PHCT.
A community nurse's analysis of a caseload indicated an apparent high proportion (20%) of the work-load is clients with multiple sclerosis.	The situation is to be monitored to assess: (a) if this compares with other practice populations and local data (b) whether needs are being met.

Several lessons emerged from the process, which should be considered by purchasers, providers and primary health care teams who intend to adopt this approach to HNA:

- The process should be agreed by purchasers and providers and PHCTs made aware of their responsibility and of any relevant timescale. A rolling programme should be agreed between purchasers and providers over a 3–5 year period for developing the HNA to its full potential.

- The consumer view should be incorporated into HNA but there is also a requirement for consumer education on the changing culture of health care and the delivery of primary care services, for instance self-care and inappropriate attendance in surgery.

- PHCTs will need assistance and coordination in the development of HNA. Information which can be prepared centrally by the FHSA or DHA should be collated in a user-friendly way and be available at appropriate times to support the process. Multi-disciplinary training opportunities for PHCTs should be arranged to introduce the principles of HNA and facilitate the development of epidemiological skills. Personnel with appropriate skills need to be made available to work directly with groups of PHCTs to develop and coordinate the process.

- PHCTs should also be facilitated in the development of team action plans and objectives to meet health needs. These plans and objectives should contain a range of short-, mid- and long-term objectives with realistic deadlines for the achievement of health gain. They should be detailed in the practice annual report and reflected in the nursing teams' annual individual performance review.

Refocusing nursing resources

Noting the constraints

Currently a named health visitor and community nurse are attached to each practice. However, these nurses do not work exclusively with one practice; neither are they always based within the practice setting. The majority are based in clinics and arrange regular meetings with the practice and/or can be contacted by telephone.

The research carried out by Dunnell and Dobbs[2] in 1980 for the DHSS remains the definitive study of the work of nurses in the community. Although the report is over ten years old, the issue of attachment of community nurses to PHCTs is highly relevant to the development of a cohesive PHCT today. Attachment in the 1980s implied that nurses, GPs and other health professionals had access to each other's services as the need arose in relation to client care. The research demonstrated that the number of attachments affected the nurse's relationship with other members of the PHCT.

Because they are attached to different practices, the attached community nurses can be working to several sets of goals and objectives. This raises concerns as to how a cohesive team can develop. Apart from being a key member of a PHCT, nurses are also part of the community nursing service and therefore have to relieve for colleagues during periods of absence. When this occurs, objectives and priorities have to be reorganized, perhaps affecting the collaboration within a PHCT.

The FCH project remit was to review community nursing and health visitor resources. Their roles are already changing. Although the health visiting service has remained mainly oriented to the 0–5 age range, they have a wide-ranging health promotion and education involvement. Now 10% of health visitor's service time is contracted for the public health function and a further 10% has been contracted since April 1994 for the provision of services to people over the age of 65. The clinical role of community nursing teams, with members ranging from nurses graded from clinical grade H to recently appointed care assistants trained to National Vocational Qualification (NVQ) level three, is expanding to meet the changing pattern of health service provision with the shift from secondary to primary care.

Inevitably, the project touched on the work of other members of a nursing team. The number of practice nurses employed by general practice has increased sharply since the introduction of the General Practice contract in 1990. Grades range from 'D' to 'H' and work ranges from general treatment room duties to advanced practitioner status. Community psychiatric nurses and community midwives also provide services for PHCTs from their respective Trusts. Practice nurses, community psychiatric nurses and community midwives have been fully involved in the project teams.

Using skills better

Great effort was put into team development, and a fundamental aspect of this was the opportunity for all nurses in the PHCT to discuss their role with other members of the team, clarify responsibilities and improve resource use. There were many examples of poor coordination or under-utilized skills.

- Mrs X visited the practice once a month to attend the diabetic clinic run by the practice nurse, and was also visited at home both by a health visitor on a regular basis and by the community nurse once a month for an injection of cytamen. After discussion about Mrs X's health needs it was agreed that Mrs X should have a key worker who would coordinate her care plan and who would refer to other nurses as necessary.

- The practice nurse had been asked by a local school to speak to teachers about the management of children with asthma. The school nurse felt that this was her role and that as a member of the PHCT she should have been involved. New programmes use the skills of both nurses.

- The PHCT were not aware of the school nurse's expertise in the area of enuresis. She is now involved with the team in developing a common protocol for the management of the condition.

In practice there will be many more episodes of care and care management which can be overseen by a key worker. At individual practice level the difference may be negligible but in the context of a locality or health authority it presents a considerable saving in staffing and expertise.

The opportunity to discuss nursing roles also included discussion of the responsibilities and constraints involved. This opportunity is rare as everyone is busy trying to achieve their own working goals. This allows myths and misconceptions to arise as to what peoples' roles are and how they carry out their duties.

A health visitor was able to present an extensive résumé of the role and function of the health visitor, which demonstrated the broad public health and health promotion aspects of the role, rather than the common perception that the health visitor works solely with the 0–5 age range. Community nurses similarly were able to illustrate their work to colleagues, showing the range of work undertaken, different aspects of nursing intervention and the complexities of dealing with particular casework, such as nursing a terminally ill patient at home including the liaison and collaboration with other agencies and workers, to ensure that the patient and carers received a high-quality service.

Building the links

The nursing team cannot develop in isolation from the broader PHCT and it must be recognized that the location of staff within the practice setting is not the complete answer to effective team working. Nurses must also have access to professional colleagues in other nursing teams otherwise professional isolation will develop – this has occurred in practice nursing. One benefit of the project has been the alleviation of this isolation, particularly in PHCTs where there is only one practice nurse.

Primary care nurses – whether they are practice nurses, health visitors or community nurses – have at least two things in common: their nursing skills, knowledge and expertise; and a wish to provide best practice patient care. There is a need to remove the interprofessional barriers which have developed between the different branches of primary care nursing, if the nursing team is to function effectively as part of the PHCT. The project has been concerned with role definition and function and the duplication and overlap which occurs in nursing teams. This concern has been to ensure that all skills, expertise and knowledge are shared and used appropriately rather than to divide the nursing team. The project has sought a shift in working practices and collaboration across all fields in primary care nursing to achieve an holistic approach to health care. The development of a team approach and the opportunity to develop professionally will empower nurses to develop new working practices and become fully integrated into the PHCT.

The following points should be considered by purchasers, providers, nurses and PHCTs who intend to develop nursing teams in the primary health care team setting.

- A health visitor and community nurse should be attached to individual PHCTs and be fully involved with the HNA, the agreement of team goals and planning service provision for that practice. All attached staff should be based wherever practicable within the practice setting. Consideration should be given to how all team members can develop the appropriate skills required to become fully integrated and involved in the planning and decision making process of the PHCT.

- The individual nurses should be members of a community nursing team focused on a group of practices to provide relief and cover for annual leave etc for each other's PHCT, ensuring continuity of care and a known contact for referrals. The nursing team should set objectives, and develop audit and outcome measures based on the team's goals.

- A network of clinical supervision and clinical specialists is a prerequisite of practice-based team working to ensure that professional isolation does not occur and to advise nurses and PHCTs on professional nursing issues.

- Promotional material on aspects of primary care nursing should be made available to purchasers and PHCTs to ensure that a greater understanding of nursing roles is achieved and that myths and misconceptions are minimized.

Conclusion

The project ended in May 1994. In retrospect the 8-month time allocation was relatively short to achieve the ambitious aims of the project. A report on the project has been submitted to the DHA and FHSA with costing implications and a timed action plan to take the objectives forward[3].

The project teams are now facilitated by the primary care facilitator and are continuing with the working practices adopted for the project. The immediate post-project evaluation is favourable with all the teams expressing satisfaction and highlighting the benefits gained from this approach to matching resources to meeting health needs.

The opportunities and challenges that lie ahead for primary care are vast. The linking of social and health care needs, the shift from secondary to primary provision and the demographic trends require that members of PHCTs are empowered to meet these demands. The FCH project has been one small step on the way to achieving this. There is still a great deal of work to be done.

> # Learning points
>
> - Health needs assessment to focus PHCT resources requires a broad multi-disciplinary, multi-agency perspective.
>
> - Health needs assessment requires training and education as a foundation for success.
>
> - The HNA should form the basis of a multi-disciplinary, needs-oriented action plan, which should be realistic and reinforced by management action.
>
> - Team discussion can clarify roles, eliminating waste and duplication and filling gaps.
>
> - Careful consideration is required to ensure nurses in PHCTs are appropriately placed and supported.

References

1   Lightfoot J, Baldwin S and Wright K (1992) *Nursing by Numbers*. Social Policy Research Unit, York.

2   Dunnell K and Dobbs J (1982) *Nurses Working in the Community*. HMSO, London.

3   Williams N (1994) *Primary Health Care Team Development Project, October 1993–May 1994*. First Community Health, Stafford.

Further reading

Pickin C (1993) *Assessing Health Need Using the Life Cycle Framework*. Open University Press, Buckingham.

26
Social and health care integration in Lyme Regis
Barry Robinson

Introduction

To many, Lyme Regis will epitomize both seaside small town and rural England. A permanent population of around 7500 is served by two general practices in an area of around 80 square miles. Many of the population are retired elderly, bringing with them the usual high demand for health care. A large summer influx of visitors also pose problems for the providers of health and social services, whilst the transport difficulties of rural Dorset compound the distance of all secondary care centres – none are nearer than 25 miles. In 1990, the local cottage hospital was closed and at that time the only other local facility was a cottage hospital in Axminster, only four miles from Lyme Regis which provided mainly longer-term medical care for the chronically sick amongst the elderly population.

Lyme Regis, as elsewhere, was faced with health and social care reforms which laid emphasis on obtaining best value for money from the limited financial resources available. But how much resource was available for the population and how might it be utilized more effectively? What was effective and what was not?

Local organizational changes were also occurring concurrently. The Dorset Health and Family Health Services Authorities reached agreement to form the Dorset Health Commission – amongst the first in a new breed of strategic health care planners and purchasers. Single directorates were established and a joint Chief Executive appointed. They made clear their objective to place primary care at the forefront of both their planning and investment and it was into this climate that the Lyme Community Care Unit was born, but not germinated.

That lay deeper in the roots of the community where amongst some of the GPs there had been the growing conviction there must be a better way of providing health care to the patients registered with them. It was suggested by me that a radical and fundamental review of health and health care provision was the only sensible way forward.

A blueprint for change

To accomplish this it was necessary at the outset to establish the agendas of those having an interest in the maintenance of health and the provision of health care. No organization, it was contended, could succeed in the longer term, unless it has clearly identified the key issues of all parties.

Four key groups were identified, and for each key objectives listed, as follows:

- Users and carers:
  - health and social care which is comprehensive and integrated with a single point of access for the citizen
  - services to be delivered as close to home as is appropriate
  - services which are citizen centred and accountable to the local community
  - services coordinated to support rather than supplement careers.

- Doctors and health care professionals:
  - work which provides satisfaction, scope for development and adequate financial reward
  - professional accountability for the services to themselves, the wider primary care team and the patient
  - appropriate, timely and adequately funded services.

- Purchasers and strategic planners:
  - strategic direction developed and implemented by providers
  - demonstrable value for money
  - contestability
  - needs assessment and evaluation of therapy as the basis for the provision of care.

- Government:
  - equity of opportunity
  - activity driven by *Health of the Nation*
  - no domination of the agenda by any single group within the service.

Philosophy, structure and function of the Lyme Community Care Unit (LCCU)

During 1991 a proposal was put to the Dorset Health Commission for the establishment of a Locality Care Agency in Lyme Regis. This new form of organization was to assume the responsibility for improving the health of the community and would contract with the Commission on this basis. The proposal was for incremental changes which would take four years to complete.

Initially, the two bodies were agreed that the LCCU would concentrate on improving services which were provided locally. There were two convincing reasons for this decision.

- It was felt that most, if not all health professionals are inherently comfortable with the provider role hence they would be willing to make some sacrifices and undergo considerable change to improve this aspect of health care.

- Although fundholding was becoming established at around this time it was felt that its emphasis on buying care with little ability to change the patterns of care which were provided was unsatisfactory.

From the outset it was the intention to examine every service in detail and to transfer to the local community everything which was appropriate. This could only be achieved if the quality standards of local provision were at least equal to that of the distant care provided. Thus preparation was needed to transfer the distantly based work and resources to Lyme community.

The business plan reflected this ambition and proposed the establishment of several new initiatives in Lyme Regis. Chief amongst them was the hospital-at-home scheme. Other ventures included the development of a home stroke management group and a mental health team with a remit to respond to all mental illness in the locality.

Given all the stakeholder and other agendas a team of health care professionals and support staff were recruited who appreciated the opportunity of working generically. They were asked to write their own job descriptions utilizing all the skills attained during their training and postgraduate careers. They were to become generalists in their chosen field; the only limit on their activity was their professional competence and their accountability to the citizen for an appropriate service. The care which they could not provide would be purchased but they would have a significant input into the purchasing process.

It was not felt appropriate, however, to delegate the planning of health care services entirely to locally based professionals. The real issue was the method by which to transfer that responsibility to the citizens. The LCCU, therefore, established a Management Advisory Group (MAG) whose function is to inform the management team of the needs, wishes and wants of the local population. It is a nominated body containing a wide variety of lay members. These range from a schoolboy through to a member of the local town council and the Community Health Council. A GP from each practice attends as do two elected members of the primary health care team. True democratic representation is not achieved but more so than with any Health Commission, or even a general practice fundholder. Without the power to hold local elections it is the closest approach to the democratic ideal; the voices of the community and the constituencies which they represent are heard.

The MAG has a second, more subtle, function. It is anticipated that the very act of meeting together to discuss and agree decisions about the provision of health care will disseminate throughout the community some knowledge about health resources and the way in which they are utilized.

Operational developments

Before discussing these in any detail it is important to define the source, amount and limitation of funding. The Unit is funded through a modified weighted capitation formula similar to that in use by the RHA. The LCCU is, therefore receiving an equitable share of the total resource available to the Dorset Health Commission and no more. A small amount is 'top-sliced' to fund the Commission and some long-term county-wide initiatives but the remainder is allocated for exclusive use by the LCCU and its community. With funding comes the responsibility to achieve health.

Hospital-at-home

During the first year of operation the LCCU concentrated all its efforts on establishing a competent, motivated team of people who began to share the vision of transferring care and resource into the community. A hospital-at-home scheme was established and protocols and clinical guidelines agreed to ensure safe and effective working. Transfer of patients in the community began after three months and by the end of the first year it was calculated that the scheme had provided the equivalent of two inpatient beds for a whole year. A small beginning but very satisfying to patients and carers alike. The GPs co-operated with this initiative, providing increased medical support for nursing and other professional colleagues. This has led to an unsurprising increase in medical work-load. Alongside the hospital-at-home scheme a mental health initiative has emerged involving a newly appointed community psychiatric nurse and part-time qualified counsellor. Their brief was to adopt as much of the mental health case-load as was thought to be appropriate. GPs co-operated by writing to consultant psychiatrist colleagues encouraging discharge from follow-up outpatients clinics for the chronic mentally unwell. The result was impressive, and within a very short space of time most of this work was being managed by the in-house team.

Diabetic care

Other appointments, such as a dietitian and chiropodist, have absorbed significant amounts of work from the GP case-load. But, more importantly, many diabetics who were formerly seen in hospital settings will now be dealt with by these clinicians working alongside a visiting medical consultant. Development of the primary care team is crucial to the longer term plan for transferring resources, patients, and responsibility back to the community. By the beginning of the second year there was a growing confidence that the logistical and data problems posed by the purchase of secondary care could be tackled.

Purchasing secondary care

The second year involved monitoring all care provided outside of the locality. Emergencies, ambulance transport, tertiary and extra-contractual referrals became the stuff of daily life. At first, there were many difficulties to overcome much of the data incapable of interpretation. By the end of the year confidence was beginning to grow that the data had turned into useful information.

The whole process required bilateral action; but secondary care providers had to be cajoled into increasing co-operation with the Unit. Initial scepticism and even outright hostility was gradually replaced by a dawning comprehension that the LCCU was permanent, and hospital providers, in particular, began to accept that their future might lie in marketing to a fragmented purchasing network and their behaviour altered accordingly. The need for change was not always welcome, but its necessity was emphasized by the hospital-at-home scheme. Fears about instability and the long-term future were expressed but despite this the hospital–LCCU relationships have improved and changes have been implemented.

The agreement with the Dorset Health Commission also began to assume a different form. Substantial purchasing shifts were signalled towards the middle of the second year's operation and these were included in the Dorset Purchasing Intentions. Two examples can be highlighted.

- For many years the lack of any reasonable quantity of day case eye surgery had been a source of dispute, and despite protestations little seemed about to change. Negotiations with the Axminster Community Hospital established a willingness to provide this service – a move away from traditional district general hospital activity. Exploring the possibilities further, there is a willingness to develop appropriate clinical protocols to involve the local optometrist in monitoring chronic eye conditions rather than a consultant ophthalmologist. Local services for local people become a reality, and quality is assured.

- Urology was another contentious area; and the LCCU have supported the establishment of a comprehensive urological service also at Axminster. A consultant-led operating service, with full urodynamic investigations, is now in place. To the elderly population, who utilize these services frequently, this is proving of major benefit.

The changing contract scene

For the LCCU the most significant purchasing shift at the end of the second year was the transfer of a significant sum of money into the unit operating budget, accomplished by negotiating a block discount from the two major providers to reflect the activity of the hospital-at-home scheme. It had been agreed that in year three these providers would still be paid on a block contract basis so that such a discount made sense. Negotiations were protracted and the final discount did not represent the true savings to the acute units; but a principle had been established which was to be of great importance.

By this time also the contract size with the local Community Trust was very small. Some professional support from senior personnel was still purchased but almost no direct patient care. Their core business had become ours and there was no intention to support the Trust's management overhead and staff when the LCCU team could provide a better, cheaper and more responsive service.

Half-way through the third year the final stage in development is eagerly anticipated. Throughout this year the LCCU has acted as the contract monitor on behalf of the Dorset Health Commission. Attendance at contract monitoring meetings with experienced Commission staff had taught us about the intricacies of contracting. For their part the Commission has been surprised and appreciative of the detailed patient-focused information which has been available to support the LCCU case.

The purchasing intentions for 1995–6 have been prepared and circulated to the Management Advisory Group. Currently, these documents flow from the LCCU clinical professionals but it is believed over time that knowledge and skills will develop in the community and the intentions will be very much the product of this group. Local information and advice will still flow from the GPs and other members of the clinical team but we anticipate that there will be an important and increasing input from public health consultants to ensure the provision of effective health care, rather than non-validated and inappropriate treatments. This should be resource releasing in itself.

Purchasing intentions 1995–6

The team members and functions carried out by the LCCU are:

- community nursing
- hospital-at-home
- community psychiatric nurse
- counsellor
- dietitian
- casualty
- outpatient clinics
- general practice support services
- physiotherapy
- occupational therapy
- speech therapy
- chiropody
- health visiting

- social worker
- community health adviser
- secondary care purchasing.

This serves as a baseline for assessing the services that are provided locally, and the changes which are taking place in those services provided by others.

Secondary care contracts this year will be set around the following criteria:

- maximum 3-day inpatient stay without specific consultant approval
- a cost-per-case for all admission procedures
- development of a new form of consultant contract for outpatient clinics which will reflect new teaching and service assessment responsibilities
- payment made only on validated invoices for which clinical details have been received
- the responsibility for accurate data lies with the provider of care.

From the beginning of the next financial year the LGCU will be managing the total Health Commission budget for the population that it serves. Significant sums will be transferred into primary care as more procedures which are both suitable and appropriate to this setting are identified. Some examples under consideration include the following.

- Investments will be made within statutory limitations in local services which can determine health. Resources will be transferred from health care into health education and information. Particular emphasis will be placed on the two largest groups of consumers – the elderly and school children.
- Public hygiene measures such as dog control and public toilets concern the local population and there is a shortage of all-weather sporting facilities locally. There will be investment in these if the evidence and the community support us.
- The transfer of General Medical Service (GMS) monies into the Unit and the contracting of interested GPs for services that they could offer. Already regular bids are sought from GPs for services which are not normally included within GMS.

The range of such opportunities to transfer care and resources is enormous. It varies from the relatively technological, such as from transfusing patients in their home, to an initiative announced by the secretarial team that in future they would be typing the letters dictated by the visiting consultants in the outpatients clinic!

Moving on

Despite all of these structural changes sight must not be lost of the important concerns.

First is the issue of increasing personal responsibility for health; and the LCCU sees this as its prime responsibility. The employment of a full-time community health advisor was only possible by the transfer of funds from secondary care and subsequent savings on local services. Her remit is to facilitate cultural change within the community and she is working with diverse groups within the locality providing valuable feedback on the care provided by the LCCU. Her prime concern is always to increase personal responsibility for the maintenance of health and to identify best practice in the provision of information and care.

The second focus must remain on providing only appropriate education and care to the citizens. Resources must be directed to evaluation and audit and greater emphasis placed on appropriateness. With these two objectives clearly in mind the Lyme Community Care Unit can continue confidently in its role of focusing on health gain for the community.

Learning points

- Stakeholder analysis is required before changes in health care priorities can be made.

- Citizen bodies must be empowered to participate in the planning process.

- Good secondary care purchasing includes sending only those patients to hospital who cannot be looked after elsewhere.

- Responsibilities for health lie with the individual citizen and the community.

27

Integrated care for asthma

*Neil Drummond, Ken Buckingham, Ian Russell, Mona Abdalla,
Sue Ross, Jim Beattie, James Friend, Joe Legge and
Graham Douglas*

Introduction

With the apparent increase in the prevalence of asthma[1-3], there have been
associated increases in deaths from acute asthma[4] and in hospital admissions[5].
These increases appear to be unaffected by the introduction of new drug preparations, and new forms of drug delivery. The British Thoracic Association[6] suggested
that up to 86% of asthma deaths are preventable, and recommended 'closer overall
supervision' as one means of improving care.

Developments in information technology through the introduction of computerized database management systems in both general practice and hospital settings, increasing awareness among GPs about the management of asthma
patients[7], and changes in the structural relationship between general practice and
hospital as a result of GP fundholding, have created opportunities for new
management strategies for chronic disorders such as asthma.

Background to the GRASSIC scheme

In 1989, a shared or integrated care scheme between general practice and hospital
was developed in Grampian for patients with asthma who had been referred for
outpatient review. This scheme uses the computerized Patient Record System (PRS)
of Grampian Health Board, which had already proven its effectiveness in coordi-
nating the care of patients with hypertension[8].

The implementation of integrated care for asthma was incorporated within a
scientific evaluation given the acronym GRASSIC (the Grampian Asthma Study
of Integrated Care), after the Aberdeenshire novelist, Lewis Grassic Gibbon.
This study was intended to evaluate, in clinical, social and economic terms, the

effectiveness of integrated care[9], peak flow self-monitoring[10] and computer-supported asthma education[11]. This chapter refers only to the first of these.

Establishing the integrated care scheme

In 1989, an integrated care scheme was implemented for patients with moderately severe asthma regularly attending outpatient chest clinics in Aberdeen, Banff, Elgin and Peterhead. Using PRS, the chest physicians review patients in this scheme annually, while interim reviews take place in general practice, usually every three months.

Patients are sent computer-generated letters at the appropriate time inviting them to make an appointment to have their asthma checked by their GP. Within the letter is a brief questionnaire, asking for information about symptoms, days of restricted activity, courses of oral steroids, general practice consultations for asthma, hospital admissions and nights of disturbed sleep. Patients are asked to give the completed questionnaire, together with, if relevant, a peak flow diary card, to their general practitioner when their consultation takes place.

Simultaneously, the patient's GP is sent a separate computer-generated letter, informing him or her that the patient is due to attend shortly for an asthma review. This letter contains its own questionnaire concerning consultations, use of β-agonist bronchodilators and oral steroids, alterations to the patient's medication since the previous review, hospital admissions, body weight and peak expiratory flow rate. The GP is asked to return all documentation to the consultant, who uses the information to update the patient's computerized record. One paper copy of the new record is sent back to the GP, and another put into the patient's hospital notes, along with any suggestions by the consultant for changes in the management plan. Previous profiles are discarded.

Evaluation of integrated care

GRASSIC was constructed as a $2 \times 2 \times 2$ randomized trial. Patients were independently assigned at random to:

- integrated care or conventional care;
- peak flow self-monitoring or conventional monitoring;
- computer-supported education or conventional education.

Thus each patient could have been assigned to receive all three innovations, or any two, or one, or none at all. Patients whose asthma was considered too severe or too difficult to manage within integrated care were excluded from randomization from that limb of the trial, but were randomized between the two remaining limbs. Patients randomized to receive conventional care continued to attend outpatient clinics for routine review of their asthma.

The Grampian Joint Ethical Committee and General Practice Sub-committee of the Area Medical Committee both approved the project. Each GP in Grampian (around 330) was contacted by letter, given an outline of the project and an opportunity to withdraw. Only one GP declined to participate, and his patients were duly excluded from the trial.

Patient selection and monitoring

Patients were considered eligible for inclusion in the study if they were aged 16 years or older, had their diagnosis of asthma confirmed by a consultant respiratory physician and experienced pulmonary function reversibility of at least 20% on treatment. Patients were enrolled opportunistically as they attended outpatient clinics for asthma between October 1989 and December 1990.

Those who entered the study were interviewed twice, at entry and just prior to their final consultation with a specialist. The initial interviews were intended to confirm that the randomization procedure had been successful and to measure potential prognostic variables. The final series of interviews were conducted in patients' homes 12 months after entry to the study, and formed the principal data collection point for social, psychological and self-management information. Information relating to the costs borne by patients during the course of the study year was collected by postal questionnaire sent immediately following their third interim review, irrespective of whether that took place in general practice or in the hospital outpatient clinic.

In addition to the Hospital Anxiety and Depression Scale[12], two further measures of psychosocial outcome were applied. The first was derived from the Asthma Self Efficacy Scale[13]. This was intended to assess the degree to which patients considered themselves able to control their asthma successfully while experiencing a number of well-recognized behavioural, emotional or environmental 'trigger factors'. The second measure consisted of an adaptation of the Living with Asthma Scale[14], originally considered to reflect the degree to which patients have adapted their life-styles to accommodate the demands or limitations caused by the presence of asthma. In the version of the scale used here, attention was focused on the interactions between asthma and 'social and physical function'.

Since the trial was located within the context of 'normal' clinical practice, and was designed to guide practical decisions rather than merely to acquire scientific information, it was considered to be 'pragmatic' rather than 'explanatory'. Data analysis was conducted on the basis of 'intention to treat': patients who did not adhere to the management plan to which they were assigned at random were still assumed to have done so for the purposes of analysis. Failure to adhere and failure to respond therapeutically were both regarded as failures of treatment. The study was designed to have an 80% chance of detecting a 10% difference (at the 5% significance level) in the number of hospital admissions for asthma.

Results

Scale of study

A total of 801 patients signed informed consent documents and took part in the study. Thirty-seven additional patients refused to take part, were automatically assigned to receive conventional management, and were excluded from data collection. Eighty-nine patients were excluded from randomization because their asthma was judged too severe to be managed effectively under integrated care. Seven hundred and twelve patients were therefore eligible for randomization, 363 to integrated care and 349 to conventional care. There were no statistically significant differences between the two randomized groups on entry to the study.

Comparison of outcomes

After 12 months, no statistically significant differences between the two groups were detected for pulmonary function, as represented by forced expiratory volume in one second (FEV1) (expressed as a percentage of predicted FEV1), nor for peak expiratory flow rate (PEFR). This similarity in clinical outcome between the groups was supported by the mean number of prescriptions for bronchodilators, and corticosteroid inhalers, and courses of oral steroid recorded throughout the year. The number of general practice consultations for asthma and asthma-related admissions to hospital were also similar in both cases.

During the study year, the distribution of sleep disturbance (a symptom regarded as being a good indicator of asthma control) was similar for both groups. Forty-six per cent of patients in the integrated care group reported no disruption to sleep, compared with 45% in the conventional care group, while 6% in both groups reported that their sleep was disrupted every night by asthma. Among patients who sometimes reported sleep disturbance, analysis confirmed that no statistically significant differences were identifiable (Figure 27.1).

Similar results were obtained for the mean number of days of restricted activity: 73% of patients receiving integrated care reported no restriction on activity, compared with 72% of those receiving conventional care. Among patients who reported some level of restriction on activity, analysis revealed a small and statistically non-significant increase among those receiving integrated care (Figure 27.1).

No differences between the groups were recorded in the results for the psychosocial outcomes assessed after 1 year. Patients receiving integrated care, however, were more likely to report themselves as being in control of their asthma 'all the time' than were those in conventional care (Figure 27.2).

Patients' satisfaction with the scheme

Patients' perceptions of integrated care for asthma were recorded at interview. Those who had experienced it were more likely to select integrated care for the future management plan (75% versus 62%) than those who had experienced

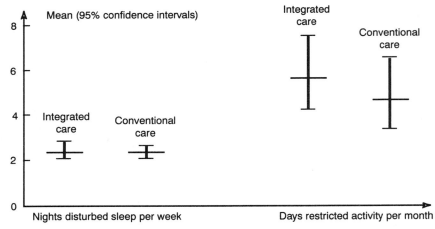

Figure 27.1   Symptoms after 12 months. Values estimated from normal regression model

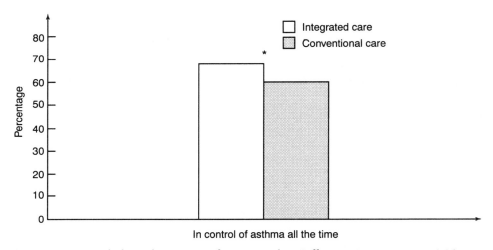

Figure 27.2   Psychological outcomes after 12 months. *Difference in per cent, $p < 0.05$

conventional care only. Alongside this was the finding that conventional care patients were more likely to perceive both advantages (47% versus 40%) and disadvantages (50% versus 37%) to integrated care. This appears to indicate that the 'potential' of integrated care for asthma is more dramatic than the 'reality' (Figure 27.3). Although integrated care patients were more likely to cite positive attributes of their GP as an advantage of integrated care, the proportion of respondents who did so was low (11%), and overall, conventional care patients were more likely to describe themselves as being 'very satisfied' with the medical care they had received for asthma during the study year (Figure 27.4). These findings appear to indicate a resistance to change among patients, many of whom had been attending out-patient clinics regularly for a considerable period and

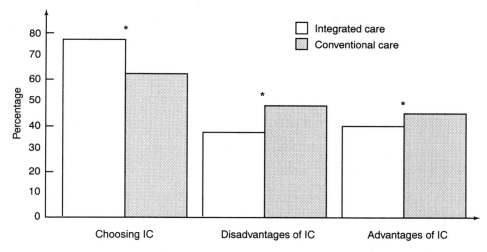

Figure 27.3   Patients' perceptions of integrated care, I. *Difference in per cent, $p < 0.05$

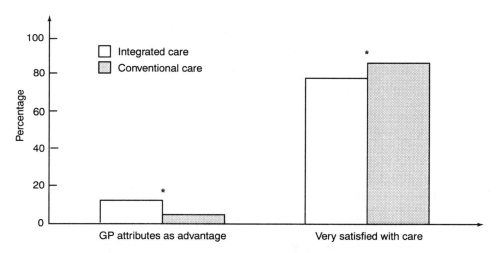

Figure 27.4   Patients' perceptions of integrated care, II. *Difference in per cent, $p < 0.05$

among whom a tenacious impression had become established that GPs, as their name suggests, are 'generalists', while consultant respiratory physicians are 'experts'.

Costs of scheme

Figure 27.5 indicates the costs of operating the Grampian integrated care for asthma scheme. Conventional care patients attended the hospital outpatient clinic an average of 2.6 occasions more during the study year than those in integrated care,

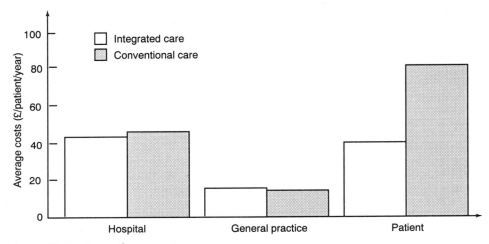

Figure 27.5   Costs of care

but also attended their general practitioner as often as integrated care patients. Taking into account the extra usage of medical resources made by conventional care patients, and all relevant staffing and material costs, the study indicates that the mean costs per patient per year are similar for both hospital and general practice services (assuming the latter are fundholders), for both integrated and conventional care. For integrated care patients, however, a large saving in overall costs was recorded, mainly through a reduction in travelling expenses and reduced periods of time devoted to visiting hospital clinics.

Support for integrated care scheme

The development of integrated care appears to have been hindered by the lack of empirical evidence supporting its clinical, as well as its cost-effectiveness. The GRASSIC project, we believe, provides that evidence in the case of asthma: integrated care patients were at no clinical, psychological or social disadvantage through being managed under such a scheme.

The co-operation of GPs is clearly vital to the successful running of integrated care. Van Damme[15] indicates GRASSIC achieved the support of participating GPs largely because it facilitated their increased involvement in the management of moderately severe asthmatics and allowed GPs to consolidate their role as 'primary' carers.

In the light of the reforms which have overtaken the NHS since GRASSIC began, the role of general practice has achieved even greater influence over the future conduct and development of integrated care. Integration is seen as a means to achieving 'seamless' health care. However, promotion 'on the ground' depends greatly upon the influence of GPs. In this respect, given the clinical effectiveness of integrated care for asthma, the costing implications for all participants (GPs, hospital medical and nursing staff, hospital management, health authority management and *patients*) are paramount.

The extent to which each of these parties will incur additional costs or accrue savings depends upon:

- circumstances in individual areas

- the choice of system selected to coordinate the scheme

- the specific conduct of the scheme

- the number of patients.

Hickman[16] presents a taxonomy of shared care consisting of six individual types based on their methods of information exchange.

Details of the costings for GRASSIC are given elsewhere[17]. Patients would appear to benefit substantially by being able to obtain care from their GP at places and times which are more convenient than those offered by hospital-based clinics. Assuming the adoption of a personal-computer-based system, fundholding GPs are likely to bear additional costs of around 30 pence per patient per year for integrated care (at 1991 prices). This is in comparison with the costs to general practice of having similar patients routinely reviewed by a hospital consultant in conventional care (for which the fundholding GP would have to pay). The costs to general practice will be reduced if special clinics for asthma patients were instigated, for which reimbursement may be claimed. The further development of nurse-run asthma clinics should enhance the cost-effectiveness of integrated care for asthma in general practice still more.

Since the completion of GRASSIC in December 1991, integrated care has continued as a clinical option for patients with asthmas in Grampian referred for out-patient supervision. To date, a total of 610 patients have participated in the scheme at some time, while 385 are currently receiving this form of shared care.

Learning points

- Integrated care for moderately severe asthma is clinically effective, cost-effective and popular among GPs and patients.

- It represents an important aspect of the movement away from hospital-provided services to the provision of quality services in the community.

- In doing so, it should enable the release of consultant and outpatient resources, in order that they may be concentrated upon those patients for whom the provision of specialist expertise and equipment is a prerequisite for health.

References

1   Alderson M (1987) Trends in morbidity and mortality from asthma. *Population Trends.* **49**: 18–23.

2   Robertson C F, Heycock E, Bishop J *et al.* (1991) Prevalence of asthma in Melbourne schoolchildren: changes over 25 years. *British Medical Journal.* **302**: 116–18.

3   Burney P G J, Papacosta A O, Withey C H *et al.* (1991) Hospital admission rates and the prevalence of asthma symptoms in 20 local authority districts. *Thorax.* **46**: 574–9.

4   Burney P G J (1986) Asthma mortality in England and Wales: evidence for a further increase, 1974–84. *Lancet.* **ii**: 323–6.

5   Fleming D M and Crombie D L (1987) Prevalence of asthma and hay fever in England and Wales. *British Medical Journal.* **294**: 279–83.

6   British Thoracic Association (1982) Death from asthma in two regions of England. *British Medical Journal.* **ii**: 1251–5.

7   Jones K (1991) Asthma care in general practice – time for revolution? **41**: 224–6.

8   Petrie J C, *et al.* (1985) Computer assisted shared care I hypertension. *British Medical Journal.* **290**: 1960–3.

9   Grampian Asthma Study of Integrated Care (GRASSIC) (1994) The effectiveness of integrated care for asthma: a clinical, social and economic evaluation. *British Medical Journal.* **308**: 599–64.

10 Grampian Asthma Study of Integrated Care (GRASSIC). (1994) The effectiveness of routine self-monitoring of peak flow in patients with asthma: a pragmatic evaluation. *British Medical Journal.* **308**: 564–7.

11 Osman L M *et al.* (1994) Reducing hospital admissions through computer-supported education for asthma patients. *British Medical Journal.* **308**: 568–71.

12 Zigmund A S and Snaith R P (1983) The Hospital Anxiety and Depression Scale. *Acta Psychiatrica Scandinavica.* **67**: 361–70.

13 Tobin D L, Wigal J K, Winder J A *et al.* (1987) The 'Asthma Self-Efficacy Scale'. *Annals of Allergy.* **59**: 273–7.

14 Hyland M E (1991) The living with asthma questionnaire. *Respiratory Medicine.* **85 (suppl. B)**: 13–16.

15 Van Damme R A E, Drummond N A,' Beattie J A G *et al.* (1994) Integrated care for patients with asthma: views of general practitioners. *British Journal of General Practice.* **44**: 9–13.

16 Hickman M, Drummond N A and Grimshaw J (1994) A taxonomy of shared care for chronic disease. *Journal of Public Health Medicine.* **16** (4): 447–54.

17 Buckingham J K, Drummond N A, Cameron I M *et al.* (1994) Costing shared care. *Health Services Management.* **90**: 22–5.

28

Tracking the financial shifts
Peter Brambleby

Introduction

This chapter explores two themes. Firstly, it shows how health care expenditure can be broken down into a matrix of specialities and age groups, using data from a former District Health Authority in East Sussex. The cost implications of certain diseases can be followed through the matrix, examining the potential for disinvestment and reinvestment, and tracking the consequences of any shifts which might occur. Secondly, coronary heart disease is taken as a worked example of how resource expenditure was tracked through the matrix and how 'an innovative scheme for reducing coronary disease risk factors was established.

Purchasing health care – the early years

Separation of the purchasing and providing roles in health care has created an opportunity for imaginative thinking and radical change in the way services are delivered. In reality, the approach of most commissioning authorities has been one of incremental change, gradually understanding and modifying the *status quo*, rather than designing sweeping new reforms from the ground up. Many would defend the incremental approach as being safest and most appropriate in a world of inadequate data on costs, activity and outcomes.

The early years of the purchaser–provider arrangement allowed for commissioners to identify clinical activity and its costs and to create contracts with providers, generally without innovation and major change, which was considered disruptive at that time. Fundamentally, the concept of health gain was not the basis for commissioning or contractual arrangements. Health gain was introduced through the Department of Health epidemiological reviews and guidelines on health needs assessment[1], the publication of the *Health of the Nation* Strategy[2], the recognition of an outcomes focus, rather than process and the public and media debate about epidemiology, economics, priorities and rationing[3,4].

Health needs assessment – the first step towards health gain

Health needs assessment (*see* Figure 28.1), the first step in working towards health gain, embraces both science and art. It combines 'hard' empirical data with 'soft' consumer feedback, quantitative measurement with qualitative judgement. *Science* includes both epidemiological and economic approaches. Between them, they identify:

- the nature and scale of health care problems

- scope for prevention and the evaluation, in clinical and economic terms, of the range of available interventions using the criteria of effectiveness and relating outcomes to costs.

In addition, attention is focused on efficiency, equity and the balance between them. As yet, economic appraisal is still a neglected science in needs assessment[5].

The *art* of needs assessment juggles central government policies, providers' historical service patterns, and purchasers' and providers' visions of the future and the views of the public, elicited through local surveys. Central government policies

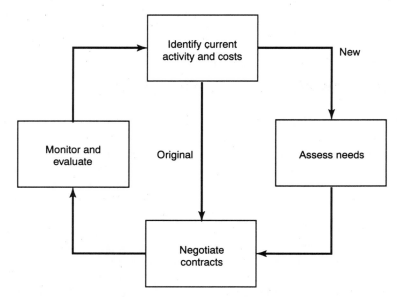

Figure 28.1   Health needs assessment – the first step towards health care. Aim: to purchase 'health gain'

include the *Health of the Nation* strategy, an efficiency index heavily dependant on activity rather than outcome, a patient's charter guaranteeing minimum standards, a junior doctors' hours initiative and a push towards community based services, amongst others. These may be at odds with the views expressed by purchasers, providers or the public. In East Sussex the population has expressed clear views about priorities for prevention and listed circulatory disease as foremost amongst the *Health of the Nation* key areas.

All these disparate views, added to the scientific evidence, are synthesized into the purchaser's health strategy and are expressed in a purchasing plan and contracts for services.

Cost mapping – a tool to establish current health expenditure

Charting current health care expenditure in terms of activity and costs is, as already described, a fundamental task for any commissioning authority. This enables a clear sense of future direction to be developed. As an old piece of twisted logic has it, 'If you don't know where you are going, you might end up somewhere else'.

As a starting point, a 'cost map' provides a summary to inform commissioners of the relative size of the component parts (Table 28.1). This assists planning and coordination by the locality purchasing managers and their partners from other agencies involved in securing caring services. It also provides a means of communicating past experience and future intentions with the public and their representative bodies. The table shows the full cost map for the former Hastings Health Authority in 1992–3 plus General Practice fundholding spending. The two-way matrix of age groups against specialities includes an acute/community division within each cell. It includes other areas of spending such as extra-contractual referrals and the Health Authority's overheads. The table provides an overall picture and enables planning of resource shifts. The right-hand column shows the percentage spend on each speciality and other areas of contracted activity.

A practical illustration of the value of this approach is that only 0.15% was spent on the health promotion unit (row 19), so a further £200 000 from 'growth money' was earmarked for this activity under *Health of the Nation*. It is possible using this matrix to look at per capita expenditure in any cell in the matrix, or any specialty or age group overall.

Other comparisons can be made – between localities, age groups, areas of relative under- or over-spend (e.g. elderly versus reproductive age group or young children), ratios of acute and community spend and allocation between specialities. As an educational tool, the matrix reinforces:

- the concept of opportunity costs
- the importance of the margin for disinvestment and re-investment decisions
- the balance between equity and efficiency
- the inevitability of value judgements in future plans.

Table 28.1 Total spending on Hastings Health Authority residents 1992–3 (including GP fundholder activity): all figures are in £000s

Specialty	0–4			5–14			15–44			45–64			65–74			75–84			85+			Row total			Grand total (%)
	Acute	Com	Total	Acute	Com	Total	Acute	Com	Total	Acute	Com	Total	Acute	Com	Total	Acute	Com	Total	Acute	Com	Total	Acute	Com	Total	
1 General surgery	78.6	0	78.6	116.5	0	116.5	1114.3	0	1114.3	1682.6	0	1682.6	1733.1	0	1733.1	2088.8	0	2088.8	740.6	0	740.6	7554.7	0	7554.7	10.57
2 Urology	3.4	0	3.4	17.7	0	17.7	140	0	140	310.3	0	310.3	471	0	471	719.1	0	719.1	269.8	0	269.8	1931.3	0	1931.3	2.7
3 Orthopaedics	73.8	0	73.8	209.2	0	209.2	903.7	0	903.7	941.5	0	941.5	1147.7	0	1147.7	3227	0	3227	1227.7	0	1227.7	7730.6	0	7730.6	10.32
4 ENT	118.2	0	118.2	403.3	0	403.3	363.8	0	363.8	165.5	0	165.5	86.2	0	86.2	92.1	0	92.1	28.4	0	28.4	1257.5	0	1257.5	1.76
5 Ophthalmology	45.7	0	45.7	32.8	0	32.8	59.4	0	59.4	173.2	0	173.2	372.6	0	372.6	588.9	0	588.9	285.5	0	285.5	1558.1	0	1558.1	2.18
6 Oral surgery	25.1	74.2	99.3	36.9	144.1	181	166.4	2.2	168.6	8.2	0	8.2	7	0	7	4.4	0	4.4	1.4	0	1.4	249.4	220.5	469.9	0.66
7 Pain relief	0	0	0	0	0	0	36.6	0	36.6	46.8	0	46.8	17.8	0	17.8	22.8	0	22.8	7.6	0	7.6	131.6	0	131.6	0.18
8 Obstetrics	0	0	0	1.1	0	1.1	2706.8	565.3	3272.1	3.9	0	3.9	0	0	0	0	0	0	0	0	0	2711.8	565.3	3277.1	4.58
9 Gynaecology	0.8	0	0.8	4	3.5	7.5	1760.9	138.7	1899.6	786.2	60.2	846.4	331.6	4	335.6	193.2	0	193.2	67.7	0	67.7	3144.4	206.4	3350.8	4.69
10 Accident and emergency	149.3	0	149.3	88.4	0	88.4	408.5	0	408.5	270.9	0	270.9	296.4	0	296.4	482	0	482	274.8	0	274.8	1970.3	0	1970.3	2.76
11 General medicine	1.8	0	1.8	0	0	0	784.1	111.2	598.3	1980.5	14	1994.5	2682	11.2	2693.2	640.8	0	640.8	63.3	0	63.3	6152.5	136.4	6288.9	8.8
12 Haematology	0	0	0	0	0	0	50	0	50	126.6	0	126.6	34.8	0	34.8	145.6	0	145.6	0	0	0	357	0	357	0.5
13 Rheumatology	0	0	0	0	0	0	92.6	0	92.6	177.8	0	177.8	66.8	0	66.8	19.4	0	19.4	7.8	0	7.8	364.4	0	364.4	0.51
14 Geriatric medicine	0	0	0	0	0	0	0	0	0	85.1	8.8	93.9	473.9	31.3	505.2	4998.4	172.1	5170.5	3919.2	118	4037.2	9476.6	330.2	9806.8	13.72
15 Paediatrics	1878.8	849.9	2728.7	567.6	275.9	843.5	47.6	0	47.6	0	0	0	0	0	0	0	0	0	0	0	0	2494	1125.8	3619.8	5.06
16 Psychiatry	11.4	12.8	24.2	0	56.1	56.1	1295.6	520	1815.6	909.8	270.2	1180	679.8	111.1	790.9	1173.8	173.8	1347.6	375.2	78.7	453.9	4445.6	1222.7	5668.3	7.93
17 Regional specialties	228.8	0	228.8	138.5	0	138.5	660.7	0	660.7	1069.4	0	1069.4	745.7	0	745.7	312.3	0	312.3	130.8	0	130.8	3286.2	0	3286.2	4.60
18 Learning difficulties	0	0	0	35.7	7.2	42.9	196.8	83.9	280.7	115.8	34.7	150.5	12	5.8	17.8	0	1.4	1.4	0	0	0	360.3	133	493.3	0.69
19 Health Promotion Unit	0	6.1	6.1	0	11.5	11.5	38.5	0	38.5	0	23.3	23.3	0	13.8	13.8	0	9.8	9.8	0	3.3	3.3	38.5	67.8	106.3	0.15
20 Drug abuse	0	0	0	0	9.2	9.2	0	227.1	227.1	0	12.6	12.6	0	3.4	3.4	0	0	0	0	0	0	0	252.3	252.3	0.35
21 HIV/AIDS	0	0	0	0	20.8	20.8	83.3	83.3	166.6	0	20.8	20.8	0	0	0	0	0	0	0	0	0	83.3	124.9	208.2	0.29
22 Disablement services	0	2.7	2.7	0	7.7	7.7	0	63.2	63.2	0	34.7	34.7	0	42.4	42.4	0	118.8	118.8	0	45.1	45.1	0	314.6	314.6	0.44

Table 28.1 *continued*

Specialty	0–4			5–14			15–44			45–64			65–74			75–84			85+			Row total			Grand total (%)
	Acute	Com	Total	Acute	Com	Total	Acute	Com	Total	Acute	Com	Total	Acute	Com	Total	Acute	Com	Total	Acute	Com	Total	Acute	Com	Total	
23 Joint finance	0	23.6	23.6	0	44.7	44.7	0	149.8	149.8	0	90.6	90.6	0	53.8	53.8	0	38.1	38.1	0	12.8	12.8	0	413.4	413.4	0.58
24 Community nursing	0	9.4	9.4	0	18.7	18.7	0	148.6	148.6	0	281.4	281.4	0	482	482	0	1012.4	1012.4	0	696.5	696.5	0	2649	2649	3.71
25 Community clinics	0	0.6	0.6	0	1.1	1.1	0	9	9	0	16.6	16.6	0	28.9	28.9	0	62.2	62.2	0	43.4	43.4	0	161.8	161.8	0.23
26 GP Access therapists	0	43.9	43.9	0	39.5	39.5	0	77.1	77.1	0	83.3	83.3	0	127.7	127.7	0	189.3	189.3	0	99	99	0	659.8	659.8	0.92
27 GP Access pathology	0	33.2	33.2	0	33.9	33.9	0	220	220	0	114.9	114.9	0	106.2	106.2	0	165.2	165.2	0	72.8	72.8	0	746.2	746.2	1.04
28 GP Access Radiology	0	15.9	15.9	0	16.2	16.2	0	219.4	219.4	0	55.2	55.2	0	51	51	0	69.8	69.8	0	35	35	0	462.5	462.5	0.65
29 Hospice	0	0	0	0	0	0	0	129.3	129.3	0	78.4	78.4	0	46.5	46.5	0	32.8	32.8	0	11	11	0	298	298	0.42
30 Long stay (non-SE TRHA)	0	0	0	0	0	0	0	124.5	124.5	0	75.3	75.3	0	44.8	44.8	0	0	0	0	0	0	0	244.6	244.6	0.34
31 ECR	360.9	0	360.9	118	0	118	989.8	0	989.8	560	0	560	264.3	0	264.3	258	0	258	51.2	0	51.2	2602.2	0	2602.2	3.64
32 Ambulance	132.6	0	132.6	88.2	0	88.2	568.3	0	568.3	294.5	0	294.5	273.6	0	273.6	369.1	0	369.1	184.9	0	184.9	1911.2	0	1911.2	2.67
33 Managerial overhead	38.1	38.1	76.2	72.1	72.1	144.2	241.4	241.4	482.8	146.1	146.1	292.2	86.7	86.7	173.4	61.4	61.4	122.8	20.8	20.8	41.6	666.6	666.6	1333.2	1.87
34 Total spend	3147.3	1110	4257.7	1930	762.2	2692.2	12 709	3114	15 823.3	9854.7	1421	11 276	9783	1250.6	11 033.6	15 397	2107.1	17 504.2	7656.7	1236.4	8893.1	60 478	11 002	71 479.9	100
35 Weighted capitation			2931			2788			8506			8578			14 225			22 516			11 866			71 408	
36 Variance (34/35 × 100)			145%			97%			186%			131%			78%			78%			75%			100%	
37 Acute/Community ratio			2.83 : 1			2.53 : 1			4.08 : 1			6.93 : 1			7.82 : 1			7.31 : 1			6.19 : 1			5.50 : 1	

Applying the cost map: coronary heart disease

In East Sussex this matrix has been used to consider the cost implications of coronary heart disease and to help identify future strategic direction.

The cost map showed that patients with coronary heart disease can present with a variety of symptoms to a variety of specialists, especially in general medicine and geriatrics, but that coronary heart disease is generally more prevalent in older age.

Block contracts for inpatient episodes were in place for all major specialities, using average costs for inpatient stays. The example did not attempt to include patients treated elsewhere, patients admitted for another reason but with heart disease as a complicating factor, or any outpatient or community based work. Even without these, expenditure was £1.374 million in 1992–3 (Table 28.2). In addition £0.5 million was spent on tertiary referrals to London teaching hospitals for coronary artery bypass grafts and angioplasties.

Whilst funds (£40 000) had been granted for a project in cardiac rehabilitation for heart attack survivors, no matching commitment existed for people with risk factors prior to heart attack and the proposal for rehabilitation was evaluated without comparisons with an alternative provider or pattern of care.

An alternative approach to health care: the HALO scheme

To redress this balance a collaborative 'healthy alliance' project was funded (£5000) the following year – a Health and Leisure Organisations (HALO) scheme. The scheme focuses on the popular and promising alternative to medication or hospital referral: *referral-to-fitness*.

The scheme aims to make 'more people more active more often', providing a supervised, safe environment for activity. Prescription of exercise has demonstrated high compliance and there are positive associations with an appropriate 'healthy' setting.

Table 28.1   Costs of inpatient care for coronary heart disease (£000)

Specialty	Age of patient (years)					
	15–44	45–64	65–74	75–84	85+	Total
General surgery	0	0	0	2	0	2
Urology	0	0	0	0	1	1
Accident and emergency	0	0	8	9	0	17
General medicine	39	250	297	46	1	633
Geriatric medicine	0	0	3	520	183	706
GP medicine	0	0	1	6	3	10
Psychogeriatrics	0	0	0	0	4	4
Total	39	250	309	583	192	1373

Hastings and Rother residents treated at the Conquest Hospital in 1992–3.
Primary diagnosis: 410–14 coronary heart disease.
Number have been rounded to nearest £ 000.

Following guidance and training of GPs and fitness instructors, patients visit leisure centres for their fitness programme. Enhancements to the scheme include out-posted practice nurses, dieticians, health promotion advisers and others.

The benefits to patients include improved physical and mental health, for GPs and commissioners reduced hospital admissions, reduced medication costs, reduced work-load in primary care, improved teamwork and professionalism and for the leisure centres increased use of leisure facilities. Indeed, many clients are retained as long-term paying members in their own right and the scheme is attractive to leisure centres as a loss-leader. The HALO scheme has advantages, not just for patients with risk factors for coronary heart disease, but also for people with stroke risk factors, established coronary heart disease, asthma, neurosis (especially anxiety and depression), alcohol problems, antenatal and postnatal mothers, and elective preoperative patients.

Health authorities have a legitimate interest in investing in continuing evaluation. They need to know the proportion of individuals who achieve their therapeutic objective (e.g. loss of 19 kg in weight, lowering of diastolic blood pressure by 5 mm Hg, quitting cigarette smoking). How many maintain that change? How does the effectiveness, and the cost compare with alternative interventions? Discussions are in hand to enable GPs who demonstrate a fall in prescribing costs to retain some of these savings for continued participation in HALO schemes and not simply to 'lose' the money in subsequent years, as at present.

Learning points

- Using the 'cost-map' or matrix enables a clear strategic view of the right balance between programmes of care, such that the resource consequences can be tracked and the funds liberated.

- In a world of limited resources disinvestment must occur to allow reinvestment.

- Once finances are identified, it is possible to invest in some of the creative and imaginative schemes which offer potential for improving the health and quality of life of the population.

- Some promising new interventions are possible and their costs and effectiveness are measurable.

- The leisure centre can become a new type of provider.

- The creative energy of imaginative new schemes has to go hand in hand with old-fashioned disciplines of monitoring and accounting for money.

- Development of the contracting process is possible year-on-year.

References

1   NHSME, DoH NHS Management Executive and Department of Health (1991) *Assessing Health Care Needs: A DHA Project Discussion Paper.*

2   Department of Health (1991) *The Health of the Nation: A Consultative Document for Health in England.* HMSO, London.

3   Donaldson C and Mooney G (1991) Needs assessment, priority setting, and contracts for health care: an economic view. *British Medical Journal.* **303**: 1029–30.

4   Renton A, Stevens A and Petrou S (1992) Economic approach to priority setting. *British Medical Journal.* **304**: 182–3.

5   Brambleby P (1993) A purchaser's guide to purchasing health care. *Clinician in Management.* **2(6)**: 3–6.

Acknowledgements

Cost mapping: Peter Finn, Senior Information Analyst, East Sussex
                 Health Authority.

                 Paul Haycox, Assistant Health Commissioner for Hastings.

HALO protocol: The East Sussex HALO Working Party, especially:

                 Mr David Robertson, Assistant Director,
                 Commissioning and Development, East Sussex FHSA.

                 Dr Sam Ramsey-Smith, Health of the Nation Co-ordinator
                 (Brighton/Hove/Lewes), East Sussex Health Authority.

                 Dr Jenny Bennett, Consultant in Public Health,
                 East Sussex Health Authority.

                 Dr David Hanraty, General Practitioner, Hailsham

And to Mrs Irene Slack for typing this document

29

An alternative to the asylum

Donald Pendlebury

Introduction

The Eastbourne and District catchment area is approximately 450 square miles and has a population of approximately 230 000, with centres of population focused in the towns of Eastbourne, Seaford, Hailsham, Uckfield and Crowborough. Twenty-five per cent of the population are over 65 years of age, 3% over 85 years with a more intense concentration of elderly along the coastal strip.

In the mid-1980s, following the re-location of mental health services from Hellingly Hospital to the parent Districts of Eastbourne, Hastings and Tunbridge Wells, there remained four wards serving the elderly population of the then Eastbourne District Health Authority.

The Authority decided to re-develop its services on a locality basis. As part of the re-development an eight-bedded unit was planned for the town of Seaford. At the same time East Sussex Social Services had decided that it was time to replace their Part three home in Seaford with a purpose-built residential home and day centre. Plans were well advanced in both agencies but to their credit they listened to the advice of the local team of professionals and the traditional after the event 'why didn't you tell us what you were going to do?' debate never occurred.

Out of the 'Partnership in Caring' programme the two Agencies developed Homefield Place, a multi-agency community resource centre to provide a seamless service to the elderly people of Seaford. Homefield Place (Figure 29.1) is jointly funded and staffed by Health and Social Services. Each agency contributed to the building costs and the complex financial arrangements are contained within the framework of the legal agreement between them.

Figure 29.1   Homefield Place

The history of Homefield Place

The centre consists of a 16-bed unit providing assessment and respite care, a 30-place seven days a week day centre and a separate, adjacent cottage unit providing seven respite beds and four day care place facilities seven days per week. The facilities provide individual bedrooms affording privacy and comfort, with emphasis on a domestic style environment throughout (Figure 29.2). Meals on Wheels service operates from the unit and freshly cooked meals on site are delivered by voluntary drivers. A laundry and soiled laundry service is also available.

The staffing of the resource centre has brought together a wide range of professional skills from different agencies. The main unit has a team of qualified psychiatric nurses providing 24 hour care, together with a staff grade psychiatrist providing five sessions per week and with a consultant psychiatrist visiting regularly, once a week. For clients requiring respite care, GPs provide medical care. Medical cover out of hours is supplied by the on-call psychiatric services with local GPs providing service for acute medical problems. Social services care staff run the day centres and are trained to deal with clients having mental health problems, physical disability and frailty. The philosophy is to provide individual purposeful activity as part of a planned programme of care, offering help and relief to carers and clients alike. The home care manager is based in the unit and as such plays an

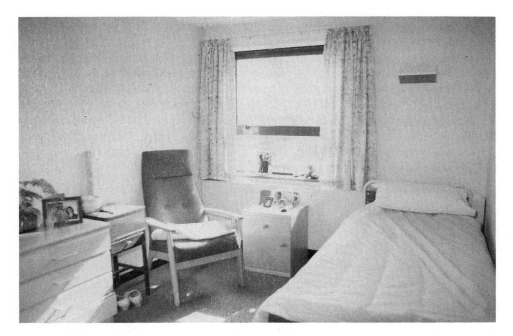

Figure 29.2   Individual bedroom

integral part in the development of the care programme and after-care plans for each client. Assessors within the community care programme, also in the unit, bring together the complex packages of care which are so frequently necessary for clients. Occupational therapists provide assessment of daily living needs together with individual and group therapy. Physiotherapy, speech therapy and chiropody services and other specialist inputs are available as determined by client need.

A Community Service Manager (CSM) for the elderly of Seaford was jointly appointed by the agencies to have overall responsibility for Homefield Place and its services.

From the outset it was recognized that staff would need to be brought together in a carefully planned way. Opportunity arose before the opening of the centre for the 'new' staff group to be involved in a 'getting to know you' through a jointly designed and developed training strategy. Now, the Operational Management group meets twice weekly with the CSM. A Joint Executive Group with Senior Managers from both agencies, Consultant Psychiatrist, GP and Commissioner meets monthly.

Later development

The past five years has seen the unit develop from those early, uneasy days to become a central focus for elderly care within the town. A League of Friends with a membership of 500–600 has developed, and the King's Fund Centre has supported the Nursing Development Unit project. These have both contributed in their own way to the improvement of service.

Carers, meeting weekly, have expressed concerns as to what would happen if they were taken ill or died while out of their home and nobody knew of their dependent person at home. Out of this a 'Carers Emergency Alert Card' was developed. The carer carries the card which states 'Someone depends on me; in an emergency contact Homefield Place'. The carer is identified on a database and relatives can be contacted or staff from Homefield respond to organize care for the dependent person (Figure 29.3).

The philosophies which continue to drive the service are:

- to provide with a local, comprehensive multi-professional service, an appropriate assessment and a range of treatments and care programmes determined by the health and social care needs of each client and carer

- to provide these services in a domiciliary, day centre or residential setting

- to collaborate with other agencies – statutory, independent and voluntary – in providing for assessed needs

- to further the development of local care networks

- to provide a focused, easy access to the services through an open referral system.

Figure 29.3   Staff member and client

Since opening, there has been an increasing request for services. Currently some 500 people are seen in the unit with a variety of service involvement, from home care and day care to respite or specific treatment programmes. Approximately 160 people are admitted annually for assessment, of whom 80% return home with support, often of a very intensive nature. Of the remainder, the majority move to residential placement in rest homes, nursing homes or Elderly Mentally Ill units. Homefield Place does not provide long-term continuing care.

There are usually 90–100 admissions annually for respite care. For the less dependent elderly this is focused within the Cottage but if the person requires nursing care they can be easily moved into the main unit. Outreach services by home helps, nurses and others continue to expand.

Homefield Place has brought professionals together, resulting in both the client and the carer receiving more appropriate assessment treatment and a care programme more finely tuned to their respective needs.

The past five years has seen the commissioning of other resource centres in the area with the opening of:

- Grangemead Resource Centre, Hailsham in December 1991 – a jointly developed unit providing 24 beds with assessment and respite facilities, and 20 day-care places, open seven days per week. There is also a rural day-care outreach service

- Firwood House, Eastbourne – a jointly developed unit opened in October 1993, providing 18 beds for assessment and respite care and 40 day-care places

- Milton Court, Eastbourne – providing 27 beds for assessment and respite and a day centre providing up to 40 day-care places, seven days per week.

Each unit has purpose-developed facilities providing a very high quality of individual rooms, some with en-suite facilities with a homely environment. Each is serviced by a multi-professional group of staff from both health and social services and provides a similar range of services to Homefield Place. It is hoped to develop a further unit in the Crowborough area in the near future.

The resource centres, as developed, have firmly located local facilities for local people within the differing communities of East Sussex. They are part of the growing network of community services and should help lead, in a sensitive way, developments in care for the elderly client and their carers into the next century. They provide a real potential to improve people's quality of life.

Learning point

- Care in the community, if it is to be done well, requires the utmost early co-operation and planning efforts by social service and health personnel.

30

Physiotherapy in general practice
Geoff Hackett

Introduction

Recent work by Hackett *et al.*[1] demonstrated the acceptability of GPs employing physiotherapists under the 70% reimbursement scheme. Analysis of the work-load showed reduced waiting times for patients, along with possible large savings to the NHS when compared with access to hospital physiotherapists via consultants.

Eliman[2] showed that GPs were at least as selective as hospital doctors in sending patients for physiotherapy and determining treatment duration.

Ross[3] demonstrated that up to 40% of orthopaedic referrals could be classified as inappropriate at the time the patient is actually seen by the orthopaedic surgeon.

Ankhorn[4] showed in a general practice in Birmingham which employed a physiotherapist, there were reduced waiting times, shorter treatment durations and large savings in prescribing, sufficient to cover the salary of the physiotherapist.

Graham-Jones and Hackett[5], in a recent review of GP referrals to orthopaedic consultants in Liverpool, suggest that direct access may reduce waiting times for consultant clinics. Official hospital data[1] demonstrate that it can cost up to four times more to treat each patient in hospital compared with general practice. In the light of the 1989 Government white paper *General Practice in the National Health Service – A New Contract*[6], such costings assume greater significance.

Examining the issues

An open prospective study of three practices, each of five partners with similar list sizes (10 000–11 000) was set up in South Cheshire and North Staffordshire. The FHSAs were consulted to ensure accurate matching of the practices in terms of size, age distribution of patients and social class. The three practices were:

- *Holmes Chapel Health Centre* (A) – A rural five partner practice of 10 800 patients in South Cheshire employing its own physiotherapist since 1982.

- *Kiltearn Medical Centre, Nantwich* (B) – A rural five partner practice 10 080 patients in South Cheshire utilizing open access to physiotherapy at Leighton Hospital, Crewe, under a scheme set up in 1987.

- *Orchard Surgery, Norton, Staffordshire* (C) – A rural five partner practice of 11 000 patients with a small branch surgery. Patients require referral to the physiotherapist via orthopaedic consultants at North Staffordshire Infirmary.

At the time of the study none of the practices were computerized but all three underwent computerization within six months of the trial completion.

The aim was to assess the quality of care, waiting times for treatment, and comparative costs in the management of joint and soft-tissue problems within the practices.

A pilot study was conducted during a four week period to confirm similar consultation rates for joint and soft tissue conditions. This involved the completion of log diaries by all doctors and provided comparative statistics of new presentations and follow up, along with diagnoses, treatments and referral rates.

Patients of any age and sex attending their GP for acute or chronic joint or soft-tissue problems between October 1988 and June 1989 were invited to join the study. The major criteria for inclusion were:

- the GP felt that physiotherapy would not be contraindicated in the management of the patient's condition

- the patient should not have been seen or treated by hospital specialists for that condition within the last 2 years

- patients did not require treatment necessitating attendance at the accident and emergency department.

On admission to the study, Form A (Figure 30.1) was completed with details of the consultation and the action taken. The patient was given Form B (Figure 30.2) on which to record information related to treatments and appointments relevant to that condition. Form C (Figure 30.3) recorded information about time lost from normal activities, transport costs, and acceptability of the treatment. Patients failing to return forms at the end of treatment were initially reminded by telephone and then by post.

How do the practices compare?

Differences in major outcome variables between groups were tested by two sample t, chi-squared, and Mann–Whitney U tests. If there was no evidence of a difference between the two practices, their data were pooled for comparison with the remaining practice. As the significant differences were substantial, a major

PHYSIOTHERAPY IN GENERAL PRACTICE
RECORD CARD A

DR G. I. Hackett
Patient details

Name   Trial number

Address   Date of birth

Telephone   Day   Mth   Year

Date of trial entry

Diagnosis

1. ....ICT code

2. ....□□□□□

Q. code

3. ....□□□□

Action taken

1. Drug prescription

2. NHS outpatient referral

                                                        Please
3. Private referral   tick

4. Other (specify)

Prescriptions issues

Drug name.   Dose.   Frequency.   Date start.   Date finish.

1. .... □□□

2. .... □□□

3. .... □□□

Signature ....Date

                                                        Day   Mth   Year

Figure 30.1   Record Card A

PHYSIOTHERAPY IN GENERAL PRACTICE
RECORD CARD B

DR. G.I. HACKETT
This form is to be retained by the patient and collected by the doctor at the end of the trial.
Please record details of consultations with specialists, therapists and visits to hospitals.

PATIENT DETAILS

NAME   TRIAL NUMBER..........

ADDRESS   DATE OF BIRTH

                                          ____ /____ /____

                                         DAY   MTH   YEAR

1. GENERAL PRACTITIONER ATTENDANCE

	D	M	YR
1.	....	....	....
2.	....	....	....
3.	....	....	....
4.	....	....	....
5.	....	....	....
6.	....	....	....
7.	....	....	....
8.	....	....	....

2. SPECIALIST ATTENDANCE

	D	M	YR
1.	....	....	....
2.	....	....	....
3.	....	....	....
4.	....	....	....
5.	....	....	....

3. X-RAY ATTENDANCE

	D	M	YR
1.	....	....	....
2.	....	....	....
3.	....	....	....
4.	....	....	....

4. PHYSIOTHERAPIST ATTENDANCE

	D	M	YR
1.	....	....	....
2.	....	....	....
3.	....	....	....
4.	....	....	....
5.	....	....	....
6.	....	....	....
7.	....	....	....
8.	....	....	....
9.	....	....	....
10.	....	....	....
11.	....	....	....
12.	....	....	....

5. OTHERS ATTENDANCE (SPECIFY)

	D	M	YR
1.	....	....	....
2.	....	....	....
3.	....	....	....
4.	....	....	....
5.	....	....	....

Figure 30.2   Record Card B

PHYSIOTHERAPY IN GENERAL PRACTICE
RECORD CARD C

DR. G. I. Hackett

Please indicate below the cost involved in attending the practitioners listed below, e. g. petrol, bus, train, taxi.

Expenses

	Cost/Visit £ p	No of visits	Total £ p
G.P.	☐☐-☐☐	☐☐	☐☐-☐☐
Physiotherapy	☐☐-☐☐	☐☐	☐☐-☐☐
X-ray	☐☐-☐☐	☐☐	☐☐-☐☐
Others (specify)	☐☐-☐☐	☐☐	☐☐-☐☐

Duration off work/normal duties....................days

Opinion of treatment

Very good   Good   Average   Poor   Very poor

Comments

....
....
....
....

Figure 30.3   Record Card C

comparison correction was regarded as unnecessary. It must be noted that some variables are interrelated.

To facilitate analysis within diagnostic groups, the international classification of disease protocol was modified to produce a 'quick code' for specific diagnostic problem areas within general practice.

Table 30.1   Diagnoses. Results are in numbers (%) of patients

Diagnosis	Practice A	Practice B	Practice C
Soft tissue	22 (12)	7 (8)	15 (11)
Tennis/golfers' elbow	4 (2)	2 (3)	9 (7)
Knee injuries	18 (10)	7 (8)	16 (12)
Ankle ligament sprains	22 (12)	2 (2)	3 (2)
Shoulder injuries	33 (18)	13 (15)	42 (32)
Lumbar sacral spine	44 (24)	31 (36)	32 (24)
Cervical spine	18 (10)	19 (22)	16 (12)
Miscellaneous	22 (12)	4 (5)	0 (0)

The response rates were high in all practices ranging from 83% to 93%. There were similar distributions of mean age (46.3–48 years).

Diagnoses were broadly similar (Table 30.1). Soft-tissue conditions were usually muscle sprains of the calf, hamstring, abdominal or intercostal area, usually the result of sports injuries or falls. The commonest conditions in the miscellaneous group were wrist hand and foot injuries with three cases of shin pain related to jogging.

Table 30.2 indicates that there was no significant difference in the prescribing rates of practices A and B whilst practice C had significantly higher rates with corresponding higher average costs per patient. However, as Practice C had the highest rate for generic prescribing, the average cost per item was lower than for practices A and B. The types of drugs prescribed were similar between the three practices (Table 30.3).

There was no significant difference between the three practices in terms of GP consultations with a mean of two visits per patient. The presence of a physiotherapist on the premises did not influence this figure.

Table 3.4 indicates that no patients in practices A and B were referred to private physiotherapists during the study period. In practice C, however, patients were

Table 30.2   Prescribing

	Practice A	Practice B	Practice C
Number (%) of patients receiving prescription	91 (49)	41 (48)	112 (84) A + B vs. C p <0.001
Mean cost per patient (£)	3.65	3.85	5.85 A + B vs. C p <0.2
Mean cost where prescription actually issued (£)	7.58	7.27	6.50
Number of items (as %) related to FPC average PACT data	–8	–20	–5
Percentage generic prescriptions	30	38	65
Cost per item (£) PACT data	6.03	5.81	4.30

Table 30.3   Types of drugs prescribed. Results are given as numbers (%) of prescriptions

Drug	Practice A	Practice B	Practice C
Non-steroidal anti-inflammatory (NSAID)	72 (79)	28 (68)	82 (73)
Analgesics	10 (11)	10 (24)	8 (7)
Both	3 (3)	0 (0)	1 (1)
Joint/soft tissue injections	3 (3)	3 (8)	15 (13)
Others e.g. gels, muscle relaxants	3 (3)	0 (0)	7 (6)

Table 30.4   Physiotherapy treatments and delays

	Practice A	Practice B	Practice C
Mean delay (days)	9	23	74 (4 NHS) 10 (15 Private)
Mean number of treatments	7.0	7.2	7.2 (NHS) 7.0 (Private)

frequently referred for private physiotherapy during the initial consultation. The number of treatments required across the practice were constant at around seven, suggesting that physiotherapists in the different settings managed patients in a consistent manner.

The mean delay before NHS treatment in practice A was similar to that for private referrals in practice C. Patients in practice B had a longer mean delay than those in A ($p < 0.001$ Mann–Whitney U). NHS patients in Practice C had much longer mean delays than those referred privately ($p < 0.003$ Mann–Whitney U).

Table 30.5 shows that although direct access patients (practices A and B) would be seen within 24 hours if specifically requested by the GP, when standard referral procedures were used, involving postal and administrative delays, 40% of patients in practice B were not seen within 3 weeks and none in practice C, compared with only 2% in practice A.

In addition, practice A referred nine patients (6% of total) to specialist consultants, with a median delay of 28 days, practice C referred nine (8%), with a delay of 93 days, and practice B two 2 (3%), with a delay of 42 days.

Table 30.5   Delays in physiotherapy. Results are given as numbers (cumulative %) of cases

Delay (days)	Practice A	Practice B	Practice C
Same day	18 (10)	12 (14)	0 (0)
Within 6	60 (32)	19 (22)	0 (0)
Within 11	132 (71)	25 (29)	0 (0)
Within 16	167 (90)	44 (52)	0 (0)
Within 21	181 (98)	51 (60)	0 (0)
Over 21	4 (100)	34 (100)	100 (100)

Finally practice A referred 11 (7%) for x-ray (median delay, 12 days); practice B four (5%) (delay 32 days); and C 15 (14%) (delay 32 days).

Table 30.6 shows that a higher proportion of patients incurred cost in practice B (84%), than in practices A (36%) and C (34%). Mean patient costs were lowest in practice A and highest in practice C.

No patients in practices A and B decided to seek private physiotherapy and the 24 patients in practice C who sought private treatment include the costs in their assessment. As these were additional charges resulting from the system prevailing in that practice and were actual costs incurred by the patient, they are included for analysis

As shown in Table 30.7, more patients in practice B lost time from work than in practice A and C. However, the amount of time lost was similar for practices A and B and much less than practice C.

More patients evaluated the treatment as being above, as opposed to below, average in practices A and B (94%), than in practice C (80%). (Chi-squared = 9.2, $p < 0.005$; 95% confidence interval for difference in percentage 3%, 25%. Table 30.8.)

Discussion

Musculoskeletal conditions account for 10–15% of all time lost from work in the UK each year[1]. Lengthy waiting times for hospital treatment directly affect these

Table 30.6   Patient costs

	Practice A	Practice B	Practice C
Number (%) of patients incurring costs	58 (36)	66 (84)	37 (34)
		A + C vs. B p < 0.001	
Mean patient costs (£) overall	0.27	7.42	16.12
	A vs. B p < 0.001	B vs. C p < (0.005)	
Mean cost in patients who actually incurred costs (£)	0.74	9.55	47.94

Table 30.7   Days lost from work or normal activity

	Practice A	Practice B	Practice C
Number (%) of patients losing time from work	30 (18)	26 (33)	22 (20)
Median days lost overall	4.0	3.0	14.0
Mean days lost in patients	13.8	10.42	27.86

Table 30.8   Patient satisfaction as numbers (%) of patients

Treatment evaluation	Practice A	Practice B	Practice C
Very good	58 (39)	25 (34)	24 (34)
Good	62 (41)	34 (46)	21 (30)
Average	23 (15)	9 (13)	13 (19)
Poor	7 (5)	5 (7)	8 (12)
Very poor	0 (0)	0 (0)	3 (5)

figures. The conditions studied in this trial are amenable to management in a general practice setting.

The use of log diaries in the practices for a month prior to the start of patient recruitment confirmed similar prevalence rates for the conditions studied. It was impossible, however, to standardize the practices for all other variables. It could be argued that the prior establishment of on-site physiotherapy in practice A demonstrates a higher motivation amongst the partners compared with practices B and C.

On-site physiotherapy (practice A) resulted in a referral rate of more than double that of a similar sized practice using direct access (practice B). This suggests that conditions of a more minor nature might be referred but as there was no difference between the numbers of treatments given in the groups studied, this was probably not the case. A likely explanation is that working closely with a physiotherapist has increased the doctors' awareness of what the treatment has to offer. This is shown by the differences in conditions referred to the physiotherapist within the three groups. In practice A, the physiotherapist had earlier stressed the importance of early referral for ankle ligament injuries, thus perhaps explaining the 12% referral in A compared with 2% in B and C.

Drug prescribing was much higher in practice C, with 84% of all patients receiving a prescription, of which 73% were nonsteroidal anti-inflammatories (NSAIDS) often in expensive, once-daily formulations. Approximately half the patients in practices A and B received prescriptions, with a similar proportion of NSAIDs. Ready access to physiotherapy resulted in lower drug prescribing with considerable cost saving. These findings are in agreement with Ankorn et al.[4], who postulated that the saving in drug costs would more than pay the salaries of the physiotherapists concerned. This was not the case in this study because practice C was able to offset some of these increased costs by a generic prescribing rate of 65%, compared with 30% in practice A. The most disturbing aspect of these data is the overprescribing of NSAIDS in a range of conditions where a true inflammatory component may be of little importance. The high prescribing in practice C (84%, of which 73% were for NSAIDS) suggests that a group of drugs – with a large number of side-effects – may be prescribed because of difficulty in obtaining physiotherapy.

Consultant delays at 71 days and x-ray delays at 41 days were unlikely to aid the management of acute conditions. Practice C (13%) referred significantly more patients for x-ray than practice B (5%) and A (6%). As patients referred for immediate casualty treatment or suspected fractures were excluded from the trial, these results confirm the findings of earlier studies, that readily available physiotherapy reduces x-ray referral with resulting cost savings[1].

The overall cost to patients in practice A was £0.27 compared with £7.42 in B and £16.12 in C. Where costs were incurred by patients in C the costs rose to £47.94 largely because 24 out of 29 patients treated by physiotherapy were done so privately. Five patients had costs over £150, even though there was no tendancy for those treated privately to be seen more often. Indeed, throughout the study, physiotherapists were remarkably constant in the way they managed their patients. Those patients incurring high costs usually expressed dissatisfaction in the comments section of the data record card. The marked differences between A and B demonstrate that the costs to the patient in getting to their local hospital for treatment are considerable.

Readily available physiotherapy (practices A and B) resulted in significantly less time lost from work. Patients off work in C lost an average of 28 days, more than double the time lost in practices A and B. Although it would be expected that patients needing to travel to and from hospital would lose more time from work than those treated in their local health centres, there was no difference between the groups. This suggests that the hospital physiotherapists were able to treat patients with minimal interruption to their daily routine.

At present, GPs who employ physiotherapists are ineligible for reimbursement on the salary. In addition, they must purchase aids such as cervical collars and splints and maintain their equipment. Payne[7] demonstrated that GPs were as efficient as hospital doctors in their utilization of such resources. It is difficult to justify, in the light of the cost savings demonstrated in this study, why such practices should not be financially supported. It is to be hoped that the current reorganizations within general practice, particularly in relation to fundholding and health promotion, will offer some incentive rather than penalty to GPs who provide improved services.

A fundholding practice of 12 000 patients would expect to pay £28 000 per year for physiotherapy services and would need to provide a full-time physiotherapist to provide the service. Some practices have obtained physiotherapy time by purchasing it from the partnership, using fundholding money to provide assessments for patients with functional mobility and respiratory problems. Providing that charges are in line with other provider units, this may result in a more efficient service for the patient and provide income for the practice, without contravening the fundholding regulations.

Learning points

- Many referrals to orthopaedic specialists are inappropriate.

- Waiting times and costs can be reduced and return to work often improved using physiotherapy services based in the community.

- Clinical outcomes are also improved and fewer drugs administered when patients are seen away from the hospital.

References

1   Hackett G I, Hudson M F, Wylie J B *et al.* (1987) Evaluation of the efficiency and acceptability to patients of physiotherapist working in a health centre. *British Medical Journal.* **294**: 24–6.

2   Eliman R, Adams, S, Reardon J A *et al.* (1982) Making physiotherapy more accessible. *British Medical Journal.* **284**: 1173–5.

3   Ross K (1983) General practice orthopaedic referrals in North Staffordshire. *British Medical Journal.* **287**: 1439–41.

4   Ankhorn L, Pratt J and Nottingham S (1989) *Therapy Weekly.* **23**: 4.

5   MRHA Research Scheme (1989) *A Study of Orthopaedic Referrals From General Practitioners to Consultant Orthopaedic Surgeons in Liverpool.* Second Report. MRHA, Liverpool, p. 550.

6   Department of Health and the Welsh Office (1989) *General Practice in the National Health Service – A New Contract.* (White Paper.)

7   Payne S, Ramalah, RS and Jones DT (1987) Open access to orthopaedic appliances for general practitioners. *British Medical Journal.* **294**: 485–6.

Index